Joseph Butler, H. R Huckin

Dialogues Founded upon Butler's Analogy of Religion

Joseph Butler, H. R Huckin

Dialogues Founded upon Butler's Analogy of Religion

ISBN/EAN: 9783337262853

Printed in Europe, USA, Canada, Australia, Japan

Cover: Foto ©Lupo / pixelio.de

More available books at **www.hansebooks.com**

The Analogy of Religion.

DIALOGUES

FOUNDED UPON

BUTLER'S ANALOGY OF RELIGION.

BY

Rev. H. R. HUCKIN, M.A.

FORMERLY FELLOW OF ST. JOHN'S COLLEGE, OXFORD,
ONE OF THE MASTERS AT MERCHANT TAYLORS' SCHOOL.

LONDON:
CHRISTIAN EVIDENCE COMMITTEE OF THE
OCIETY FOR PROMOTING CHRISTIAN KNOWLEDGE;
SOLD AT THE DEPOSITORIES:
77, GREAT QUEEN STREET, LINCOLN'S INN FIELDS;
4, ROYAL EXCHANGE; 48, PICCADILLY;
AND BY ALL BOOKSELLERS.

1873.

THE Christian Evidence Committee of the S.P.C.K., while giving its general approval to the works of the Christian Evidence Series, does not hold itself responsible for every statement or every line of argument.

The responsibility of each writer extends to his own work only.

CONTENTS.

	PAGE
PREFACE	5
INTRODUCTION	13

Part I.

DIALOGUE I.
ON A FUTURE LIFE 25

DIALOGUE II.
ON REWARDS AND PUNISHMENTS 63

DIALOGUE III.
ON THE MORAL GOVERNMENT OF GOD . . . 82

DIALOGUE IV.
ON A STATE OF TRIAL OR PROBATION . . . 120

DIALOGUE V.
ON LIFE CONSIDERED AS A STATE OF MORAL DISCIPLINE 141

DIALOGUE VI.
ON THE DOCTRINE OF NECESSITY 174

DIALOGUE VII.
ON THE GOVERNMENT OF GOD: A SCHEME BEYOND OUR COMPREHENSION 205

Part II.

DIALOGUE I.
On the Importance of Christianity . . . 225

DIALOGUE II.
On Miracles 247

DIALOGUE III.
On Objections to the Scheme of Christianity 270

DIALOGUE IV.
On Christianity as a Scheme imperfectly comprehended 294

DIALOGUE V.
On the Appointment of a Redeemer and Mediator 308

DIALOGUE VI.
On the Want of Universality in Revelation, and of the Supposed Deficiency in the Proof of it 310

DIALOGUE VII.
On the Positive Evidence for Christianity . 378

DIALOGUE VIII.
On a Subjective Proof of Religion . . . 439

PREFACE.

THE history and design of this book may be briefly stated. The great work of Bishop Butler is now regarded with mixed feelings by various writers. By some it is stigmatized as obscure and unsatisfactory; to others it appears satisfactory, but still obscure. The character thus assigned to the book has diminished the number of its readers. People are under a reasonable apprehension, that it is mere waste of time to study what is obscure, when the same can be found clearly expressed elsewhere. This, however, is much to be regretted: for no writer has combined, in greater degree, philosophical acumen and judicial fairness with a thoroughly religious tone of mind. And no work can be found, stating so completely, yet concisely, the principal grounds upon which natural and revealed religion claim the obedience of mankind.

It must, however, be acknowledged, that the

charge of obscurity is not altogether groundless. The treatise *is* difficult; and, in some places at least, the difficulty is increased by defects of style. Yet it is a mistake to suppose that the book could be made easy by simply recasting the sentences and rearranging the paragraphs. There is, as Bishop Butler truly remarks, an intrinsic difficulty in the subject; and, if any student of Christian Evidences expects to find a royal road to the solution of the question, he will certainly be disappointed.

For, in the first place, the facts, to which the inquiry appeals, are somewhat out of the ordinary course of experience, or (to speak more precisely) the aspect, under which they are viewed, is not such as arrests a casual inquirer. In the limited and somewhat selfish estimate, which we form of passing events, our tendency is to inquire into the probable consequences to ourselves and to our fortunes of that which we experience; or, if from the nature of the case, such considerations are excluded (as, for example, in geological inquiries), we are apt to content ourselves with a historical survey of the past. But the point of view adopted by the student of Christian evidences is this: Do nature and the history of the world furnish us with any evidences of *design?* in other words, How far are we justified in inferring *intention* or *purpose* from the apparent adaptation of means to ends?

Now this mode of regarding the facts of experience is not general. In some instances, indeed, the *design* appears so obvious, that we are constrained to observe it. In others, however, and these by far the most numerous, such is our familiarity with the marvellous, that it ceases to appear remarkable. The argument from design, resting upon ten thousand apparently unimportant facts, requires the mind to be forcibly directed to them before its cogency is perceived.

It has been asserted, that in order to form a scientific estimate of the importance of *law* in the natural world, a special training is necessary; and hence it is argued that unscientific men cannot have a correct idea of scientific theories and scientific objections. Without asserting that the uninstructed mind cannot perceive signs of design, we may fairly assume that an intellect, unaccustomed to dwell upon the almost endless traces of design in nature, is by no means adequately trained for the system and method of Bishop Butler; much less fit is he whose first principle is, that there *shall* be no signs of design.

The constant references to this argument, with which the Analogy abounds, are likely to be little regarded by those who are not familiar with the grounds on which it rests. For Bishop Butler does not pause to *prove* the principles on which he argues, but simply *assumes* them. It is obvious, then, that they, who reject the argument from design, cannot obtain satisfaction from the treatise: they will find it obscure, because it tacitly assumes what they reject. And they, who are not familiar with the details of this argument, will find the method perplexing, because it takes for granted what they have yet to learn.

Another source of obscurity should be mentioned. Bishop Butler scarcely ever mentions the names of those against whose views he is contending. In reading the Analogy for the first time, we might imagine that the writer was simply combating the difficulties which had arisen in his own mind. Yet Butler was a wide reader, as well as a profound thinker. They, who are well acquainted with the literature of the seventeenth and eighteenth centuries, have observed that the Analogy bears witness, in the refinements and intricacies of its arguments, to corresponding refinements in preceding and contemporary writers. Thus it happens, that, while combating a general principle, he frequently pauses to limit his assertions, in deference to what may have appeared to him a fair objection on the other side. To a similar cause may be assigned the apparent eccentricity of method, which marks some portion of the Second Part of the Analogy, in which he passes suddenly from speculative to practical considerations, and argues against those who treat religion with levity and ribaldry.

These defects, if they are to be reckoned such, have led to the reproduction of the Analogy in its present form. The object of the writer has been to maintain, as far as possible, the order and method of the original; and, at the same time, to connect together, by more obvious links of reasoning, those parts which labour under the obscurities here specified. The Dialogistic form suggested itself, as best adapted to draw out, in natural sequence, the various points as they arise. In this attempt the writer is conscious that his familiarity with the original has proved a drawback, inasmuch as he is aware that many points, which appear to him simple and obvious, may present a very different aspect to others. But he was compelled to choose between a prolixity which might render the book repulsive, and a conciseness which might leave it obscure. And where the meaning of his author is not transparently clear, he has, after much anxious thought, preferred to confine himself to what appears to him to be the intention of the original treatise.

The great development of scientific investigations during the last half century has opened many questions, of which the age of Bishop Butler knew but little. With great diffidence the present writer has, in a few places, introduced this new matter into the work. It was indeed impossible to avoid reference to these questions. To discuss them fully is the work of a lifetime, and to view them in their bearings on religion forms one of the most vital duties of Theologians in these our days. In a work like this, they can receive only a passing notice; and such a treatment must be but partially satisfactory to those who consider that they are reconcilable with the Christian Scheme, and to those who see in them a subversion of our faith. The writer will here only express his conviction that the works of God cannot be at variance with one another; and that, could we comprehend the whole of His purpose, we should find no contradiction between Science and the Christian Religion.

Once more : the salient points of Biblical criticism have in one place entered into the discussion. The few lines, which could be devoted to a matter of intense importance and much difficulty, obviously express most imperfectly the bearings of the question. Still the writer hopes that he has not asserted anything which transgresses the laws of fair criticism, nor weakened the cause which he has at heart, by omitting what might have been introduced within the limits prescribed.

It is necessary here to observe that, in the course of the discussion, opinions are expressed and concessions made, which, under the circumstances supposed, were unavoidable. It may occur to some that these concessions should have been withheld; that the dignity of the Gospel history has been injured ; that inspiration has been too slightly insisted upon ; that some vital truths appear to be impugned. But it must be remembered that in such a discussion the disputants must meet upon some common ground, consequently many points, which to the writer appear legitimate and inevitable inferences, so soon as the Gospel scheme is acknowledged, are held in abeyance while that scheme is itself in question. Without such concessions the whole discussion must have degenerated into a mere formality, and the progressive force of the argument would have been entirely destroyed.

The matter of the last dialogue is mainly derived from Dr. Newman's Grammar of Assent. The present writer desires to express his deep obligation to that treatise. He read it after the greater portion of this book was prepared for the press: and his study of it has tended to increase his sense of the imperfection of his own work. He would ask those of his readers, who desire to see how powerfully the historical argument for Christianity can be stated, to study the last two sections of Dr. Newman's book. The portion here adapted supplies an important element in the argument from analogy; but the whole two sections contain the most powerful contribution to the Christian Evidences, which the present generation has produced.

LONDON, 1873.

INTRODUCTION.

RATIONAL objections to Christianity emanate from two sources, widely different in their nature and principles. Some men satisfy themselves that the order of nature in no way implies a God; they reject the arguments derived from the appearance of design in the universe, on the ground that the agency of a mind in the operations of nature is an idea, based upon an insufficient acquaintance with the material universe: they argue that this idea enters in, as explaining the laws of the universe, only through ignorance or impatience; but that were men content to accept only what was experimentally proved, the progress of science would soon convince them that the *unknown*, to which they give the name of God, is, not improbably, to be discerned in the course of time by scientific demonstration. They refuse to allow any weight whatever, however small, to the almost universal consent of mankind, or to the testimony of ancient times on this point; and they repudiate all arguments of an abstract nature, under the title of metaphysical refinements. Those who hold such a belief are, in the strict sense of the word, *Atheists*. The present treatise is not directly concerned with them, although the main argument may, perhaps, be extended so as to refute their assertions.

The other class of objections assumes this form. The belief in a God, the benevolent and all-wise Author of the Universe, is acknowledged to be reasonable. But the main doctrines or ideas, which stand prominent in Christianity, are thought to be in conflict with the true ideas of wisdom and benevolence which are essential to the nature of God.

In consequence of this supposed conflict between reason and the Christian religion, it is not unusual to find men forming a system of religion for themselves upon hypothesis; in other words, they lay down certain principles, which, they imagine, must of necessity guide the Divine mind; and when they find that the Christian religion does not coincide with conclusions drawn from their principles, they are offended at it. The plan upon which they proceed is briefly this.

It is justly argued, that the only form of

religious belief which a rational man can accept, is that which represents God regulating the universe so as to produce the greatest amount of good. Up to this point the inquirer is thoroughly at one with the Christian believer. But here the divergence commences. The Christian believes that the arrangement of the universe, *which he perceives*, is *on the whole*, in spite of many *real* difficulties and *apparent* contradictions of the law of benevolence, *the best possible*. He acknowledges that there are difficulties, but he considers that these are only *apparent*, arising from his inability to comprehend at once the whole of the past, present, and future ages of the world, or to see how the general well-being of the whole may be promoted by the suffering of a part. He sees that the principles, which in one age reign among men, are often repudiated with abhorrence in another, and this from an increase of knowledge and enlightenment; and he draws the inference that, were the eye of his mind as clear, and its range of vision as extensive, as he hopes it may be at some future time, he would be able to recognize in the order of the universe such signs of wisdom and benevolence as are worthy of a God perfectly wise and good.

This is the course adopted by the Christian, and may fairly be described as of the essence of Christianity. The objection levelled against it is, that it leaves many things doubtful, which the reason induces men to attempt to solve, and that it requires men to acquiesce in some conceptions of the Divine government which seem to contradict the Divine attributes. Another charge which is brought against it, of sanctioning, at least in principle, all the vain imaginations which have found shelter under its protection, may be passed over with one remark. The truth of a principle is not impugned, because it has been abused, or exaggerated, or misapplied.

But the former objection to the Christian religion deserves our attention. It may be fairly asked, If the Christian scheme is defective, what substitute do the objectors propose? This is a fair demand as regards them, for they start with assuming the existence of such a God, as, even by their admission, Christians theoretically confess to be the object of their worship; and, *assuming such a God*, they are bound by their principles to *define his manner of working*. As a matter of fact, some do not acknowledge this obligation, but are satisfied with criticizing. Others, however, are more logical and candid. They are ready to define their notions of the agency of a Supreme Being. And their description amounts to this. Their reflections upon the nature of God lead to the belief that He will govern the world after the most perfect manner. What that perfect manner is, it remains to determine; and it appears that the following scheme, more or less consistently held to, is the ordinary result.

A *perfect* being must be *perfect* in his operations. A perfectly *Holy* Being must love perfect *holiness*, and promote it among His creatures. A perfectly *loving* being must show *mercy* to all, of whatever character. Combining these principles, the *à priori* or ideal theory of religion presents us with the following astonishing results.

God must have made all creatures as perfect and as happy as they are capable of being; it is not possible that He should put them in positions of hazard or danger, where they may probably, or even possibly, fall; or at all events, if He does allow them to be tempted, He will effectually provide for each person acting rightly, and so as to promote the general happiness; no difficult matter, it is thought, for Infinite power to effect, for it is perfectly easy to establish in each person principles strong enough to prevent wrong-doing, or to set before the mind, on each occasion, motives on the side of virtue, strong enough to counterbalance all temptations on the other side. The idea of a moral government carried on by rewards and punishments is rejected, as being a circuitous way of bringing about the desired result, and is thought to contradict the great principle of benevolence, which requires as its end the happiness of all.

This is a general sketch of the principles which, in more or less completeness, underlie the religion of reason. The degree of assent which they receive is exactly measured by the divergence, on the part of those who receive them, from the principles of Christianity.

What is remarkable about these speculations is, that they are founded on ideas which the most rigid believer accepts. That men are created to act virtuously, and that the object of their Creator is to produce as great an amount of happiness as possible, and that these two objects coincide, is confessed on all sides. There is no ground in the Christian religion (however much some of its adherents perversely assert the contrary) for the belief, that God *intends* or *purposes* the misery of any created being. It should be borne in mind that the doctrines of a religion, and the opinions of a portion of those who profess it, are by no means necessarily the same.

That God is Love is the foundation of the Christian faith; but the exact manner in which that Love works its way, the agents which it employs, and the means by which it effects results—with these the Christian confesses himself to be only partially acquainted; and the result is that divergence of opinion which has been here exhibited.

But it may be asked, Is there not any common ground upon which the Christian, and the believer in God, who is not a Christian, may meet in order to test the respective merits of their creeds? There is such a ground; and it is not a little curious that the Christian should appeal for the corroboration of his belief to a source of information which he is generally supposed to avoid. That ground is *experience*. The Christian invites his opponent to submit their respective creeds to the test of *facts*.

The form which this argument will take may be stated very briefly. If the universe and all that it contains is the work of God, then we may expect to find, in the various parts of it, signs of unity of origin. A comparison of various portions of the system of the world will probably give evidence, by marks strongly or slightly defined, of the workings of one undivided mind. It may indeed be difficult in places to trace this unity of design; but this may be, and, as we shall see, probably is, because we have not sufficient facts to judge by, or have not sufficiently examined those facts which we possess.

But if, upon the whole, there is sufficient resemblance between the workings of the physical side of nature and its moral aspect, and, again, between the moral system, which the nature of man appears to indicate, and that system which we call religion, to form a presumption that they both spring from one common origin, we shall be supplied with the following chain of argument.

Nature exists as a *fact*. Religion also exists as a *fact*, whether it is a fact in accordance with reason or no. Morality, or the laws of human conduct, also exists as a *fact*. Are these three independent, or have they any connexion with each other? If they have no connexion, we should expect not to find any broad or general similarities, however we might sometimes be able to illustrate one from the other. But if there are any grand systematic resemblances between these three facts, we may infer, with more or less probability, the truth of that which is more abstruse from that which is plainer and more evident to our faculties. And this presumption will be strengthened by the following considerations. Suppose we meet with a point or doctrine in religion difficult to comprehend or believe, such as the government of the world by rewards and punishments, we may appeal to the facts of history. There we find that " perhaps the one and only scientific conclusion which can be drawn is, that in the long run it is well with the good, in the long run it is ill with the bad." That is, the natural government over man points to such a law as religion states to be the principle of the Divine mind. So that even the difficulties which are thought overwhelming, may occasionally be found to be the strongest arguments for the truth of religion.

This mode of reasoning is natural and proper. It is the plan which we should have adopted, if the Christian religion had proclaimed only one fact, that men are immortal. As soon as that fact is certified or rendered probable, it at once introduces the thoughts into a field of infinite contemplation. It opens questions as to the relation of the present to a future life. We can hardly imagine that, if the soul is immortal, its progressive existence here, its growth in knowledge and experience, all the minute influences that day by day and hour by hour are at work to influence it, will go for nothing. To a person with this amount of knowledge, and this only, it becomes essential to discover some mode of reasoning by which he may resolve some of his difficulties. The obvious course is to apply the facts of his own experience, and those of the collective experience of mankind, to the question.

Now, in deciding upon the events of his own life, he would doubtless prefer to have absolute certainty. Probably all people at the outset expect to attain scientific certainty in practical matters. A very little experience assures them that they cannot. They are forced to put up with presumptions. It is the very condition of their existence. They wish for absolute assurance; they can only have probability. If they wait till they are absolutely certain, they will cease to act at all. What we call certainty is after all only a strong presumption. This is abundantly evident in matters of practice. No one in entering upon any course of action can be *sure* as to the result. All that he can know is that, if he makes due allowance for probable contingencies, he is likely to succeed in what he undertakes. In order to estimate these contingencies he compares one thing with another. He sees what are the points of resemblance; and if he sees that probabilities are in his favour, he will act.

In questions of science men are able to suspend their judgments. They may be content to pass out of life in doubt as to their conclusions; but, as a rule, they will convince themselves on one side or the other. But, after all, their conviction amounts only to this, that the probabilities on one side are very strong. We may be satisfied that the sun will rise to-morrow, even though we do not see it; and we are justified in so thinking. Still our only ground for this certainty is that it has done so always before—a fact, to which the universal testimony of mankind bears witness. And we have learned to look upon this as absolutely certain. Still it is only from a comparison of circumstances similar in what, as far as we know, are their essential features that we have arrived at this conclusion.

Probability, therefore, which is the guide of life, is the result of a comparison of things like one another. In proportion as they resemble each other we are justified in expecting similar results. In thus arguing, as we do every day, we are, unconsciously to ourselves, arguing from analogy.

The analogy of religion is the resemblance between *nature,* supposed to be the work of an intelligent Creator, and *religion,* which is asserted to be a revelation from the same source. And, in arguing from one of these to the other, we meet with numerous points of likeness, some more, some less complete. Taken all together they form a powerful chain of argument, amply sufficient to justify men in acting as if religion were absolutely and incontrovertibly true. There will be found to be similarities so great as, taken by themselves, to make the scheme of the Christian religion probable, and extremely *like the truth.* Some points will undoubtedly remain obscure; and we could scarcely expect it to be otherwise in a subject which confessedly deals with matters to a great extent beyond the regions of ordinary experience. But it should be borne in mind that, if religion be even possibly true, it is incomparably the most important practical subject which can present itself. And it is a point of practical prudence not to require, in a practical subject, arguments more convincing than those with which we are willing to be content in matters of less importance.

DIALOGUES

FOUNDED UPON

BUTLER'S ANALOGY.

Part I.

DIALOGUE I.

ON A FUTURE LIFE.

A. I have been, for a long time past, turning over in my own mind the question, Are we immortal beings? It is a point of such vital importance, that I feel there can be no happiness for me until I can resolve my doubts on this matter. I would willingly believe it, if I could. Could I once be satisfied that I am to live after my death, I should feel the cares and trials of this life much more tolerable; but my reason refuses to be persuaded, and the arguments against my immortality seem to be irresistible.

B. I am sorry to hear you speak in this manner, and as I quite agree with you, that the belief which you desire to hold on this subject is of the utmost importance in enabling us to shape our course through life, and is calculated to make the ills of life, when they befall us, much more tolerable, I should very much like to hear what are the difficulties to which you refer. Perhaps, if you will state them to me, I may be able to render you the assistance of my own reflections in resolving some of them. But, before you do so, will you answer me this question?—What kind of conviction do you desire?

A. I should wish to have an absolute certainty upon the matter.

B. When you are called upon to act in a matter of business, do you wait for absolute certainty before you act, or are you satisfied if the reasons for acting in one way are stronger than those which point to the opposite course?

A. I confess that I am usually compelled to be satisfied with the latter.

B. If the matter is one of very vast importance, should you decline to act at all upon such a presumption?

A. No; but at the same time I should be extremely cautious how I decided. I should require stronger inducements to act, in proportion to the importance of the question at issue.

B. Very true; but suppose the question were of this nature. If by adopting one course there were a possibility of your attaining a great advantage, and by adopting the other you would be placed in possession of a very much smaller one, would you not in reason be in a way compelled to adopt the one which promised the greater advantage?

A. Certainly.

B. Now let us suppose two courses of action set before you, and that in neither of them you could attain absolute certainty as to the result; but that the one offered as its possible result incalculable gain, the other enormous loss; if you were compelled to adopt one or the other, and no middle course were open, would you not desire to act upon even a slight probability in favour of the one which promised such extensive advantages, or should you require absolute certainty before you decided to act?

A. Of course, if I saw the least probability in favour of the former course of action, I should unhesitatingly adopt it.

B. So, then, if there is a probability that you are an immortal being, you would live with regard to your immortal existence rather than look only to the immediate present?

A. I should.

B. If, then, I can show you that the objections which are raised against the doctrine of immortality are not so strong, even in a very small degree, as the argument in favour of that doctrine, you would confess yourself compelled to believe yourself immortal?

A. I admit it.

B. We agree, then, that this is a question of probability, even as almost all practical matters are. Will you now tell me why you think that you are not immortal?

A. I see all living things subject to death: plants—animals—men. They live for a certain time; after a certain number of years, or days, or minutes, they cease to flourish. Plants wither, animals lose their faculties of sense and perception, which grow weaker and weaker, and at last vanish altogether. The body ceases to live and decays, and passes away into dust. This appears to be the law of nature. What reason have I for inferring otherwise with respect to myself? If I am to argue from what I see around me—and I know not what else there is from which I may argue—it appears certain to me that, like all other creatures, I must perish at my appointed time.

B. Let me ask you what you mean by "yourself." Do you mean your body, or do you mean something which is not your body, but invisible?

A. It appears to me that I mean both. To identify myself I must take in the idea of both these.

B. Does not science make plain, that the body is in a perpetual state of change and decay? Do not the elementary components of blood and bone continually alter, so much that it has been said, on a rough estimate, that none of the tissues of the body, as it now exists, are the same as they were seven years ago?

A. I believe it is so.

B. Is the body the same as it was seven years ago?

A. It appears not.

B. Are you the same that you were seven years ago?

A. Undoubtedly I am. I know and am sure that I am not some one else.

B. Are you quite sure that you have not been unconsciously changed into another person?

A. I am quite sure of this. I have a complete memory of things which occurred to me in childhood, and I can entirely identify myself with what I was then. I feel indeed that my mind has developed, and that in that sense I am altered from what I was. But while I know that my body has entirely lost its original tissue, I know also that I myself am the same that I always was.

B. Does not this make it evident that, when you speak of yourself, you do not mean your body, but something different from your body, whatever that may be?

A. It seems so.

B. Well, then, bearing in mind that what constitutes each man's self is something different from his body, let us return to the question of a future existence. You say that death, which all creatures undergo, seems to be an end of them. Suppose you had never witnessed a death, or heard of it, I suppose you would not expect to die yourself?

A. Assuredly not.

B. If you had only seen that children grow by degrees into maturity, that they pass from utter helplessness into full vigour, would you say that it was a law of the human race, that the same persons should exist with greatly different powers and capacities of thought, enjoyment, and suffering, at different periods in their life?

A. This is self-evident.

B. And does not the same law extend to

other species? Do we not see grubs turn into butterflies, worms become flies, birds emerge from eggs? And is not the change between the conditions, circumstances, and mode of life, quite as great in some of these cases, as it is possible to imagine?

A. I think it is.

B. Well, then, putting any ideas of death out of the question, would not the order of nature lead us to argue that we too might, and (death being unknown) probably would, live in a state of existence as different from the present as any of those to which we have referred?

A. Perhaps so; I am not sure. Possibly we are now in the last stage of existence, and, like the butterflies of which you speak, shall come to an end as they do.

B. How do you know that they come to an end? That is an assumption. Do you not see that you are now not reasoning, but depending upon your imagination? But you have just now stated that you wished for certainty; and to obtain this you must not allow your imagination to run away with you. But, leaving this, let me ask you another question. If our bodies are not ourselves, what will you dignify with that title?

A. I suppose, the mind.

B. That is so indefinite a word, that I should be glad if you will make it clear what you denote by it.

A. Well, on reflection, I think what I mean by *myself* is that part of me, whatever it is, which leads me to act, and by which I am conscious of happiness or misery.

B. Unfortunately this is still indefinite. Yet I believe you will find it difficult to get a clearer definition. We agree, then, that by our capacities for action, for enjoyment, and for suffering, we are made acquainted with what we call *ourselves.*

A. I grant it.

B. These faculties are ours before death; therefore we shall probably possess them after death.

A. How? By what reasoning will you establish such an extraordinary assertion?

B. It is by no means extraordinary. Why do you suppose the sun will rise to-morrow? Why do you think that to-morrow will be as to-day?

A. Because it has been so, as far as our experience and the records of history convey us; and we are assured that the course of nature is uniform. On this principle only are we justified in believing that anything whatever will continue to exist a moment hence.

B. Most true; and therefore I assert that, because we possess these powers of acting, enjoying, and suffering now, we shall possess them afterwards.

A. But not so surely, if death is the destruction of such powers.

B. You mean, I presume, that it is probable that death is the cause of their destruction, and not that any other cause operates to destroy them at the moment of death?

A. I do not understand.

B. I mean this:—If at death these faculties are destroyed, they are either destroyed by death, or by something else acting at the moment of death. Now, I ask you whether you do not suppose that death itself is the cause of these powers perishing?

A. Of course I mean, that death destroys them.

B. If it could be shown that death certainly was not the agent which destroyed these powers, you would then feel a moral certainty that they would not perish *from any other cause* at death?

A. I should.

B. And, I suppose, if it can be shown that

c

death is *probably* not the destroyer of these faculties, you will consider it *probable* that they will not be annihilated at death?

A. It appears that I must so consider it.

B. Why do you think that these faculties will perish at death?

A. Because at death they cease to exist.

B. Pardon me; you should add, "as far as I can see."

A. Of course I intended to convey that idea.

B. But you must recollect that most people would understand you to mean that, because you could not perceive them to operate, you were therefore certain that they had perished. Now, what is death? All that you know about it is that body, flesh, and bones disappear, and are resolved into their constituent elements. But is this any proof whatever that the faculties of the mind are *destroyed?*

A. I certainly thought it to be such.

B. Not unless you mean to assert that the power of willing and of acting, and the capacity of enjoyment and suffering, have their origin simply and solely in these portions of elementary matter so curiously compacted together, which we call the *body*. I am perfectly aware that there are people—and those, too, men of learning and judgment—who profess to hold this opinion. It is not difficult to understand the principle upon which they are led to argue in this manner; but it is difficult—almost inexplicable indeed—to understand how they can allow themselves to be convinced by such arguments. The principle upon which their reasoning proceeds is simply this:—Whatever knowledge the senses convey to them is capable of being tested experimentally: with more or less of certainty, the information so acquired can be tested and reduced to general laws. That which impresses the senses is *matter;* sometimes solid and easy to be perceived; sometimes so refined, that the most delicate instruments are required to assist the senses in perceiving it. And hence it is concluded, that as the effects of matter, before the discovery of its qualities and hidden operations, were falsely attributed to some supernatural agency, so now matter, and matter only, is the agent by which all effects are produced; that the most refined thoughts, the most devoted and generous actions, are simply identical with certain operations of matter; that though this matter appears in many cases to be quite unconscious, yet if it be skilfully arranged, and mingled in proper proportions, it will by such chemical combination become conscious; and that, as the various elements are more elaborately and curiously compounded, additional degrees of consciousness will of themselves arise. Further than this, as the minuteness and complexity of the structure increases, this consciousness increases also. First, there is total insensibility, without animation or life of any kind; then, comes something which we call *life*, which consists only in the capacity of growing; then, as the complexity of the structure is increased, we discern a power of *motion*; at another stage, motion is developed into a faculty of *perceiving* outward objects, and receiving pleasure and pain from them; in the next place this complex arrangement of elements, without sense, acquires a power of distinguishing for itself what is likely to give it pain or pleasure, and of avoiding or seeking this; and, finally, it is developed into a being which not only compares and chooses, but is capable of loving and hating, of enduring sufferings, not because they are necessary, but because it appears to be right to endure them; it acquires, by a power inherent in itself, an admiration for certain things which it calls honourable, or beautiful, or virtuous. And these things must in themselves be certain forms of matter; because, if there is nothing else but matter, it is idle to talk of these ideas being anything else but that which alone exists, viz., matter. So that will, emotion, desire, are nothing else but forms of matter. If matter is the only thing which exists, there can be no ideas which are not derived from forms of matter. Now, the principle upon which this reasoning proceeded was, as you remember, that nothing is to be believed which cannot experimentally be proved. But the great test of experimental knowledge is that, in some degree, at all events, the laws which have been deduced by observation should be capable of being applied to produce similar results. Has science been able, in any—the smallest—degree, to produce results at all justifying these conclusions? Is there an instance of life or motion, much less of thought or feeling, and still less of any moral qualities, having been produced by the aggregation or putting together of elements? If not, we are just in this position, that we may as reasonably suppose such phenomena to be the result of agencies totally unlike those which we call material, as that they are produced by matter acting, we know not how, upon itself. But this is a distinct question by itself; and, though it must be decided on its own merits, we will, with your leave, pass it by for the present, in the hope of reverting to it at another time. This, I am led to expect, you will allow me to do, because your difficulty, as I understood it, was not whether you had a soul, but whether that soul was immortal, or likely to live after the death of your body. Was it not so?

A. It was so. Still, the point on which you have touched is one of such moment, that I shall hold you to your promise of reverting to it.

B. I will not fail you. For the present, however, the issue is this:—Granting that soul and body are distinct, is there any presumption that, when the body ceases to live, the soul ceases to be conscious? You have stated it as your belief that, if the soul does perish, its destruction must be the direct result of death, and not of anything else which accompanies death. Will you tell me what you imagine death to be?

A. It is an unknown something, under the influence of which the power of motion ceases, warmth quits the body, the limbs and members cease to be conscious, and after a while decay ensues.

B. An unknown something! Is that your definition of death? You will not, I presume, object to my changing the order of the words, and calling it " something unknown "?

A. By all means, if you please.

B. Can you tell me what it is that gives us the power of feeling, thinking, and acting?

A. I fear that I am quite in the dark on this point.

B. Can you inform me upon what the power of exercising these faculties depends?

A. I do not think I can.

B. If you saw a stone at rest, would you say that it could not be moved?

A. No; because I know that it could be moved.

B. If it were to lie at rest, and be worn away by the rain and wind and the various influences of the atmosphere, and never move from its place till it were dissolved into dust, would you feel justified in saying that it never could be moved? or could you assert that, because it was firmly fixed on its foundation, the power which could move it had ceased to exist?

A. No; I could only say it was not in operation.

B. Now consider the case of death. It is something unknown, as you have stated. When, therefore, you see a body deprived of motion, animation, and consciousness, all that you can assert is, that that which had given it these faculties or powers was in abeyance. In the case of a swoon there is a temporary cessation of these agencies. In the case of death the cessation is perpetual, as far as you know. But, after all, you have only arrived at this: that the cause of these faculties has ceased to *act*. You have no right to assume that it has ceased to *exist*, unless indeed you are willing to be satisfied with the following form of reasoning: that something unknown, viz., death, has annihilated something else unknown, viz., the cause of sensation, action, and thought; which would be to me a most strange and unsatisfactory solution of the difficulty.

A. I fear you are quibbling and playing with words. If your argument is valid, it leads to the conclusion that I can know nothing at all about the matter.

B. Perhaps it does. It seems, at all events, to point to this: that arguments, based upon experiment or observation, are not of any value to prove or disprove things which are not subject to either form of inquiry. And the nature of death is a question of this kind.

A. But may we not argue from observation as to the effect of death?

B. Certainly, if you can find any basis of comparison between the sensible world and the matter in question. But, try as you will, you will find yourself utterly foiled in establishing your argument, that death destroys the faculties of living beings. That your senses fail to detect their operation is true; but it is a pure assumption that they cease to exist because you cannot detect them. If you say it is *impossible* they should exist, that is an assertion which you cannot substantiate. If you say that they do not exist, because you cannot perceive them, you are making the same kind of assertion as if you were to declare that the planets are not inhabited because you cannot see living creatures moving in them. Perhaps the planets are not inhabited, but the proof of this depends upon arguments very different in their nature from this mere assertion: physical laws may compel us to admit this to be the case; but no physical laws can apply to that of which we confessedly know nothing.

A. There appears to be something in what you say.

B. And, moreover, if you wish to apply the argument from observation, it will lead to this: the wonderful development of the powers of the mind which we observe, and which is frequently not attended with correlative development of the body, would lead us to infer that possibly our powers may be capable of a further development in another existence, when the body which, through its weakness, is more frequently a hindrance than an aid, has been removed, or changed and transformed into a more glorious condition.

I dare not at present add to what I have said an argument which to me seems the strongest of all, but which to you would carry no weight. I think I can trace signs of foresight and design in the works of nature, and, though I cannot expect you to admit it, yet I will put it hypothetically. Suppose there were design in the universe, and that all the apparent coincidences which even you cannot deny, by which this notion is strengthened in my mind, were really proofs of design, then it would be quite reasonable to infer that, as we have gone through great changes and developments hitherto, and are yet, even the wisest of us, far from having attained to the highest possible perfection, so we may probably continue to advance after our bodies have lost their powers of sensation.

A. I cannot deny your inference, whatever I may think of your hypothesis.

B. Let us proceed to some other considerations. What do you mean by destruction?

A. I mean the separation of something compounded into its elements. Thus, when water is decomposed into its constituent gases, I say that water is destroyed.

B. Could you destroy those constituent elements?

A. No: they are proved to be indestructible, being simple elements.

B. So, then, that which is uncompounded is indestructible. Is our consciousness simple or compound?

A. I cannot tell what you mean.

B. Can we suppose that what we call "ourselves" should be part of it here and part elsewhere? Can part of our proper selves be in London and part in New York?

A. That is impossible: for, if it were, we might have different ideas, diametrically opposed, at the same time.

B. Our consciousness seems, therefore, to be indivisible; hence, by the argument, it is indestructible. Our bodies may cease to be actuated by it, but it cannot be destroyed.

A. This appears to be an old-fashioned metaphysical argument, and carries no conviction to my mind.

B. I did not expect it to convince you. Still it is an argument of some kind or other, be the value of it as small as you please. And, if it be true, it will follow that the body, which can be broken up and destroyed—which is, in fact, perpetually being resolved into elements, while we ourselves are, to say the least, unconscious of any change in our powers of perception and of action—is only a portion of matter, incapable of action except it be united with a living and conscious power. That power appears to belong to some impalpable being, which we call "ourselves," and which, as far as we can judge at all about it, appears to be simple, and therefore indestructible. And the connexion between the body and this unknown and invisible existence, though it is more intimate, is no more *necessary* than is my connexion with the chair upon which I sit. If I stand up I am no longer connected with the chair. And if my limbs cease to act and to obey my will, or even to be under its influence at all, the most that can be said with certainty is that the connexion between the will which moves and the body which is moved exists no longer.

A. If you are right, science is wrong, and misleads its followers.

B. Not so in the least. Follow scientific processes, and you will arrive at scientific results. Bring imagination into play, as those most assuredly do who perceive in the motion of a muscle or a fibre the reality of a thought and an emotion, and you destroy science by the abuse of its processes. All that I ask of you at present is not to deny the possibility of mind and matter being distinct, and to see how the results thence deduced receive any light from the rest of nature.

A. I will endeavour to do so; but still I wish you would furnish me with some more special reasons for admitting so much as I here concede.

B. Supposing that each man's "self" is material, how large do you think that portion of matter, which constitutes that "self," will be?

A. I cannot possibly tell.

B. You cannot, I presume, then, possibly tell whether it is larger than the chemical atoms, which Dalton's law assumes to exist?

A. I cannot.

B. Can you tell where it is seated?

A. I cannot.

B. Is it in the brain or the heart? for it would seem it might be in either, because an injury to either destroys the evidence of its existence, and therefore in your view destroys its actual existence.

A. It would appear that it resides in both.

B. It must be a very large portion of matter, then?

A. Of course it is: it is the whole human body.

B. Pardon me, it cannot be that; because we know a large portion of the body may perish, as arms and legs, and yet the man's self be unaltered.

A. I was mistaken; it is the vital organs.

B. Literally translated, that is, the organs which contain life. I can only admire the ingenuousness of the definition, "Life exists in those members wherein life resides." But, though your logic is not good, I will pass it by. Tell me in what organs our life resides; for, though life is not altogether to my mind synonymous with consciousness—for, as far as we can perceive, life may exist without the consciousness of individual existence—still it will be something to learn in what part of us life resides, and how large ourself, supposed a portion of matter, must really be. To make the reasoning clearer, tell me, Is all the heart necessary for life? If it is a vital organ, then by what you have just said it must be.

A. In one sense it is necessary that the heart should be entire in order that life should exist, for I am not aware that life has been discovered in any vertebrate animal of which a portion of the heart is destroyed. But, on the other hand, I cannot deny that some portion of the heart may become inoperative, and yet the reason and the will be unimpaired.

B. Am I to understand that some portion of the heart is more necessary to life than the others?

A. Assuredly.

B. Well, then, as we have been compelled to give up some portion of the body as not necessary to consciousness, such as the limbs, so now we must allow that some portion of the heart is not absolutely requisite. I mean that we might conceive a person existing and thinking without the operation of some portion of his heart, and that, were it possible to remove that inoperative portion, still existence would continue.

A. We might conceive it to be so.

B. Might we also imagine the heart to be uninjured, and yet consciousness not to exist?

A. We have no need to imagine it, it is the case; for death may arise and yet the heart be entire and free from disease.

B. Then surely the principle of life does not reside in the heart. I suppose that we must look for it elsewhere. Is it situate in the brain?

A. I think it is. At all events, if the brain be injured, consciousness ceases.

B. Will injury to every part of the brain destroy consciousness?

A. No; but injury to some part of it will have that effect.

B. Well, then, that portion must, according to your idea, be the "self" for which we are seeking.

A. On reflection I cannot admit that; for death may come and yet the brain remain intact.

B. If, then, neither heart nor brain is the sole seat of life, it will be found to reside in both, so that the self, regarded as a material being, is placed in at least two portions of the frame. If that is the case, the indivisible self is made up of divisible elements; and these two portions of the self are as distinctly separate, as if one were at New York and the other in London. How comes it that they are never at variance?

A. Because they always, during life, naturally operate upon one another.

B. And what causes them so to affect each other? This action must necessarily proceed from one to the other.

A. Not so: they act simultaneously.

B. If I understand you aright, consciousness is a function of both these. Will you inform me what you mean by a function?

A. I mean a necessary action pervading them both.

B. Do you not see that you have introduced another factor, if I may speak mathematically, and that factor is, after all, the point in dispute, viz., life? It is a "tertium quid," at once the result and the cause of the action of the various portions of the organism; so that, you have only pushed the inquiry a stage back, and are again involved in the same difficulty, viz., that life is the result of an agency, of which you can examine the results, but cannot define the nature. However, suppose you were able to analyze the organism completely, and at last, by a process of exclusion, discovered that life depended upon a single element—an uncompounded cell—what proof have you that that cell—a particle so minute that the most powerful microscope was unable to detect it—ever loses its consciousness? For anything you know, it may exist and think, and have a power of willing when the rest of the body is reduced to dust.

A. It may possibly do so.

B. But let us leave this, and proceed to more

positive arguments. We have seen that very much of our bodies may be destroyed and yet our consciousness be unimpaired. Why should we not argue that all of the matter of our body may be destroyed in like manner, and yet consciousness remain? It is only following out an argument supplied to us by experience. Let me ask you what you suppose the sense of sight to consist in? Is it your eye which sees?

A. No: my eye is only a complex lens so arranged as to transmit rays of light.

B. In other words, your eye is an instrument by which you see. Similarly, your tongue is an instrument by which you taste; your fingers instruments by which you feel; your legs instruments by which you pass from place to place. If you lost a leg, you could supply its place by an artificial one. Is it not possible that, if our knowledge were more extended, other artificial instruments might be given us to supply the natural members by which the various functions of the body are performed? The truly marvellous inventions of science lead to such a conclusion. This makes it plain that a great portion of our bodies is only adventitious matter, useful to us for various purposes, but by no means absolutely necessary for us.

A. You are drawing inferences too hastily. It is quite true that, in the act of seeing, our eyes serve only as lenses, by which we are made acquainted with the existence of external matter; but it is by no means clear that artificial glasses could serve us in the place of eyes.

B. It is by no means necessary to my argument that this should be proved; all that I intend is that, *so far as we are able to trace* the action of our senses, the various members serve us as instruments which present external objects to our powers of perception. As far as we can see, there is no ground whatever for imagining that the members of our body perceive, in any other way than it may be said, that glasses, which make clear objects otherwise obscure, perceive. A telescope reveals to us the existence of stars, of which we know nothing by unassisted vision, and a microscope opens our gaze to a world which is absolutely concealed from natural eyesight. And these are only instances of matter external to us, affording knowledge of that which is concealed from us. Suppose that a man born with unimpaired vision loses it afterwards, that does not deprive him of his consciousness, even though it prevents him from acquiring any further knowledge of the external world by the organs of vision. You must bear in mind that we are not arguing to prove that our body is unnecessary for the acquisition of knowledge, but only to show that the body is not the individual "self" which constitutes the reality of our existence.

A. But still, if you deprive a man of the members of his body, he ceases to be possessed of the faculties which those members impart.

B. Even there I think you are mistaken. What do you say of the phenomena of dreams, in which a man is often, in imagination, re-instated in the possession of those faculties which he has lost? This is a plain proof that the power of consciousness is not dependent upon the actual possession of the limbs and members by which he has gained his knowledge of external things.

A. This does, in truth, seem to be an argument of some weight.

B. Again, the power of willing, which is the distinctive possession of reasonable beings, does not in any sense depend upon the possession of limbs and members. A man with an artificial leg, properly adapted, is able to move it, though it is only dead matter, and entirely devoid of any power of willing. And so, just as a microscope and a stick are instruments, which we employ for the exercise of our will, the body and its members are likewise instruments, useful for the attainment of the objects of our choice. And there is no more reason to consider the one as constituent elements of our consciousness than the other.

A. But, granting this, I should infer from it a result which you would not be willing to concede. If these arguments lead us to conclude that we are immortal, we must also allow that the lower animals, who are possessed of like members, are also immortal and capable of eternal happiness, for there is nothing here asserted, which will not hold equally true of other animals besides man.

B. Your objection does not appear to me to be any difficulty. If by immortality you mean simply a future existence, then I reply that neither you nor I are competent to decide whether, in another stage of existence, it might not be in accordance with the economy of nature that there should exist creatures possessing faculties such as those which the brutes now possess, without any capacity for rational and moral action ; in other words, without any consciousness of right and wrong, of what is just, holy, and pure. If, on the other hand, you mean to imply that the brutes would, in a future existence, have to develope into rational and moral agents, then I answer that you cannot tell what latent powers brutes are possessed of. You have no ground whatever for assuming that the lower animals might not develope into higher forms of activity. Your own science declares—without sufficient grounds, I think, for the assertion—still it declares that such a development is possible. A child exhibits fewer symptoms of reason than some of the maturer animals, and yet, if it live long enough, it will, in all probability, attain to the possession of faculties, quite incommensurate with its attainments in infancy. As a general rule, it is placed for years in a position where its possible development in virtue and religion receives little stimulus; a large portion of the human race actually die without having had an opportunity of exercising their faculties in this respect at all. It is therefore absurd to argue from experience that animals may not live after their death, and develope to degrees inconceivable to us. And it is still more nugatory to employ such an argument to disprove the possibility of human beings living after their death.

A. I am willing to allow that the objection was inconsiderately urged.

B. I will forgive you, and, in return for your candour, I will waive the "argumentum ad verecundiam" which I have urged. Suppose that there were something in your objection, it will not apply to the following considerations. Can you not distinguish in man any qualities not shared by the brutes?

A. Yes; I think I can. The brutes seem to live by the senses and for the senses. They seem to exist purely in a state of sensation, being guided by their external senses, and apparently incapable of any other emotions. But man, though he, too, lives by sensation, possesses also faculties of thought and reflection. When the senses have conveyed impressions to him, he appears to be capable of reflecting and pondering upon the knowledge thus acquired, without any reference to the means by which he gained it. He seems to be able to abstract himself from the things of sense, and to be capable of deriving the most profound enjoyment from the contemplation of impressions, which are not sensations, but have been transformed into realities away from the region of the senses.

B. Is there any proof or ground to suppose that the dissolution of our body is in any way connected with a corresponding destruction in our power of reflection? Are there not instances of men, afflicted with a mortal disease, who, in the very instant preceding death, are known to be in possession of these powers to their fullest extent? And as it has been shown that we cannot argue from the relation between the body and conscious principle, that the destruction of the one involves the annihilation of the other, so we have reason to infer that, if the faculties of reflection are unimpared, even in the very instant preceding dissolution, they will probably remain unaffected in the instant succeeding death. There are cases when we might suppose that the reflective powers were ceasing to exist, as when men pass through stages of drowsiness to a deep sleep, wherein all the conscious faculties appear suspended; but they revive when sleep departs, and hence experience teaches us to reject our first impressions. But here we have instances of their continuing in full energy up to the moment of death; and, therefore, *à fortiori*, we have no ground to believe them destroyed by death. For what reason have we to imagine that the reflective powers are destroyed, when, in the very moment preceding death, men act and think and speak,—when their affections are in full play,—they are able to discern character, and take a deep interest in the topics which occupy the thoughts of those about them? when, even to the last gasp, they are capable of the highest mental enjoyment and suffering; feelings of so intense a character that they are a far stronger evidence of life than any amount of bodily strength can possibly be. Why are we to suppose that any disease will destroy the reflective powers, when progressive disorders, such as we refer to, do not in the least impair them up to the moment when they become mortal?

A. But, even if it do not destroy them, it will surely suspend them.

B. There is not the least presumption that it will do so. The very fact of their existing in full vigour up to a time when the body is on the point of losing all sensation (as in the case of Socrates, a large portion of whose body was actually dead, while his mind was intensely active; and in that of others, especially those who die of diseased heart), is a presumption that they may continue to be in unimpeded activity after sensation has ceased. Thus death may supervene, and yet the mental energies continue to be exercised. If, then, experience cannot render us any reason for supposing that the fact of death necessarily affects our powers of reflection, in the same way as it seems to affect our powers of sensation, and if there are instances of fatal diseases reaching a climax, and yet not affecting in any degree the mental activities, we have a presumption, that death and the annihilation of our reflective powers are not identical; we have also a probability that those powers are not even impeded; that they continue in full energy, irrespective of the operation of death upon the material frame.

And now I will ask you to pardon me, if I follow out these reflections a little further. It may seem to you that in what I am about to say, I am transgressing my own canon about yielding to imagination. The subsequent course of our inquiry, if you will have patience to follow it out, will, however, justify my inferences.

Death may be to our present existence what our birth into this world is to our state of being previous to our birth. It may be a continuation and a development of our present life. Just as our birth introduces us into a higher and more advanced state of life, so it is possible that, when death comes upon us, we may find ourselves released from various circumstances, which hinder our progress in knowledge and wisdom. The conditions of our existence here, its wants and necessities, form a material check upon our progress. We are limited in the sphere of our activity; we are compelled to minister to the cravings of our body; we are subject to weariness and distress and sorrow. These may possibly be altogether removed, and all that impedes us here may then be cleared away. The beauty of the outward form indeed decays, just as the delicate fibres and gorgeous clothing of the flowers of the field pass away. But the analogy between the two here ceases, for the flowers possess, so far as we can see, no powers of will and perception; and this, which is the especial attribute of man, renders the supposed analogy between the flowers and him imperfect. The ground of all our argument is, that we have capacities of perception and of action which they do not enjoy; and these, as we have seen, are, as far as we can judge, not necessarily affected by death.

In our present life we live in society; we may possibly do so after death. The advantages which we here enjoy, depend in a great measure upon the capricious action and opinion of society. It may, perhaps, be the blessing of a future state to exist in the immediate presence of the Highest Intelligence, and to derive our happiness from Him; yet that happiness may come to us in a way altogether as natural as it does now. The laws which regulate our existence now are natural; but who shall say that they are the whole of nature? The laws of nature are only partially known to us. There are conditions of existence in the world which were unknown before the invention of the microscope; there are probably others affecting millions of creatures which our senses fail to detect. And it is as probable that there are conditions of existence in higher spheres undetected by us, as it is that there are planets which we cannot perceive. Unless we are ready to deny the latter, we have no right to question the former. And since the improbability of the existence of minute forms of life, before the invention of the microscope, is now seen to have been no valid argument against their existence, so our ignorance of the existence of higher beings than man is no ground for assuming that none such exist. And these higher beings may correspond to what man becomes after death. A veil may be removed from their eyes, and they may see clearly things which to us are obscure; they may apprehend the reasons of things which to us are unintelligible; they may have a comprehensive faculty of knowledge denied to us. And when we consider how infinite is the ignorance of the wisest men, how in proportion to the scope of their knowledge they are ready to confess its limitation, this probability becomes greatly increased.

Thus I have endeavoured to remove one stumbling-block which stands upon the very threshold of religion. The doctrine of a future life is a fundamental one; without it religion is inconceivable. The arguments which I have urged are by no means demonstrative, but still they may serve to show that a future existence is not only not impossible—that it is even probable.

A. You say one stumbling-block: are there others?

B. There are indeed. We may be immortal, and yet not accountable beings; we may live now and hereafter, and yet that existence may be conceived to impose upon us no duties or obligations. Our future life may be imagined as in no sense depending for good or evil upon the present. Without a belief in immortality, no man would be religious; but men may believe that they are never to be annihilated, and yet pass careless, wretched, and godless lives. If you are inclined to continue our conversation, I shall endeavour to prove by similar arguments that the essential doctrines of the Christian religion are in accordance with the analogy of nature, and that the supposed conclusive proofs against them will tell as strongly against that visible course of nature, which our eyes perceive and of which we can have no doubt.

DIALOGUE II.

ON REWARDS AND PUNISHMENTS.

A. After much careful thought upon our last conversation I am constrained to admit that you have made out a probable case for a future existence. But here a difficulty occurs. You seem to assert that that future existence will be a continuation of the present. If so, I should infer that we shall go on thinking, gaining experience, and changing as we do now. But religion asserts that we shall in that future life receive reward and punishment for what we have done in our life on earth. This I cannot believe.

B. Why can you not believe it?

A. Because God is a merciful and good Being; and how can such a Being inflict misery upon His creatures?

B. If I understand you, you find a difficulty in believing that God will punish any one?

A. Certainly.

B. Do you see that that implies that He will not reward any one?

A. Pardon me: it is quite consistent with my idea of God that He should reward, but not that He should punish.

B. The idea of rewarding implies that actions are requited according to their deserts. Does it not?

A. It does.

B. Do all actions in this life deserve reward?

A. Certainly not. A murderer or a thief deserves punishment.

B. On what ground?

A. Because he does wrong.

B. "Wrong" is a very indefinite word. Will you define your meaning?

A. Well, then, because he injures society.

B. Surely, then, if those who injure society deserve punishment from society, those who offend against the law of Infinite Goodness deserve punishment from Infinite Goodness?

A. They may deserve it; but I cannot reconcile it with the idea of Infinite Mercy that it should inflict punishment.

B. I am afraid we are dealing with abstract arguments, and we agreed only to be guided by facts.

A. But can you find any facts to help us?

B. Let us try. You allow that there is a Creator of all things?

A. Yes: that I have already conceded.

B. He is the Creator of men, and of the conditions under which they exist.

A. He is.

B. Here, then, is a fact. A child is born into the world; as he grows he gains knowledge and experience; and among the objects presented to his experience is, we will say, fire. What does he learn about fire?

A. That it will warm him if he is at a safe distance from it, and that it will burn him if he goes too close to it.

B. Suppose he puts his hand into a candle, what happens?

A. Of course he suffers pain and is injured.

B. That is, the pain is a natural consequence of his action. Suppose I say pain is the punishment attached to such an action: should you object to the word?

A. Certainly: it is only a natural consequence.

B. A natural consequence! Do you mean a consequence imposed by nature?

A. Yes: it is the same thing.

B. And what do you understand by nature?

A. I mean, that series of events of which our senses and other faculties inform us.

B. And what gives to nature its laws? Are they self-imposed?

A. They are inherent in nature.

B. What makes them inherent in nature?

A. Nature herself.

B. So, then, nature is personified. Matter, I imagine, made itself, and imposed laws upon itself.

A. I see you are laughing at me.

B. Indeed I am not. I never was less inclined to laugh. I am only trying to interpret your meaning. We must go back to experience. Have you ever thought of what you mean by a law? To me a law seems to imply a lawgiver. If I take any law, such as gravitation for example, I cannot conceive of it otherwise than as universally imposed upon nature, and implying an intention. All matter, as it seems to me, was *intended* to be subject to this law. Uniformity, so far from implying an absence of mind, seems to imply the action of a mind. Of course you may say it does not; but, so far as my experience extends, I know of no activity which does not originate in a mind; and those who assert that it may perhaps not so originate, assert simply a theory based upon no facts of experience. But this we agreed was not a scientific process.

A. We did.

B. Law, then, is a creation of mind.

A. On second thoughts I think I see a fallacy in your argument. A law of nature is only the expression of the fact that certain consequences are always found connected with certain antecedents. Thus I assert that it is a law of nature that a stone falling from the hand will, unless impeded, go in a straight line towards the centre of the earth. By this I mean that in all *observed cases* it is found to be so, and nothing more.

B. Very well. Now, if I assert that, on a certain day not recorded in history, it was observed that stones *fell upward*, and away from the earth, what will you say?

A. I should at once deny the fact, and say you could not prove your words.

B. Well, I will content myself with saying that they *will* fall upward to-morrow.

A. And I with saying that they will *not*.

B. On what ground will you deny the possibility?

A. Because nature acts uniformly.

B. How do you know that?

A. By experience. Such a fact as you predict never has happened, and therefore never will happen.

B. Observe, now. Experience might possibly have assured you that it never had happened; but that it never will happen is a truth which, though true, depends upon an act of *faith*. Do not start at the word. It is precisely an act of faith to believe that nature will act uniformly; just as much an act of faith as to believe that, because there appears to be *design* in nature, there is really design. In each case you have an act of faith, superinduced upon experience.

A. But, supposing this to be so, how does it tell upon our argument?

B. In two ways. First, it proves that the idea of Law is not simply what you assert, an aggregation of experiences. It is that and something else. Secondly, it shows that to refuse to see design, where design appears to exist, would be a mode of action which would make it impossible to hold the belief that nature is uniform in its operations.

A. But are there not instances in which it is impossible to trace design?

B. Perhaps there are, at least with our present faculties. But are there not also instances in which the uniformity of nature seems to be infringed?

A. Yes; but greater knowledge of nature explains those apparent anomalies.

B. And in the same way a fuller knowledge of the will of the designer will probably explain anomalies in the sphere of design. It is true that, in dealing with the impalpable facts of *mind*, we are less aided by our senses than in reasoning upon the palpable facts of what we call *nature*. But the same reasoning which excludes design, viz., apparent instances of the absence of it, would logically forbid you to believe in uniformity.

Now, I say that, seeing how many apparent instances there are of design, and seeing that, so far as our experience of action goes, it always proceeds from a will, we have a right to assert that all nature is regulated by a will.

A. And what follows?

B. This: that, when we see a result following upon an antecedent, we have a right to assume that that result is purposely attached to that antecedent; and that where pleasure or pain follow any action, they were intended to mark that that action should be practised or foregone. These pains and pleasures are natural punishments and rewards.

A. But in the case of human laws we see pains and penalties attached to the laws, and inflicted individually by the judge; whereas this idea of yours, of natural rewards and punishments, seems to exclude the idea of a judge, and thus loses the special characteristic of law. If, indeed, when a man did wrong, fire came down from heaven and burnt up the offender, there would be something in it; but in these cases the punishment appears to be irrational, the administration of it unfair, falling alike upon the innocent and the guilty, on the ignorant as well as on those who know the consequences of their actions.

B. You say the punishments and (to supply the correlative idea) the rewards are irrational. You mean, I presume, that you do not see the judge, or that no person appears in these cases?

A. That is what I mean.

B. Now, I will ask you to attend to this. Do you consider it essential to human laws that they should be executed by a judge?

A. I certainly do.

B. But suppose a legislator established a code of laws, with rewards and punishments attached, should you consider that the nature of law would be excluded, if he so contrived that the laws should execute themselves? Would it be a proof that the legislator did not intend the rewards and punishments to be inflicted, if they actually inflicted themselves without the intervention of a judge?

A. Well, I confess I should think it an instance of extraordinary wisdom and forethought on the part of the legislator, and a remarkably simple method of procedure.

B. Well, this wisdom, forethought, and simplicity of operation we attribute to God, when we assert that He has so created the universe as, by its ordinary course, to work out His will in rewarding and punishing.

A. But is it not, sometimes at least, an unjust proceeding? Does it not occasionally punish the innocent and reward the guilty?

B. No doubt there are difficulties connected with the material universe which we cannot explain. But these perhaps may receive some alleviation if we consider how very little we really know of the tendencies of things. They may further be resolved by the consideration, that, if God has chosen to rule the world by general laws, it would involve an inconsistency in our ideas of Him to expect Him to be constantly rescinding those general laws by special interference, to say nothing of the fact that men would soon come to think little of the laws, and to look constantly for intervention on their special behalf; and thus the orderly scheme of nature would pass away into a series of Divine interpositions. And, further, we must recall to mind that we have agreed to be guided by the balance of probabilities, and not to withhold our assent because everything is not made clear to us.

A. In this, at least, you are right. I do believe that, in the great majority of cases, the laws of nature do not act unjustly; and for the others I am bound to waive the difficulty which I have raised. Will you proceed?

B. Let us turn from purely material questions, such as the purposes for which fire is intended, to what after all concerns us much more nearly, I mean moral questions. Now, my assertion is that, in this sphere, we have ample reason to argue from *present* to *future* rewards and punishments. At the commencement of the discussion you waived the question of rewards, and only took objection to the punishments. Now, let us take a glance at human life. Do you think that most of our *enjoyments*, and much at least of our *sufferings*, depend upon ourselves?

A. No one but a necessarian of the most unpractical type would deny this. I do indeed know of men—and those Christians, as well as others—who say that we have no power to do or to forego any one of our actions. But, for my own part, I feel that I have capacities for foreseeing the future, and a power over my will, which, taken together, place my happiness and misery in this life very much in my own power.

B. Is this freedom and foresight sufficient to form a guide to your life?

A. Amply sufficient.

B. Suppose you knew that a certain course of action would perhaps end in misfortune, what, as a prudent man, would you do?

A. I should avoid it.

B. On what grounds?

A. Because I should feel that the pain was attached to the action, in order that I might avoid it.

B. Attached! By whom?

A. By nature.

B. Again that very ambiguous word!

A. It was an inadvertence; by the Creator.

B. So be it. And is not pain of the nature of a punishment?

A. It is.

B. And pleasure of the nature of a reward?

A. Assuredly.

B. So, then, if in our lives here we find that certain actions bring pleasure, and certain others, pain, as their foreseen consequence, we are quite justified in asserting, that in this world, at least, the God of nature rewards and punishes men according as they obey or disobey the laws of His creation, according as they attend to the index which He has given them of His will.

A. It seems so.

B. This is a proof that God not only dispenses pleasures and pains, but rewards and punishes actions. God, therefore, is presented to us by His creation as a governor; that is, One Who rewards and punishes. But, if He does so now, what is there incredible in the idea that He will do so afterwards? Why should we make God inconsistent? Why should we divide His attributes? Why should we say that a God of mercy cannot or will not (for it is the same thing) punish men *hereafter*, when the whole course of the world proclaims that He does so *now?*

A. Still I cannot but feel that the idea of goodness implies a desire for the happiness of His creatures.

B. Far be it from us to deny so beautiful a conception. In the same way a good man desires the happiness of all about him, and, so far as lies in his power, affords the means. But we know this, that, in spite of that beneficent desire, men will turn what is intended for their good into evil. They will be selfish, and cheat, and defraud, and be jealous of one another. And mark this:—If man be a free agent—if he be not such as those, of whom you lately spoke, would (contrary to their own consciousness) make him—a mere machine—the idea of the goodness of God can only imply this: that God wills man's happiness; that He gives him the means and the faculties for happiness; that He supplies him with warnings and natural restraints, to keep him in the right course; but that if, in spite of all this, he chooses to defy God's law, then, just as when he defies the powers of nature, he is ground to powder—so in this case, he will bring upon himself the consequences which the opposition to the law of righteousness involves.

A. It is an awful idea, and, I confess, somewhat differently expressed from the views which I often have heard, of an angry and revengeful God, delighting in the punishment of the wicked.

B. Ah! my friend, how often has the truth suffered from some ill-judged and unwary expression! It is, indeed, too common to hear this repulsive representation of a revengeful God held up before the minds of men. But, remember that the idea of a God of goodness implies that He is of too pure eyes to behold iniquity. What if it be not He, but ourselves, who by our own act exclude ourselves from His presence? Is that conception a whit less awful or appalling than those coarser representations of God's vengeance, with which in ruder times, or to ruder minds, the preachers of righteousness have endeavoured to recall the vicious from their ways? But, pardon me for thus digressing. I see you have further difficulties yet to solve.

A. I have indeed: a difficulty so tremendous, that I fear, lest every argument will fail to resolve it. The punishment of sin after this life is declared by religion to be final. Is it possible that, where infinite mercy is an attribute of God, it can ever be His will to inflict perpetual punishment upon His creatures?

B. It is, indeed, an awful thought; and I, like you, have often desired that I could believe otherwise. I have often pondered over the passages in which the word "eternal" is used of punishment, and have tried to extract a less dreadful meaning from them; but, alas! if punishment is not eternal, neither is happiness. The two stand or fall together. Still, we may bear in mind that, if the certainty of immediate punishment is not sufficient to deter men from crimes—if the probability of pain in this life is not enough to keep men from incurring it—it may be that, as their sense of goodness becomes dulled, and perhaps obliterated, the actual condition of misery will be insufficient to bring about repentance. There *may* be a condition in which truth and the soul have become actual strangers. But these are only surmises. Let us again see if, in the course of nature, there are no analogies to help us towards the solution of this awful question.

A. What analogy can there be between time and eternity?

B. None, perhaps; but the question of *finality* may perhaps assist us.

A. What do you mean by finality?

B. I mean a condition in which no repentance avails.

A. But is there such a condition?

B. Assuredly there is. Consider this:—Do we not know of cases where men pursue a course of crime? For these crimes they know that there is a probability of suffering: still they practise them. The days go on. No punishment, or apparently but little, follows. They are intemperate, or live impure lives, or allow their passions to master them. And the more they continue so to act, the less do they fear the consequences. Suddenly and in a moment the punishment comes. A blighted life, ruined health, and irremediable misery is their lot. They may repent and be truly sorry; but there is the punishment, in spite of remorse —fixed, perpetual, and intense. What is this but, so far as this life goes, finality of punishment?

A. This is, indeed, a sad truth gathered from experience. But then these punishments, though terribly severe, are not disproportionate to the offences.

B. Are they not? What will you say, then, to those instances where these punishments follow upon offences committed in the days of youth, before the judgment is matured, or experience of the course of nature has assured men of the possible consequences of their actions?

A. They do seem disproportionate.

B. And yet they occur; experience proves it. And such cases are intensely mysterious; and I would add that no explanation can solve the mystery of punishment. But this I say, that, looking upon this as a practical question, it is only reasonable to expect that, if only out of mere prudence, men avoid actions which they are told, upon the authority of others, involve terrible and irremediable punishments as their results, they will be equally careful to avoid actions which may possibly affect their happiness for ever.

A. Ah! you are treating this as a practical question; but mine was really a speculative difficulty. You have indeed afforded me reasons for believing that punishment may be *final* and actions *irremediable*. But I wished to be able to believe in a God all merciful, to Whose beneficent nature punishment was a thing opposed.

B. And by so doing you were practising a mode of thought which we repudiated. You were trying to create a God of your own, and you were refusing to be guided by the experience of the universe. But, now we have looked at the course of events in the world, and have found that, if the material universe and the soul of man come from the same hand, we have a right to believe that some actions are punished, that some are even punished finally, so far as this world goes; and that, if religion asserts that the punishment or (let us call it) the effect of some actions is perpetual, such a result is only in accordance with present experience. And we ought not to forget this, that the doctrine of eternity of punishment does not, so far as we know, assert that any *individual* action will incur eternal condemnation.

A. But does not the Bible assert that for a particular sin, called The sin against the Holy Ghost, there is no forgiveness?

B. The sin against the Holy Ghost, spoken of in Scripture, is not defined as an individual act; but we have sufficient reason to believe that it consists in a *continued and determined* refusal to believe the highest truths; which refusal, supposing what we call the highest truths to be true, implies the deliberate preference of darkness to light. And even an atheist, if he believes that there is such a thing as truth, would probably concede, that the negation of truth and the belief in falsehood are beyond measure debasing and degrading to the human soul. And if, as we have shown, there is a probability of an existence after death, there is also a probability that the negation of truth would be the most intense degradation, and, therefore, the most severe punishment to a soul, conscious that there is a truth towards which it ought to aspire, but from the knowledge of which its own actions have excluded it for ever.

A. You must allow me time to think over these things: they seem at least plausible.

But the line of argument is different from what I expected, and I cannot tell how these matters will appear on reflection.

B. Here, then, let us part for the present. I will only add one word. The doctrine of future punishment is indeed essential to religion. But those who are satisfied of the truths of religion, and who practise what religion enjoins, have little concern with it; because to such men religion speaks not by threatenings, but promises. A Christian, worthy of the name, has no occasion to think of God as an Avenger, but as a loving Father, Who gives him assistance in his needs, and offers rewards of incalculable extent. But even the idea of reward rarely enters into the thoughts of the Christian. The principle which guides him is that of love, and his state of mind is said to be one of peace; and that peace may be defined in the words of one who was not a Christian, as "an unimpeded activity of all the faculties of the soul upon an object appropriate to them."

DIALOGUE III.

THE MORAL GOVERNMENT OF GOD.

B. Have you reflected upon the questions discussed in our last conversation?

A. I have; and I should feel well satisfied to accept your conclusions, did not I find a further startling difficulty, which seems very hard to meet.

B. Will you tell me what it is?

A. Certainly; for I came for that very purpose. If God is a governor and a judge, He must govern and judge according to some fixed code of laws. It would be entirely destructive of the idea of God to suppose Him capricious in His decisions, which would be the case if there were no discernible law in His dealings with His creatures. I say, that if His creatures could not in any degree detect the principle upon which the Creator acts, He would be to all intents and purposes a capricious Being. A judge who passes judgment on no discernible principle, a governor who rules without a fixed law, is an arbitrary person, and in no way deserving of that love, which you spoke of as the state of mind under which the true Christian exists.

B. I think what you say very reasonable. But surely you do not mean to imply that such a description is an appropriate one of the government of God?

A. I would willingly think that it is not. But I read an ingenious and able book the other day, the tendency of which was to show that no intelligible principle of Divine government is discernible either in nature or society. The writer declared that the contradictions to any assigned law of operation were so numerous, or rather innumerable, that they amount in every case to a positive disproof of the existence of the law.

B. It must have been an ingenious work. Could you give me an idea of the line of argument?

A. It was simply what I have stated. The writer produced various doctrines of causation, and against them set the instances in which the supposed law was broken through. He gave various cases, for example, in which animals which swim in the waters have incipient organs adapted for other conditions of life; of serpents, which have incipient wings, and land animals with incipient fins; and showed that, if these were a proof of design, then the framer of nature was convicted of making mistakes.

B. And he argued from this, I suppose, either that there was no design, or that God was fallible, and left you which alternative you preferred?

A. He did so.

B. Well; it was rather a bold assumption, except on the ground that the writer knew all that existed or will exist; all the possible changes and varieties of which nature is capable, and which it is intended to undergo. But how does this bear upon the present matter?

A. I will tell you. It occurred to me that in forming a judgment of the dealings of God with man, we assume that there is a certain law by which He acts. We take for granted that God governs the world according to principles of morality. Now just as the exceptions to the general *physical* laws, which we think we have discovered, annihilate those laws, so the exceptions to what we call the *moral government* of the universe disprove the existence of such a government. Religion declares that the world is morally governed: facts declare that this is not the case.

B. I think I see your difficulty. You think that the idea of right and wrong is a creation of the brain of man, and that there is no fixed and definite quality in the nature of things corresponding to it.

A. I do.

B. Now consider. There are two questions here involved, let us keep them separate. One is, Is the idea of right and wrong naturally inherent in such a creature as man? The second is, Is this or that particular opinion as to what is right or wrong necessary, or is it a creation of man's imagination and association?

A. Will you make the distinction between the two things somewhat clearer?

B. I will try to do so. If we consider the history of the world, we shall find a constant variation, in every age, of ideas which are approved or proscribed. The opinions of each age and each nation are stamped upon their institutions. One age considers slavery a necessary condition of society; another asserts that slavery is an abomination, to be utterly detested by mankind. One nation approves of polygamy, another looks upon it with horror. In such questions it is evident that the opinions of men differ as to *what* is right and *what* is wrong, but it is equally evident that all ages have considered that there *is* a right and a wrong. In other words, it is quite plain that since no age or nation has ever existed without a distinction between right and wrong, these ideas are natural to man. The idea of virtue and vice, however it may differ in its form, is an essential constituent of human nature.

A. It seems so.

B. And being such, it is evident that the Creator has implanted it in man.

A. Pardon me, it only shows that men naturally make a distinction between what is beneficial to society and what is injurious.

B. Yes; but they do so by the very constitution of their nature. It is perfectly true that men have differed very widely in their opinions as to what is right and wrong. But you never heard of a society of men to whom right and wrong, in some shape or other, were not familiar ideas. And these ideas, however crude, indefinite, and incorrect, have materially influenced the history of the world: I might say, with justice, have moulded its course, in so far as man is concerned. It cannot be said, then, that there are no signs of, at least, an incipient moral law in the condition of mankind. All men acknowledge that there is a right and a wrong.

A. I think they do. But this does not by any means prove that God is a moral governor of the universe.

B. No; but it goes some way to dispose of the objection, as you have urged it, that the exceptions to a moral law were more numerous than the instances of its operation. Here is a fact, wide as the universe, that, however men differ upon details, they naturally and unanimously acknowledge something of the nature of right and wrong. The exceptions to this rule are so few, and, if examined, of so doubtful a character, as to be of very little value, regarded as constituents of a probable argument.

A. Perhaps it may be so. I am quite aware that the mind is easily misled by one or two apparent exceptions to a general rule; and that if we read of a people in the centre of Africa who know no distinction between right and wrong, we forget, that even if the partial and imperfect acquaintance of travellers with a people, whose language they knew but slightly, and into whose habits and feelings they had but little opportunity of entering, were thoroughly reliable, a single exception, such as this, would have to be classed under the head of things unnatural and monstrous.

B. The fairness and candour of such an admission is much to be commended. Allow me to say, that if all men would come to the discussion of philosophical, moral, and religious subjects in so temperate a frame of mind as this, I do not believe they would ever go away dissatisfied.

A. Pray do not compliment me on my candour; my admission is only purely reasonable. But I have a further objection to make to what you are upholding as to the *evidence* of God's moral government, and that is, the fluctuations of the ideas of moral good and evil. If a thing is wrong at one time, it cannot be right at another; if God is governing the world according to moral laws now, He was not so governing it at the time when the opposite opinions were rife.

B. I do not think you fully appreciate the position which religion takes up with regard to this question. Religion asserts that God governs the world by general laws; and that, though He does not preclude Himself from suspending the action of those laws at His supreme will, yet, on the whole, the laws which God gives are self-acting. Moreover, religion asserts that man is a free agent; and that, though he does receive divine assistance if he asks for it, he is in a great measure left to determine his rules of conduct by the light of his faculties, which are the gift of God, and adequate to the object. The result of this free agency of man is that he does not always choose what is plainly beneficial to him: in fact, he often chooses what he knows to be injurious, even in cases where the common knowledge of mankind declares him to be in error. In other cases, less clear, he is equally liable to be misled by present desires, or a wish to avoid discomfort and annoyance. By means of these declensions from the laws of his nature, by the force of example and association, and by the other influences which operate upon man in a state of society, various opinions, contradictory to truth and justice, arise and sway mankind. This is the view which religion takes of the origin of perverted notions of right and wrong.

A. It appears reasonable enough, so far as it goes; and the inference you would draw from it will be, that, though there is one right opinion on every subject, the free will of men distorts it into various errors: and that whereas God has desired that good should triumph and evil be destroyed, He does not so interfere with the actions of men as to prevent the reverse happening, if they deliberately prefer evil to good.

B. That is in part my meaning; but still I assert that there are signs sufficiently plain to convince us that virtue is approved of by the Author of nature, and approved of to such an extent, that if men would accept the evidence which lies before them they would cease to make a question on this point.

A. And what is the evidence upon which you depend?

B. Is it not certain that a life of virtue is attended with more satisfaction than a life of vice? do we not ourselves experience a feeling of calmness, quiet, and satisfaction when we have done what we believe to be right, or avoided what we believe to be wrong?

A. We do, I confess; but does not that feeling arise from the absence of fear? if we acted otherwise we have an apprehension that society would avenge itself, if at last men discovered our motives? and this apprehension of discovery is what causes the uneasiness of a vicious man.

B. No doubt this apprehension is an element in the feeling which we are describing; but it is not all. There are some actions which produce satisfaction, and others which cause disquiet, without the fear of detection entering into the consideration of them. Acts of disinterested kindness are frequently attended with satisfaction, even in the most criminal. There is a story told of two soldiers on a campaign, the one robust and sturdy, the other weak and delicate. In a cold winter's night, as they lay side by side, the strong man observed the weaker shivering with the cold, and stripped off his own great coat to cover the weaker. The strong man, it was afterwards discovered, was a forger and a murderer. Do you suppose that it was the expectation of reward which influenced him? Was it not rather that the act of disinterested kindness brought its own reward?

A. But might not his motive have been the sense of superiority which his greater power of endurance gave him?

B. In analyzing any motive you will find very many converging influences; but what I want you to observe is that, analyze it as you will, you will find much difficulty in getting rid of some sense of satisfaction attendant upon virtue, and discomfort attendant upon vice. And even if the motive were, in the ultimate analysis, seen to be purely a self-regarding one, yet I do not see how that would prevent it being an argument of the purpose of the Creator. If it be proved that, by acting disinterestedly, men are acquiring for themselves satisfaction and pleasure greater than they would attain by mere selfishness, this would show that such actions were approved by the Creator.

A. But all men do not acknowledge that virtue brings more satisfaction than vice. Some men, or most men, even though they try to be virtuous, declare that it is an arduous and cruel work, and others boldly give their vote on the side of vice.

B. Well: it is almost impossible to weigh the relative pleasures and pains which accompany vice or virtue: at all events, it is impossible to find an arbitrator to decide between their respective claims.

A. Ah! but I fear I cannot let you off with that reply. There is a kind of judge whom we can find, a most unwilling one, and therefore the better for our purpose. I speak of those men who, having lived vicious lives, are persuaded to turn to virtue. These men have experienced the sensations both of vice and virtue. Now whatever they may tell us of the comfort of a virtuous life, it is plain from their confessions that their life is full of grief and pain. While they lived viciously all things went on satisfactorily. They went through their round of pleasures without hindrance or anxiety. But now that they have turned to virtue they find themselves continually drawn to what they believe to be wrong: their life is a constant battle against temptation. They have not even the satisfaction of the approbation of the world. Instead of sympathizing with them, it points the finger of scorn at them; it heaps up against them their former sins and transgressions; and they themselves are rendered additionally wretched by the consciousness that they deserve its censure.

B. All that is a true picture. It has only one fault as an argument, that it overlooks entirely the true and obvious reason for all this discomfort.

A. And what is that?

B. Why! do you not see that all this wretchedness, all this inclination to yield to temptation, is to be attributed, not to *virtue*, but to *previous vicious courses*. They attend upon reformation, but they are consequences of vice. You have no more right to blame virtue for them than you have to attribute to temperance the horrible sensations which the inveterate opium-eater experiences upon giving up his habit. Vicious courses will have their revenge: body and spirit alike suffer from them; but those men who relinquish them in time have a long up-hill road to traverse before all the cravings of their passions, hitherto unrestrained, can be brought to order. But with your permission, leaving this argument for what it is worth, we will pass on to another. What do you consider to be the characteristic of virtue and vice?

A. I think that what is meant by *virtue* is a deliberate acting upon principle to promote the general cause of good.

B. Do you consider vice as a deliberate acting upon principle to promote the general cause of evil?

A. No; I believe that vice for the most part consists in a deliberate want of forethought. It is possible that some men love evil for its own sake, but such are very few; and it is also possible that some men, through want of education or from other causes, do what is wrong without being aware of it. But, on the whole, vice consists in a culpable want of forethought.

B. We are not very far wrong, then, if we say that virtue and vice are of the nature of prudence and imprudence.

A. They certainly are of that nature.

B. Now, can any thing be plainer than that prudence, as a rule, is rewarded, and imprudence punished, in this life? We are enabled, by our faculties, to appreciate that the world is governed by fixed laws; we can reflect upon the good and evil consequences of our behaviour, and if we neglect to act upon our reflections, there is a tolerable certainty that we shall not do so with impunity.

A. That is true in the long run, no doubt. But I fear your argument will prove too much. Vicious people, as well as virtuous people, make use of forethought; they work patiently and deliberately to obtain a bad end; and they succeed. So that prudence is rewarded on the side either of virtue or of vice.

B. Yes; but it is rewarded in consequence of its resemblance to virtue. In so far as a man has an evil end in view he is undoubtedly vicious; but in so far as he exercises patience, self-restraint, and watchfulness over his actions, and is willing to forego every enjoyment or profit which may interfere with his purpose, so far he is, not indeed virtuous, but adopting the qualities of the virtuous; and if he succeeds, it is owing to those qualities which are in themselves admirable, and only evil in their application. Even then it remains to show that such a man enjoys peace of mind and contentment, after he has attained the end of his long discipline. As a rule such men are not satisfied; their tempers and dispositions are soured; and the close of their life is not attended with calmness or content.

A. But are not virtuous actions often punished, and vicious ones rewarded, in the world?

B. Not that I am aware of.

A. Consider this. Society is the creature of God, and the principles, which on the whole are found to be necessary to the wellbeing of society, may be assumed to be the laws of Providence. Now, do not we find in society that persecutions are inflicted upon the good, and applause given to the bad?

B. We certainly do; but then you must remember that men are not persecuted as benefactors to society. Persecutions arise from an erroneous idea that the principles and actions of the persecuted tend to the injury of society. It is very true that the truth is often oppressed in this way, not because it is truth, but rather because it is believed to be false. And, again, society applauds vice, not as vice, but because it has assumed the garb of virtue.

A. I do not quite see this.

B. With regard to virtue, it is quite evident

from contemporary history that the Apostles and early Christians, who professed a life of austere virtue, were punished, not for this, but on the principle "that they were turning the world upside down." In addition to this, we learn that all kinds of vices of the most atrocious character were attributed to them: nothing was too bad for "the most pernicious sect of the Christians." This evidence is as good as any other, as it proves that the persecution was in the supposed interests of order. Or, again, take the persecution of Galileo: Did it not originate in the idea that by his opinions he was likely to destroy the truth, and bring all his followers into peril of extreme misery? So that that, too, arose from the notion that what he taught was antagonistic to virtue. On the other hand, the rewards and favour bestowed upon a rascal, like Titus Oates, were bestowed because it was thought that he was working for the general good.

A. But even granting what you say to be the case, that men only punish virtue and reward vice when they mistake them for their opposites, does it not appear that nature often bestows her favours on the vicious, her frowns upon the virtuous, and this, too, by way of direct consequence of either?

B. This is another aspect of the question, and requires careful consideration. You mean to say that virtuous actions are not always naturally rewarded, and that pleasure often attends what is acknowledged to be vicious?

A. I do.

B. But you must make a distinction. Every faculty of our nature is intended to be used, and when employed its exercise is attended with pleasure. This is our guarantee that it is intended to be used. But occasions may occur in which the exercise of the faculty would be injurious. Nevertheless the pleasure attending its exercise would still be experienced; and though it would be followed with pain exceeding the pleasure, the immediate exercise of the faculty is pleasurable. When, then, you say vicious actions are often rewarded and virtuous actions punished, it is necessary to specify what you mean. Is your meaning that virtue, as virtue, is often punished, and vice, as vice, often rewarded? or that vice is often attended with pleasure, and virtue with pain?

A. I believe I did not make the distinction; and what I intended to convey was the latter of the two propositions. Still, I should like to hear your disproof of the former.

B. Well, then, I assert that virtue, as virtue,

is rewarded. And I see a proof of this in the inward satisfaction and happiness which virtue causes—a satisfaction so great that in many cases it is quite enough to compensate men for any misfortunes. It does not matter how that satisfaction originates, whether from a consciousness of promoting the general good, or fulfilling the law of God, or from an instinct: it is an undeniable fact. You hear men say that they have the satisfaction of knowing that such and such a matter was not occasioned by their fault; and this is an instance, though in a low degree, of the inward happiness of which virtue is the cause. And, on the other hand, it is plain that, in many cases, vice causes misery and inward disquiet, quite irrespective of the fear of discovery and punishment. Criminals have been known to inform against themselves, declaring that no punishment would compare to the gnawings of remorse; and though such cases are, perhaps, not frequent, they are an indication of the state of feeling of which almost all men are more or less conscious after wrong-doing.

A. I think your argument may be met in two ways: by denying the fact that most men do feel such remorse, and by explaining both the pleasure and the pain, of which you speak, as a growth of the principle of self-love. A man may say, "I do not believe that the pleasure of virtue or the pain of vice exists, except in so far as men expect advantage or fear punishment in consequence of their acts;" or he may say, "This feeling of satisfaction arises from the consciousness that, by the exercise of friendship and benevolence, we have placed ourselves in a position of superiority over others."

B. With regard to the first objection, that men do not feel remorse, it is an assertion and no argument; and if it were, it would be contradicted by the second. I will appeal to experience against you, whether remorse is not a common feature, or even a general rule, with those who have acted viciously; and with regard to the assertion that men act from a hope of advantage, I will ask you what advantage does a man expect to reap by going among the poor and miserable, and relieving their necessities?

A. I suppose he expects their gratitude.

B. But he knows that among such persons he will probably find more ingratitude than gratitude.

A. Why, then, I suppose he looks forward to reward in a future life.

B. Here, again, I can only say that you are asserting what you cannot prove. No doubt, many people do hope that by such acts they are pleasing God, and they are right. But the motive which actuates them is, for the most part, that this is simply their duty, and in the acts of kindness which they do, there is no thought of the reward which is to follow, but simply the exercise of a religious principle within them.

A. And yet very many people cease to discharge this duty where no gratitude follows, and they see no visible success attend them.

B. I have never contended that there is not much weakness in human virtue, nor that mixed motives can be entirely excluded. My argument is, that there are sufficient proofs of disinterestedness among men to show that the pleasure of virtue does not arise from selfish considerations. Pure benevolence is a very precious jewel, and is rare and costly. Still from the less pure instances, we are able by analysis to ascertain what is the essential quality, and that is *not* selfishness.

A. But may it not be unconscious selfishness?

B. Do you mean that people act virtuously, because it gives them pleasure to do so; but that they do not know that this pleasure leads them to be virtuous?

A. That is what I mean.

B. If so they are not selfish. If it is possible to act under the impression that you are simply doing good, and without any motive or design to give satisfaction to yourself, you are acting without selfish motives. But after all, what your last objection amounts to is simply, that in every energy attended with pleasure the motive to action is the pleasure, which is not the case. There are numbers of actions, selfish and unselfish, which are attended by pleasure, but the pursuit of which arises from another motive besides the pleasure. It is a fallacious mode of reasoning, to argue that because every action successfully performed causes satisfaction, the only or the principal motive to act was the desire of that satisfaction. But leaving this, I will only remark that, as you allow that the satisfaction of virtue is so great and palpable as to induce many people to seek it, in spite of apparent difficulties and pains which lie in the way of its attainment, this is a very strong confession that virtuous action is in itself preeminently desirable. And if it is so much to be desired, I do not see how we can avoid inferring that nature, in other words, the

Creator of nature, has intended us to pursue it. But I see other arguments of great weight in this matter, to prove that virtue is naturally rewarded, and vice naturally punished.

A. Pray, produce them.

B. If the voice of nature is to be found speaking anywhere, it is in the unconscious tendencies of large bodies of men. Now, however much men may be inclined to selfishness or sunk in vice, it is certain that they have an instinctive admiration and love for unselfishness, generosity, kindness, and virtuous actions generally. This is evident from the fact that eminent justice, fidelity, love of country, and the like, are rewarded by the approbation of men, both good and bad, so long as those qualities do not interfere with their own success; and not only with the approbation, but even with substantial marks of approbation, in the way of honours, rewards, and dignities conferred upon them. On the other hand, such is the feeling which men have respecting tyranny, oppression, and cruelty, that the sequel of these evil qualities frequently exasperates nations into revolution. And if you will consider the history of revolutions, you will find that among their causes, the actual misery endured by the people, is as nothing compared with the exasperation awakened by the sight of the injustice and oppression which precede them.

A. I am quite willing to concede that much of the spirit which influences revolutions is sentiment. Men magnify their wrongs, dwell upon mistakes in their rulers as if they were crimes, and act thoroughly unreasonably, even though they have justice on their side. But ought we not to attribute these things to a kind of mania, which seizes upon men acting in masses, and spreads like an infectious disease?

B. Granted that it is so, you must explain what gives rise to the mania. You compare it to a disease. Are you prepared to say that the objects and aims for which nations rise in revolution are evil? I ask this, because though no one would be surprised to hear me, a defender of things established, make the assertion, such an opinion coming from your side of these questions would be remarkable.

A. No; I do not think that the objects and aims of revolution are generally evil. Looking through the history of nations, so far as I am able to judge, I should say that injustice and oppression have been the principal causes. A hatred of tyranny and of the attempt to enslave the bodies and minds of men, has led men to band together to promote such things as liberty, fraternity, and equality; and though, under these names, many foolish and many unjustifiable acts have been done, I do not think we ought to refuse to see a natural movement towards good things.

B. Well, whatever may be thought of your estimate of revolution, I have no reason to complain. You assert that the masses of mankind, when aroused, are aroused on the side of what is in itself good, however undesirable the means which they employ to express their sentiments or gain their ends. You are, therefore, at one with me in the assertion, that men naturally admire what is right and detest what is wrong.

A. Yes, but you and I perhaps differ in our definition of right and wrong.

B. Do you consider justice, truth, honesty, fair dealing, public spirit, patriotism, generosity, and kindness, as things good or bad?

A. Good, certainly.

B. Do you believe falsehood, treachery, cruelty, dishonesty, and harshness, to be virtuous or vicious?

A. As certainly they are vicious.

B. Then I think you and I will not differ much in our definition.

A. Ah, but I call things good, because they tend to the good of society, and bad, because they injure society. You, on the other hand, call them so, because you imagine people have an intuitive perception of them.

B. I will not dispute the metaphysical question. It matters nothing to the present argument *how we estimate* virtue and vice, if, as it appears, we are agreed as to *what they are.* If that which appears beneficial to society at large has such power to sway the passions of multitudes, it seems only an additional argument, that the Author of Nature has so ruled that men shall approve what He intended for their benefit. The arguments seem to me all to point one way. Whether we look to the natural tendency of actions, or the sentiments which accompany them, or the opinions of mankind, all seem to point to a declaration of Nature on the side of virtue and against vice. To go into every detail would occupy too much time, but I honestly believe that every single argument which can be fairly adduced would be found to tell on my side.

A. I do not yet think you have fairly disposed of the fact that sometimes virtue is punished and vice rewarded.

B. Well, I can only say, that if there are

cases in which we find virtue suffering, and vice triumphant and happy, you may fairly infer from the general course of things that such cases are exceptional. And, perhaps in a world guided by general laws, such exceptions are inevitable. If you will say that, because not every case of virtue is found to be happy, or, rather, prosperous, therefore you cannot believe that there is a preference for virtue over vice in Nature, I will assert that you require proof for your belief, greater than you will find in any question with which you have to deal.

A. But the exceptions are so numerous, that I have a fair right to dispute, whether the happiness of virtue or the prosperity of vice is the rule or the exception.

B. I cannot help thinking that you are confounding two things, *happiness* and *external prosperity*. Now, if there is one thing more certain than another, it is that these two things are not synonymous. Prosperity does not make happiness, nor adversity unhappiness. I will go farther, and say that you will find as much misery among those who are externally prosperous as among the unprosperous. Mental happiness is a very different thing from bodily comfort; and *that* you will find among virtuous poor people, quite as strong as among virtuous wealthy people; in fact, the sympathy, generosity, and kindness, which are found to exist among the poor, might well be a pattern to others in better positions. And the admiration which they have for good qualities frequently contrasts very remarkably with the critical, half cynical, judgment of the rich upon humane and earnest men. And the happiness and contentment, the simple pleasure, which they feel in helping one another, is an evidence of the natural effects of virtue in very critical cases.

A. Well, I suppose experience alone can decide these questions. But I own myself disappointed that you can bring no more convincing arguments of the moral government of God.

B. I have not said that all my arguments are exhausted; so far, I have only been arguing against your objections. I have tried to show you that you have not sufficient ground for assuming the absence of moral government in the universe. As a rule, men admire and respect virtue and nobleness of disposition; they never reward a vicious man *because* he is vicious; they never punish a virtuous man *because* he is virtuous. The more you mass people together, the more you will find that the *principles* which they *avow* are good, though selfishness and passion mar them in the carrying out. In *this* sense the words "The voice of the people is the voice of God" are seen to be true. But in all this, you will observe, we are only on the very verge of the religious question. We have not mentioned what Christianity avows as to the moral government of God.

A. I do not understand you. Is there anything more to be proved than that God favours virtue, and hates vice?

B. Yes; very much more. Religion asserts, indeed, that goodness is pleasing to God, and vice hateful; that God is a righteous Judge, who rewards virtue and punishes sin. But religion also tells us that the present state of things is imperfect, and that, in a future life, all the discrepancies and difficulties, which seem to mar the present, will be corrected; and that then vice and virtue shall shine forth in their true colours, and all inequalities shall be resolved.

A. And will you undertake to prove this from nature?

B. No! I will not; but I can show you that nature points in the same direction as religion. My argument amounts to this, that the tendency of virtue is to overcome vice in this world;

and that, therefore, if religion asserts that in another world it will actually be victorious, nature argues on her behalf. But I do not undertake to say that nature by herself would of necessity force this doctrine upon minds not prepared to receive it.

A. This is indeed widening the field of inquiry. But I fear that, if you have only partially convinced me hitherto, you will find it much more difficult to establish this point. However, please to proceed in your inquiry.

B. I do not agree with you that it will be more difficult to establish this point satisfactorily, and I am well-pleased to have arrived at this stage of the inquiry, because here we have analogies to help us, which, at present, we have not made use of. Will you help me, or will you contest every stage of the argument?

A. I will follow you, hoping to be convinced.

B. Do you really mean that? Then I have little fear you will be satisfied. Hitherto I have had to deal with you as a most determined opponent. Now listen. Are rational or irrational creatures the stronger?

A. Physically speaking, irrational creatures

are the more powerful, but the quality of reason enables those possessed of it to gain the supremacy.

B. Is this always the case?

A. No; for reason must have scope to operate; it requires time to bring its forces to bear, and opportunity for their exercise. If a number of men were cast naked upon an island occupied by wild beasts, it is probable they would all perish under superior force; although, were they enabled to use the resources of their reason, they would discover means to resist and overcome the brute animals.

B. And should you decide, then, that in such a case reason or physical strength was superior?

A. I should say that naturally reason was superior; accidentally, brute force.

B. So, then, it is possible for a particular quality to be in itself superior to another, and yet be overcome through lack of opportunity for its exercise.

A. Quite possible.

B. Apply the argument to virtue. It is possible that virtue may be intended to be superior to vice, and yet be overcome through lack of opportunity.

A. Certainly; it is possible.

B. Now what is it that forms the strength of reason?

A. The power of union and co-operation.

B. In this respect virtue and reason resemble one another. Each acquires strength from co-operation. The only difference is, that men use reason in opposition to one another; while virtue is, by its very nature, a bond of union. Men, who possess reason, use that reason to outwit one another. The virtuous never desire this; they wish to promote the interests of all alike; they have no desire to supplant or to deceive one another. Is not that the case?

A. It appears to be essential to the idea of virtue.

B. So that if virtuous men could unite throughout the world, their special object would be to promote the cause of virtue. They would have no elements of discord amongst them, no disturbing forces to mar the harmonious co-operation of the whole. Suppose, now, such an union could take place in the world, what would be the result?

A. They would form an invincible commonwealth, against which no other union could avail. For I see plainly that in any other union selfish motives would creep in and undermine the power of the whole. If virtue is, as by its idea it appears to be, a perfect unity of sentiment, or at least such an unity that it would always prefer to surrender any individual tastes and opinions to the general welfare, I do not see how any society founded on other principles could withstand it.

B. So that if even a smaller number of perfectly virtuous men were combined against a larger number of men not possessed of virtue, the union natural to the one would in the long-run prevail over the divided counsels and selfish aims of the other.

A. But yet this seems, though excellent in theory, to be at variance with facts. Do not the most crafty and unscrupulous states overcome those which are less so?

B. I grant it. But, from the very form of the question, you will see that it is not a case in point.

A. How so?

B. You ask me whether the more unscrupulous does not prevail over the less so. Now, the question is between perfectly virtuous and perfectly vicious states. As things are, it is admitted that in the best there is a vast amount of selfishness, personal ambition, and disregard of the general weal, so much so that at times the strength of the whole is sapped by the rottenness of a part.

A. Then such a state as you imagine is impossible?

B. I suppose it is. Not only are really good and virtuous men subject to all kinds of imperfections: the circumstances of the world will never allow a state to be formed of only the best men. We are forced to content ourselves with mixed states; we never can have all offices and positions apportioned out to good men, who are exactly suited for them. There will always be the ambitious struggling by every means to gain the chief power, and the selfish or idle shrinking from labour and responsibility. Offices will always be apportioned in accordance with the predilections of the powerful; and hence every state must of necessity be a spectacle of opposition and contention; although in some cases the virtuous leaven of public spirit will obviate the worse evils of the system.

A. You speak rather despondingly: still in the main you speak correctly. Is there no remedy?

B. Not till rulers are all virtuous, or virtuous men are rulers: not till all men have learned to look upon selfishness and malice and ambition as the source of their misfortunes. Then, and not till then, will a remedy be found.

A. And that will never be.

B. Yes, my friend, it will be, but not on earth. The time will come when "the people shall be all righteous, and shall inherit the land for ever." There will be a day when the strivings of the ambitious, and the plottings of the crafty, the selfishness of tyrants, and the recklessness of multitudes, shall no more be known. We shall see it, but not now. That which is now depressed by isolation, but which by its nature tends to union, and in union finds strength—that of which here and there we see the beginnings, but which is like a rich flower, choked by the overgrowth of weeds,— that virtue shall one day blossom into its perfection. When the voices of earth are silent, the virtuous shall stand in a perfect kingdom before their King, each with his own work and with unimpeded powers to accomplish it; each taking by wise appointment the post allotted to him, and rejoicing in the knowledge that all is well; not striving to go beyond his neighbour, and yet not sinking into apathy or sloth. This is the state of virtue triumphant—the beauty of holiness—the city of God.

A. Dreams, my dear friend, dreams! Plato

hoped for it, and saw a type of it in Sparta. Sir Thomas More had visions of it. But these were mere imaginations; and yours, however beautiful, however much to be desired, is as far off as theirs—and farther.

B. And why did Plato dream of it? Whence came his imaginations, think you? Imperfect, fanciful, unreal they were, I grant you. But were they not the conscious aspirations of a virtuous soul, trammelled indeed by the weaknesses of his age and nation—but pointing to a fulfilment by their very existence? If there had not been a natural tendency in virtue to raise such ideas, they could never have existed.

A. But yet such visions are no arguments. If they were, would not all the ravings of superstition, all the fancies of heathen nations, as we call them, claim to be considered as truths, and demand our assent? And if so, see what portentous results, what utter confusion, would result. Above all, what an utter destruction of a part of your thesis, upon which you have as yet not touched, but which, sooner or later, you will have to set before me, would result. You will tell me that Christianity demands from me undivided assent. Why should I not prefer Mahometanism to Christianity on such principles? That religion declares that all the glories of a heavenly kingdom are reserved for its faithful followers. And how will you prove to me that I must reject it?

B. The claims of various religions depend upon evidence. Even could it be shown that the moral character of Mahomet's religion were as high as that of Christ, it would still remain to decide between the historical evidence of each. At present that question has not come before us. We are on the ground of natural religion. And if I have adopted the language of the Christian Scriptures, it is that I may show that the principles which they imply, are not opposed to reason. Those principles are the conclusions towards which unaided reason tends. They have, therefore, a *primâ facie* claim upon our assent. We have seen that it appears as if God rules the world on principles of morality. We have seen that, on the whole, virtue has a natural beauty and attractiveness about it. It tends to happiness; it is admired, reverenced, and, in many cases, rewarded. It is never, as such, hated or persecuted; it has a tendency to unite mankind, to content them, to elevate them. And if the Bible speaks of it with approbation, if it seems to soar into the regions of imagination in depicting the ultimate triumph of virtue, it does so on grounds of reason—it carries on and completes the ideas of wise men. Nature supplies the outline, and the Bible fills in the lights and shades, and gives completion to the picture.

A. All this requires much reflection. I am not altogether so sceptical as I may seem. Your reasoning has had its weight with me: but it is hard to give up one's doubts. I believe I have urged my arguments as far as they will go; and at least you have shown me that the dogmatism with which I started was somewhat premature. Give me time; other difficulties start up before me. If you will answer them, every additional argument will have its weight, and it may be that you will satisfy my scruples altogether.

B. Ah, my good friend, I will not damp your ardour. But let me say this: You, whose life is earnest and virtuous, do not find your trials in the temptations of the world. May it not be that, to such minds as yours, the doubts and difficulties which you experience are intended for a discipline to you? Let me ask you to weigh this well, and perhaps it may assist you to resolve some of those questions with which your mind is troubled.

A. I will bear what you say in mind, and another day, if you will, we will resume our argument.

B. With all my heart. Good-bye.

DIALOGUE IV.

ON A STATE OF TRIAL OR PROBATION.

B. I am very glad to see you here to-day. It is such a long time since our last conversation that I began to fear you were utterly wearied out; and I blamed myself for my own dulness in not interesting you.

A. You have no need to do that. I am deeply interested. But in many ways your mode of argument is novel to me, and it takes much time to digest and arrange the results of our conversations. Frequently I am inclined to agree with a great deal you say; but then I discover something which makes me pause; and so I take time to sift out what I reject, or am not persuaded of, from what I approve.

B. In this case, then, I must fear that you have found very much to object to in our last conversation.

A. It is not so much *that* which has engaged my mind, as a certain deficiency in your argument, which presents an impassable stumbling-block.

B. I am afraid there may be many deficiencies. The difficulty of arguing in the way we have been doing lies in the fact, that many of your principal obstacles are only known to me through the minds of others. To me the arguments in favour of religion appear so much stronger than those against it, that the full force with which many questions present themselves to a doubting mind, is perhaps hardly apparent.

A. Yes; that is just the case. You seem to argue so much as if you were certain of your conclusions, that I am often inclined to tax you with a want of appreciation of real difficulties. My own mind is so passion-tossed on many of these matters that I turn, like a weathercock, wherever the wind blows.

B. I will not say that I wish for your sake I doubted more, because that would be untrue; but I should really feel grateful, if you will point out when I dogmatize too much.

A. That is just what I am about to do. You have been arguing about some surface facts of religion, but you have forgotten, all the while, the great underlying difficulties.

B. I grieve to hear such a charge. So far as we have gone, I have argued from the idea of a beneficent Creator. This indeed I have assumed as acknowledged by you; for I think you confess, that the appearance of order and a purpose in nature point evidently to the operation of a mind; and there are signs enough that such a mind is beneficent.

A. This I acknowledge; though you should remember that it is a great concession on the part of a sceptic in these days of free thought.

B. I know it is: but it is on this principle that you started.

A. Well, not exactly; though, on the whole, the line of argument has at least proved that such an idea is not inconsistent with reason. However, allowing, as I do, the signs of good-will toward men in the ordering of the universe, I accede to your proofs of the existence of a moral governor.

B. Then I do not perceive what you have to complain of.

A. Why, you argue that, as such, a God of purity and holiness must be on the side of virtue. You have shown fairly enough that there are signs of this. You have also, not unfairly, set out the probability of God's punishing evil-doers, and rewarding the virtuous, from arguments drawn from the actual course of nature. But the one great difficulty of all is utterly forgotten.

B. What is that?

A. Religion asserts that we are not only under a moral governor, but also that we are placed by Him in a state of great difficulty and danger. Can anything be more unreasonable?

B. On what ground is it unreasonable?

A. You ask me to believe, that a God of love and of holiness deliberately places His noblest creatures in a position, where there is every probability that they will fail, and, having done so, will be punished for their failure.

B. I think you rather overstate the case. Further investigations will, I trust, show to you, that the probabilities of *failure* do not so grievously preponderate over those of *success* in attaining to virtue as you imagine.

A. Still, such is the case. Confessedly we are in a state of trial and difficulty. How we came to be in it no one knows; and how we are to escape from it is almost as difficult to ascertain.

B. And you would, therefore, infer that the idea of our being in a state of trial, and responsible for our actions, is untrue?

A. Most assuredly I should infer this.

B. You think it hard that the hindrances to virtue in this life should have any influence upon our future condition?

A. I do.

B. Be it so. Now you and I have lived a certain number of years, and have acquired a certain character of mind. How did we acquire it?

A. By circumstances, by education, example, and the opinions of those about us, as well as from other remote causes which I cannot accurately determine.

B. Can we get rid of our mental character?

A. Not readily.

B. And shall we find it easier to do so a few years hence?

A. No: it grows more difficult each year.

B. When you were ten years old it would not, I imagine, be unfair, in some sense, to speak of your life after thirty as your future life?

A. I see no objection.

B. Well, then; more or less, your life after thirty is a result of your earlier years. The circumstances in which you were then placed, the education which you received, and the associates with whom your lot was cast without choice of your own, have had an influence upon your character, which nothing short of a marvel can eradicate.

A. All this is very true.

B. And, according to the character of your mind thus formed, you are happy or miserable, volatile, careless, painstaking, or impetuous. These conditions of mind you cannot put away; but they have a marvellous influence upon your happiness in this life.

A. I do not deny it.

B. Let us take another point of view. Are there not numberless circumstances, the importance of which we cannot estimate at the time, which influence our future life?

A. Yes, certainly. I suppose that deliberate sloth or idleness in ·youth, or, again, dissolute behaviour and intemperance, bear their own bitter fruit as prolifically as any weed that infests your garden.

B. Your observation is most just. To put it very briefly, I suppose you will acknowledge that future prosperity in some degree, future happiness (in this life) almost entirely, depend upon *prudence,* using that word in its widest and best sense of forethought and consideration?

A. All this I grant: and what does it prove? That, if a man will not follow the dictates of reason and common sense, he must expect to suffer for it. But what is all this to a state of trial?

B. You do not do justice to the facts which you have allowed. They prove much more than that. In the first place, they show that there are many things, not self-evident, in practice, to which a man must submit if he would be happy.

A. I do not quite follow you.

B. Well, I suppose to be idle and do what he pleases seems the most delightful life to a school-boy: whereas, to be under discipline, to apply his energies to his tasks, to do a great many things not pleasing to him, are necessary for his future well-being?

A. They are.

B. This, then, is one point established. In the next place, we see that a certain character of the mind is formed by circumstances, and that, if that frame of mind be of one colour, it conduces to happiness; if of another, to unhappiness.

A. This seems also to be true. However, I am not sure that you are not proving too much. But I will not at present stop to inquire whether that is so or not.

B. Now let me ask you to substitute the word *virtue* for *prudence*, and the *life after death* for the *present life*, and state the result.

A. Well, I will not decline. So far as your

argument applies, it amounts to this: *present prudence* is essential to *future well-being in this life;* *present virtue* is essential to *future happiness* in the *life after death.*

B. And what say you to the conclusion?

A. Let me consider. Upon reflection, I do not see that you have explained the benefit of a state of trial.

B. But surely at present that is not the question. Our present object is to see whether the idea of a state of trial is *unreasonable.*

A. Is it fair to draw a comparison between prudence and virtue? Are not the inducements to practise the *one* infinitely stronger and more plain than they are to practise the *other?*

B. Possibly; but then you should consider that, on the whole, the former take effect at a much earlier stage of our existence than the latter.

A. That is very true.

B. However, perhaps it will be better if you state at length some of your particular objections to a state of probation.

A. It appears to me that we are possessed of various affections and feelings which crave for satisfaction. These various emotions are naturally awakened by the presence of certain external objects. The natural inference is that these objects were intended to arouse those emotions. Is not that so?

B. Certainly. We have these emotions, and they are naturally aroused at the presence of their appropriate objects. Those objects were intended to awaken them.

A. But religion declares that we ought to eradicate our natural desires, and to live as if the external objects did not exist.

B. I must demur to that. Religion does not require us to eradicate our moral nature. It only commands us to use this world as not abusing it. And this is no more than reason requires in the management of our temporal affairs.

A. But men succeed in this world without doing violence to their natural affections.

B. Yes, and men attain to virtue without doing violence to their moral nature.

A. But religion, or at all events the Christian religion, leads its votaries into all kinds of austerities. It encourages them to forego the natural duties of home and family, and this by the very injunction of its great Apostle, and at the command of its Founder.

B. I will not pause to argue the passages from Scripture to which you refer. I might, indeed, show you that the same Person Who seems to require the surrender of home and friends and family for His sake, explains His words by saying that whoever loves father and mother more than Him is not worthy of Him.

A. But does not St. Paul counsel the surrender of all for Christ?

B. Most true, but he says no word about monastic discipline and solitary life; and, more than this, he practised neither.

A. But yet you will not deny that he approves of great self-denial?

B. And do not you also approve of self-denial?

A. Of course I do, only it must be with a distinct purpose, and not as in itself meritorious.

B. Then, to my mind, you have but little to complain of in St. Paul; for, if you read his writings carefully, you will find that the self-discipline which he approves has always a very distinct purpose.

A. And what purpose is that?

B. That question will be better answered by considering what are the objects of self-denial in reference to the present life. But, before we go any farther, I should like you to be thoroughly satisfied that you have not made a hasty concession. It is better to clear the ground as we go; and from the easy way in which you allowed the expediency of self-denial in this life, I am afraid you will regret your haste.

A. No. I am satisfied with Milton's assertion respecting fame, that it leads men

"To scorn delights and live laborious days."

B. Is, then, fame the only thing which requires self-denial?

A. No, but it is the type of those things which require it. Success of any kind—prosperity, health, vigorous thought—all these require great sacrifices from men, and without self-denial they are not attainable.

B. And yet all the while such men are subject to the same emotions and surrounded by the same external circumstances as other men. But they know that, if they give way to these, they will fail of the objects which they desire. What shall prevent us from saying, then, that men are exposed to dangers in their temporal capacity, and that these dangers form a condition of trial and probation to them, analogous to the condition in which we are placed with reference to a future life?

A. But you are taking an extreme case. A man who is to attain to a high degree of success must be eminently self-denying, but a very moderate degree of self-restraint serves for an ordinary life; whereas religion requires extraordinary self-restraint from all.

B. I do not think you speak justly about the requirements of religion. The early Christians, to be sure, underwent great privations, but this was from special circumstances. What religion requires from its votaries is not an extraordinary, but a very moderate self-restraint; not greater, in fact, than many men put upon themselves for the sake of a very moderate degree of success. Of course dissolute and worldly people imagine that the self-denial is enormous, but so do dissolute and unsteady young men consider the self-restraint, which would probably afford them health or a competence, intolerably irksome and utterly unattainable.

A. I rather think your theologians would complain, that you are setting a very low standard of practice.

B. And if they do, I can answer that the degree of caution which leads to moderate success in our temporal concerns—that is, which enables a man to steer clear of troubles and misfortunes, and to pass through life without attaining the extremes of what is called either fortune—does not deserve to be very highly commended. There is a *low* standard of religious practice and a *high* standard, and corresponding to these there is a *low* standard of care and foresight in human affairs, and a *high* standard. And there is nothing in religion to forbid the idea, that there are various degrees of perfection and rewards proportioned to the extent of the obedience to the Divine will on the part of men.

A. But just consider this. I am told that people will suffer for faults not their own. Faults in education, errors arising from bad example, and superstitious practices inherited from our ancestors, over which we have no control, are classed among matters for which men are to be made to suffer. Is this just?

B. Just or not, such a degree is only on a par with what experience teaches us.

A. How is that?

B. I thought we had disposed of these questions. However, we will take them in their order. Will you state your particular objections separately, or shall we take them all together?

A. It will be more satisfactory to take each

one by itself. Is it just that people should be punished for faults in education?

B. Why, half the misfortunes in life arise from bad training. The principles inculcated by degraded and vicious parents produce a lamentable condition in their offspring. The instances in which children rise above these debasing influences are so rare as almost to deserve the name of supernatural, even from those who do not acknowledge Divine interposition.

A. But is *that* just?

B. We do not complain of it. There are enough influences on the other side, if men will only make use of them, to rescue them from unhappiness. That they *will* not use them is considered on all hands a crime, and punished by society as such. And if it is not unjust in society, why should it be unjust in God?

A. Because God is a purely good Being.

B. In other words, your estimate of God is, that He ought not to show Himself upon the side of virtue; but, if so, the course of nature cannot have come from Him.

A. I do not see the force of your argument.

B. Is it not plain that if God never manifests any disapprobation of vice, but deals with the virtuous as with the vicious, He cannot be the Author of that course of nature in which, as a fact, virtue on the whole tends to happiness, and vice to misery?

A. Well, then, let us pass on to the case of punishment being inflicted upon those who err from bad example.

B. In that case, we need hardly call in the act of analogy. The two cases are identical. The result of bad example in this life is always misery, frequently despair, not rarely death.

A. But what will you say to superstitions, which are only religion carried to extravagance?

B. That, by the way, is not a fair account of superstitions. As a rule, they involve all kinds of abuses, wicked licence, and gross immorality, not to speak of fraud and deceit. They substitute external rites in the place of virtue. I should compare superstition to fraudulent principles, and perverted ideas as to the laws of justice and equity in dealing with our fellow-men. So long as they are confined to mistaken opinions, the consequences are not represented as so appalling as when they take the form, which they almost invariably assume, of a degradation of the moral perception. In that case, whether with reference to our present or our future prospects, the result may well be looked upon as terrible in the last degree.

A. Pardon me if I ask you to explain your meaning.

B. I mean to say that, by the influence of perverted ideas, carried out into practice, men grow up gradually into a state of turpitude, in which they eventually are unable to discern what is really to their own advantage; they acquire principles of conduct which make them unendurable to society, and society punishes them, with a rough and ready justice, for their ignorance of right and wrong. And yet these men, to all appearance, are not responsible for their own condition; they suffer for the faults of others; the bad principles which they have derived from others are punished in them. Thus the course of nature in this world is very much analogous to what religion teaches us of the operations of Providence in regard to a future life.

A. All this I confess. But my original difficulty remains, that the ordinance of Providence is unequal in its operation.

B. Unequal it may seem to us to be. But yet we are not justified in charging God with injustice, because, as I have often said, we are only capable of looking on a part of the whole dispensation of things. Besides this, it is possible that the account which religion gives of the source of all this apparent inequality may be the true one after all.

A. What is the explanation which you refer to?

B. I hardly like to enter upon it here, because it belongs to another part of the subject. Still, as it may throw a light upon some obscurities, I will venture to introduce it. Religion says that man is in a fallen condition.

A. Oh! I know what you mean. The story of Adam and Eve, and the serpent and the forbidden fruit. I don't see how that will explain punishing people for ignorance and bad example; because, if we accept the notion of the Fall, Adam and Eve fell deliberately.

B. It is as I feared; the introduction of this topic irritates you.

A. Not in the least; but I think it is nothing to your point.

B. But I was not, at the moment, referring to the mode or causes of man's degradation. I was thinking of a passage in which it is said, "God made men upright: but they have sought out many inventions;" and what I wished to convey was, that our liability to temptation may very possibly arise, in a great measure, from our own inclination to follow the feeling which happens to be strongest within us at the time; and that, in the course of time, the selfish feelings have come so to preponderate over all others, that what, in the first instance, was but a *gentle stimulus* to activity becomes a *violent desire*, which carries all before it, and pays no heed to the checks and restraints which wisdom and prudence attempt to exercise.

A. I think that is not an unfair representation of the process through which the majority of minds pass.

B. In that case you will see that, though man's nature is faulty, it is not God, but man himself, who has made temptations difficult to resist. There is nothing in the circumstances of his life to *compel* him to succumb under temptation. On the contrary, a reasonable amount of thought will restrain him from running into error. Whether he will exert that reasonable forethought is another question, not to be discussed here.

A. I shall not be satisfied till I see the advantage of a state of trial. Of what profit is it to me to know that I am liable to make mistakes, and to suffer for those mistakes? My own experience would tell me as much. But how it is to instruct me in religion, or to elevate my moral nature, certainly does not appear; and, unless you can persuade me that such is the use of a state of trial, I had rather believe that the whole resemblance between the doctrines of religion and the course of nature, is a pure accident and a freak of imagination, no more real than the old idea that fire must be the origin of all things, because the flickerings and changes of the flame resemble the mutability of all human affairs.

B. I am not without hope that we shall find some explanations of a state of trial which may satisfy you, at least in part. But, at present, all we have attempted to establish is, that this doctrine is not unreasonable. In ordinary life our happiness or misery depends in a great measure on ourselves. Unless we employ the necessary means to avoid the one and gain the other—means not altogether pleasant, nor such as we should choose for ourselves—the result is failure—grievous, painful, irreparable failure.

A. So far your argument is unanswerable; and to this extent I accept your conclusions. Happiness on earth is a condition not given to us accomplished, but to be acquired: it cannot be attained, if indeed it is attainable at all, without difficulty: the acquisition of it is attended with danger of failure, as is proved by the actual failure of a large number to acquire it. Men need attention and self-denial, which they can exercise if they will. Now, if there is a' future life, as we have conceded provisionally, it is not altogether unreasonable to expect similar conditions for the attainment of happiness therein.

B. But this is all that we undertook to prove.

A. It is: but it is meagre fare after all. You must find me more solid satisfaction than this, or you will have done little for me.

B. Be it so. To-morrow we will continue our investigations. But permit me to add to what I have said, that we have only touched upon the surface of this subject. The analogy between nature and religion is so very great in this matter, that every day will present you with striking illustrations of the mode in which trial comes in as an element of our daily life. And I am satisfied that the more you reflect upon it the more you will find reason to recall the words you have just spoken, that, in default of further evidence, you will consider the resemblance a mere accident, and no proof whatever of the identity of the Author of Nature with the God of Religion.

A. I will bear in mind what you say, and

try what my own experience declares upon this subject. I confess I see a dark shadow beginning to loom over the whole question—a phantom which I know not how to lay. How soon we shall have to deal with it I know not; but what we have done to-day will be enough to occupy me till we meet again.

DIALOGUE V.

ON LIFE CONSIDERED AS A STATE OF MORAL DISCIPLINE.

A. A VERY interesting question has engaged my attention since yesterday; but, judging from previous experience, I suspect you will not allow yourself to be drawn into a discussion upon the subject. I have been trying to discover how mankind, considered as the creatures of an all-good Being, and primarily, at all events, inclined to aspire to the imitation of their Creator, can have sunk into the state of trial in which they actually are found.

B. You are right. I should be most unwilling to enter into the question, especially at the present stage of our argument. In the first place, I do not see what advantage such an inquiry could be expected to produce. It is just one of those speculative questions which perplex without satisfying the mind. To attempt to reason out, on *à priori* principles, the intentions and purposes of God always leaves the inquirer unsatisfied. In the next place, it is confessedly beyond the scope of our present conversations, which aim at comparing the facts of human life, as known by experience, with the doctrines asserted in religion. And, thirdly, we have not yet considered the question of the credibility of revelation, in which a sufficient explanation of your present inquiry is found. But may I not hope that you will be satisfied with a cognate question, which incidentally may throw some small light upon this matter?

A. To what do you refer?

B. Shall we not, think you, find ample scope for inquiry in the question, " For what purpose are we placed in a condition of trial?"

A. Certainly; if you will answer that question I shall be very well satisfied. To me it appears a more difficult question than the other. I cannot conceive what advantage there is in being exposed to the danger of failure in duty, when such failure is to be visited with grievous consequences.

B. May I ask you, then, what idea you form of a future existence?

A. I picture to myself a condition in which men will be free from all weakness and faultiness. The faculties, which here they possess in imperfection, will be made perfect. The painful, laborious acquisition of knowledge, which forms the weak point in the purely intellectual side of human nature, will have ceased; memory will not be fallacious; processes of reasoning will cease to be necessary, and all knowledge will be by intuition. The power of grasping at one view a vastly extended range of truth will have been acquired: and though absolute science, perhaps, must be impossible to any but the All-Wise, our acquaintance with the principles and purposes of the universe will, as compared with our present knowledge, deserve to be called infinite.

B. So much for the intellect. I will only interrupt you so far as to point out one word which you have perhaps unconsciously used—the word "acquired:" to that we may have to recur. I cordially accept your view of our intellectual condition; and what will you say of the moral side of human nature?

A. In a future state all our emotions and affections will be exercised to their full extent, but without conflicting with one another. There will be no opposing interests to excite and irritate the soul—no envyings, quarrellings, or contests for supremacy. A due proportion will be observed between the various portions of our nature; passion will give way to principle in every department of our souls' energies; a general regard to the welfare of the society in which we then shall exist will actuate us, so that selfishness will disappear from the elements of our nature. Thus love, truth, disinterestedness will be the moving principles of our lives.

B. I have forborne to interrupt you in the lofty description of a future state which you have presented. Whether you are quite consistent in admitting emotion and yet excluding passion may be a question. What think you?

A. By emotion I mean simply a movement of the soul towards an object; by passion, a violent, and therefore perilous, impulse.

B. With that explanation I am satisfied. There is, however, one point which you have omitted. What feelings or dispositions will exist in the individual soul towards the God of all spirits?

A. Unmixed and perfect love.

B. But tell me. However purified the soul may be, God will still be infinitely above it. It will not comprehend all His counsels: it will not even then know all His decrees. Are there, then, no additional dispositions to be assigned to the soul in reference to God?

A. I had not thought of this.

B. Do you not think we may fairly assign to the soul, without detracting from its exaltation, a loving awe of the Almighty, a loving submissiveness to His authority?

A. I think we must.

B. And now we are in a position to proceed with our inquiry, "Of what benefit is a state of trial to man?"

A. You have entrapped me into a somewhat rhetorical flight respecting a future life; but I was not aware you were going to employ it against me.

B. Surely not. Pray retract anything you have said, if you think fancy has run away with you.

A. No, no; I do not mean that. But I cannot quite understand what your line of argument is going to be.

B. That will very much depend upon you. Still, I have a general idea of what the line of my argument will be; and as this is not a trial by jury, and I trust I am not a special pleader, I will willingly explain my present object. The question before us is, "How is this life related to the life after death?" Is not that so?

A. Yes.

B. Religion declares that it is a preparation for it, does it not?

K

A. It does.

B. And you wish to know how it is a preparation?

A. I very much wish to understand this point.

B. The idea which religion inculcates is that it is a state of discipline for that future life. Will you tell me what you understand by discipline?

A. I take it to signify a state of preparation—a condition in which instruction is given, faculties are trained, and faults and eccentricities toned down.

B. And now do you understand why I asked you for your ideas of a future life?

A. I suppose you are going to show how the circumstances of this life afford opportunities for instruction, training, and the removal of faults from the character.

B. You are partially correct; but to do so we must be able to compare the circumstances of the present with the future life, and then to compare the opportunities of discipline afforded for the two states of existence respectively.

A. I do not quite follow you. In order to your analogy you ought to be able to express it mathematically, thus: as $A : B :: C : D$. Now I see what your third and fourth terms are. The latter ratio will run thus: So are the opportunities for discipline in this life to the future state. Thus your C will be opportunities for discipline in this life, and your D will be the state after death. But now, if you draw out the first ratio, A : B, I do not see what your first term will be. The second will be the present life.

B. Let me see if I cannot help you. A future life will be the maturity to which the present tends. Let us call B the mature state of the present life, and then, perhaps, you will be able to say what A is.

A. It must stand for the condition of childhood and youth.

B. You are quite right. Do you now understand why I have elicited from you an idea of what a future life will probably be?

A. I think I perceive your drift. You are going to trace a resemblance between the state of childhood as a preparation for manhood, and our state in the present as a discipline for a future existence.

B. That is my idea. Do you think it feasible?

A. I can hardly say at present, till you open out your argument.

B. What do you consider to be the advantage of the periods of childhood and youth?

A. I should say they were a time of growth from ignorance to knowledge, and from a condition of emotion and passion to fixed principles.

B. Excellent! Now, do you think that the knowledge of a man in mature life is as much greater than his ignorance in childhood, as the combined knowledge of all things would be greater than the information possessed by any man alive?

A. No. I certainly imagine that even the most learned man has but a fragmentary knowledge; his amplest information is but a mere point in the infinite ocean of space and time.

B. Well, then, if any one objects to us that it is not fair to draw any analogy between mature manhood and infancy, we are prepared with an answer to him, are we not?

A. Yes; we should say that his very objection shows how ignorant he is of his own ignorance.

B. Well, with my consent, we should not say that, because we might offend him, and then he would be found a child in quite another way.

A. How is that?

B. Why, he would be irritated, and refuse to listen to our reasonings, and put them aside scornfully as the fancies of idiots and dreamers; and so he would become more and more a child, and, as he grew more unreasonable, would establish for us a second point, that even a wise man, who has used this life to acquire self-restraint, is very little better than a child; for if anything crosses him he is irritated and unreasonable, which are the characteristics of a child.

A. Well, I think with you that the majority of men are mere children, when their passions and inclinations are concerned; they seem entirely unable to exercise any self-control, or see anything but what lies just before them in the high road of their inclination.

B. And yet, I suppose, you will allow that, if men made a proper use of the days of childhood and youth, this wretched want of self-mastery would not exist?

A. Yes; for I see some men—not a very numerous class indeed, but still some—who have managed to bring their natural passions and emotions under proper discipline.

B. And should you say that such men were the most miserable or not?

A. I should say that, on the whole, they are the most happy men.

B. And yet do you not find men, possessed of

the greatest self-restraint, who are yet worn out with anxiety by the cares of life? I mention this, lest some one should say to us afterwards that we are not fair in our arguments.

A. If I rightly understand you, you refer to those men who have subdued all their passions, not under reason, but under one ruling passion, as ambition. I should not call those men self-disciplined.

B. And shall we say that these are the only men who are not self-disciplined?

A. I think we must include the majority of men in this category.

B. Are we to assume, therefore, that childhood is not fitted to be a state of discipline for manhood, because the majority of men do not find it so?

A. Certainly not. We are to assume it to be what its nature proves it to be, and that is a condition peculiarly fitted for a discipline for mature age, however small be the use which men make of it.

B. And do you see what this proves?

A. What?

B. Does it not show that if any one should object that this life cannot be a state of discipline for the next, on the ground that religion and facts both agree in declaring that men do not make it so, we must reply that the same objection will lie against the idea of childhood and youth being a state of discipline for manhood, which they plainly are?

A. It does prove that.

B. Having now settled these questions beforehand, we are in a position to discuss the matter of principal moment to us.

A. What is that?

B. Why, that this life is a fit discipline for the life which you depicted at the commencement of our conversation to-day.

A. I understand.

B. And do you not think that the best way to do this will be to inquire how far childhood and youth are fitted to be a discipline for manhood?

A. Certainly; I think that that is the only possible course.

B. And do you think this is a very easy inquiry?

A. Why not?

B. Is it an easy thing to trace the growth of character, the fading of passions and emotions, and the substitution of principles in their room? It is not like an experiment in chemistry, where you may actually realize by the senses, in a short time, results which perhaps have cost the discoverer years of patient inquiry. Here experiment is out of the question, and we can only draw inferences from our own experience. Do you agree with me?

A. I certainly think that inquiries into mental and moral phenomena are less real, less to be relied on, than those in physical science.

B. We will not dispute as to the respective certainty of the two departments of thought; it is sufficient that you concede that it is far more difficult to arrive at a certainty in mental than it is in physical science. Shall I commence the inquiry?

A. Pray do so.

B. Shall you agree with me, if I say that he was right, who said of human life that "one thing is set over against another"?

A. You appear to be making game of me, and asking me a riddle.

B. I ask your pardon for my obscurity. Is it true, then, that human nature is adapted to the circumstances of human life?

A. Perfectly true.

B. And does it not follow from this that the faculties of mind and body in man are actually suited to his position in this world?

A. No doubt they are: even Mr. Darwin grants this.

B. So far as my present argument goes I trust I shall not be found at variance with so keen an observer as Mr. Darwin. And are not these faculties capable of great improvement?

A. Of the very greatest.

B. So much so, that it is at least imaginable, that the degree of excellence attained by a man in this world is not the greatest possible: is it not so?

A. Yes: otherwise the doctrine of progress would have no meaning.

B. I am glad to find my ideas so modern. Well now, this human nature (if you will pardon my vague scholasticism), which is capable of so indefinite a growth, does grow in this world to a certain extent; and the process of its growth may be described as a passage from habits to principles. If you test the development of your own nature, you will find that originally you were subject to single impressions and single emotions. For example: in early childhood you saw, it may be, a tree in the garden; and when you were close up to it, you saw that it was huge, tall, and knotted; at a distance it appeared smaller, lower, and smooth. By a number of such observations, most of them quite unconsciously performed, you acquired the habit, which you now possess, of judging accurately of distances, of size, and the other phenomena of vision, by the eye. You, who are an artist, will be able to realize how you acquired this habit of accuracy, because you have had to go back over the process, in order to appreciate the rules of your art.

A. I am satisfied that accuracy of eye, even the ordinary precision by which every one judges of height and distance, is a product of habitual comparison unconsciously exercised.

B. Is not memory a habit of the same kind?

A. I should hardly have dared to compare the two, because the habit of judging of height and distance is so much more common than precision of memory.

B. Are you not confounding excellence in each case? This is just one of the instances to which I referred when I spoke of the difficulty of judging facts in these inquiries. You seem to think that memory is a much rarer faculty than the power of judging by the eye.

A. And do not you think it is, also?

B. What are we to say to the power of language? Every word we use implies a process of comparison and observation; and not only of these, but also of memory. It is a very remarkable exercise of memory to attach to each thing which falls under our observation its appropriate name; and to be able, at will, to recall the thing at the mention of the name, or the name at the perception of the thing. And I really believe that you would find that memory is more universal and more accurate than the faculty of judging by the eye.

A. I confess I was mistaken.

B. So that in questions connected with the senses, as well as in purely mental operations, men are capable by practice, or, which is the same thing, by the acquisition of habits, of growing to a much higher state of perfection than that in which they are first placed.

A. This seems certain.

B. Let us now turn to what we may call the moral or active side of human nature. Do you think that the same observations hold good here?

A. Most assuredly they do. The first stage of existence is one in which there are all sorts of inclinations and propensities. Children are always under the influence of what we may call passions, or, more strictly, emotions. If it were not for these they could not live. As they grow older, the constant repetition of acts produces habits; and the more often they act in a particular way, the more decided does the habit become.

B. But, tell me, do you think that men can become virtuous without acts?

A. No; I do not.

B. It is not enough to make a man virtuous for him to form pictures of virtue, and run over them in his mind, is it?

A. Oh, no! Some of the most ostentatiously active preachers of virtue have been found to be sadly wanting in practice.

B. It is quite evident, then, that, for the practice of virtue or any excellence, the opportunity of acquiring habits must be afforded. Men must be placed in such a condition that they may act repeatedly in the same way. More than this, they must have perpetual inducements so to act; for, if not, they will not perform the actions, and so will not acquire the habit of virtue.

A. All this is very true.

B. I said just now that the course of human life is a gradual change from passion to principle. Do you now understand what I intended by those words?

A. I do.

B. And do you think I have made out my case?

A. I think you have, so far as you have gone. But, tell me, are the passions, as you call them, non-existent in the mature man?

B. Non-existent is scarcely the right word. The seed ought not to be called non-existent when it has developed into the tree with all its leaves and branches. Yet the tree is not more different from the seed than habits are from emotions. However—to answer your question—it cannot be denied that, as habits of action grow stronger and more confirmed, the feelings from which these habits spring grow less powerful. For example: what is the natural impulse on perceiving distress?

A. To feel compassion for it.

B. Is that all?

A. To relieve it.

B. Suppose you set yourself constantly to relieve distress in others, does your sense of pity grow more or less acute?

A. Undoubtedly the sight of distress is less painful to those who are inured to it.

B. And yet it is by no means necessary that they should be less willing to relieve it.

A. No. They may be just as willing, as others who are new to it, and they certainly are far more capable of relieving it.

B. Let us take another instance. What is the natural result of perceiving that you are in danger?

A. First, alarm; and, secondly, a desire to escape.

B. Suppose you are constantly placed in a similar state of danger, does your alarm continue as vivid as at first?

A. No; we get inured to it.

B. And are you less able to avoid the danger than before?

A. I suppose I should be far better able to meet it than when I first met with it.

B. So that in this instance as well, although the emotions which arouse you to action have grown weaker, the habits which they give rise to are so firmly fixed in your constitution, as to remove the necessity for the keenness of the emotions. Let us take one more instance before we go on. The first time you were brought into contact with death, did it not shock you much more than it does now that you have seen the constant inroads of death among your friends and acquaintances?

A. Certainly. I well recollect the blighting and appalling sensation with which I heard for the first time of the death of a relation. He was a person whom I scarcely knew, but the fact of his death threw a gloom over me for days. The idea of a separation such as *death,* hiding him utterly from all who knew him, was awful and incomprehensible to me; but, now that I have seen friend after friend taken away, though I grieve for the loss I suffer, I have almost entirely lost the terrors which I first felt at the thought of the approach of death.

B. And yet you have learned to adapt your life to the fact that death is universal. I am not now speaking with reference to a future life. But you have arranged your affairs, made various preparations against the contingency of sudden death; but, besides this, you have gained a settled habit of mind adapted to a condition so uncertain as the present life. Is this not so?

A. I believe it is.

B. And thus we see that passive impressions, however made upon our minds, by admonition, example, or experience, tend to produce actions, and actions lead to habits. Habits once formed react upon our nature; they keep under and restrain contrary inclinations; they remove apparent difficulties, and thus what appeared difficult and repulsive becomes pleasant and attractive, and men acquire a new character, and a new condition of life, such as nature did not give, but in the acquisition of which it acted as guide.

A. All this seems beyond question.

B. Can you imagine any other way by which men could be prepared for the career of mature life, except by the gradual acquisition of habits?

A. No, I do not think I can; for, even if we suppose that men were created with faculties fully developed, it is a very great question whether they would be as well suited to the circumstances of life as now they are. For example, their sense of sight would be most deceptive; and although in children, whose faculties are undeveloped, this is of small importance, inasmuch as the care of others provides for them, it would have a much greater effect upon creatures whose powers of mind and body were in a high state of development. But this would be of small importance compared with other dangers to which they would be exposed.

B. Will you tell me to what you refer?

A. I mean dangers arising from their ignorance of their own powers compared with those of nature—ignorance of the means by which various ends must be attained. Then, again, the habits of body and mind would be brought into exercise upon unsuitable occasions, because even a perfect nature is not a simple thing, but a complex whole made up of principles, not indeed antagonistic, but different, and suited for different circumstances.

B. If I understand you aright, you are of opinion that men in their mature state are quite unsuited to deal with the world, unless they have gone through the natural training of childhood and youth.

A. Yes; to introduce a full-grown man without preparation into that complex condition which we call society, would be very much the same thing as introducing him into a new trade without instruction. He would have to learn the use of the various instruments, the nature of the substances with which he had to deal, the modes of treatment suited to each; and even then he would without doubt make a great many unsuccessful attempts before he was even moderately skilful, and probably after all would be a very far inferior workman to one of less natural ability, but practised in the occupations from childhood.

B. And in the same way, I suppose, a man born with all his faculties developed, would be far less able to cope with the world than one who had gradually grown up to it, and learned where to forbear and where to insist—what is of vital importance, and what is indifferent?

A. Exactly so; and, besides, we must bear

this in mind. Knowing what men are, and how they are liable to be deceived and misled by circumstances, it is highly probable that, in consequence of their ignorance of the world in which they live, they would make grievous and fatal mistakes, and render society far less endurable than it is now.

B. All this is very satisfactory. I do not think we shall have much difficulty now in seeing that childhood and youth are a necessary preparation for manhood, and that without them the present condition of the world would be utterly unendurable.

A. Yes; but you seem to forget that all this undermines one of the prime doctrines of your religion. Your story of Adam and Eve, full-grown man and woman, falls to the ground, crumbling under your involuntary assaults.

B. I do not see that. Adam and Eve were not, strictly speaking, born into a state of society; the very condition of their origin necessitated that they should not be dependent on the care of others, which is the essential of childhood. Moreover, the story is so far consistent, that the world into which they were born was one on which sin, misery, and death had not set their seal; they had not the same temptations, the same struggle for existence which their descendants have to endure. However, I am not now arguing for the truth or falsehood of the history of Adam. What I have said is, I think, sufficient to meet your present objection.

A. Well, I will allow it to pass : only recollect it is a point reserved.

B. So be it. Now let us continue. You grant, do you not, that childhood is a necessary discipline for mature life?

A. I do.

B. And that you cannot well conceive how, without some such discipline, life could be made endurable?

A. This also I grant.

B. Now let us turn to a future life. You have said that such a life must be conceived of, as the consummation of this. Whatever is here imperfect must there be perfect, and nothing that is not a plain growth of evil in this world need be considered as excluded from the future life. Is not that your description?

A. Yes, certainly; I consider that all our faculties, adequately trained, will have their exercise in a future life. I do not see why we should consider that that life will be other than a state of society.

B. Then, if so, it must appear no unreasonable doctrine that our faculties may have the opportunity of adequate training in this life, and that we shall be able to acquire such a character as will fit us for such a society.

A. Assuredly not.

B. Now, suppose that men were created in this world without any tendency to pursue wrong courses, with no bias towards evil, would there be any necessity for a state of discipline?

A. I should have thought not.

B. Consider it in this way. The very notion of an active being, like man, is that he should have emotions to incline him to act. Is it not?

A. Assuredly.

B. Every emotion implies its contrary, does it not?

A. I really cannot say.

B. If we are inclined to act in a certain way, may we not be inclined to act in the opposite way?

A. That seems to be implied in the idea of inclination.

B. One of these ways is right and the other is wrong. Now, whatever be the means by which we distinguish between right and wrong, it is evident that, if we may be inclined to choose what we know to be right, we may equally be inclined to choose the opposite. If we choose the one, constantly and deliberately,

LIFE AS A STATE OF MORAL DISCIPLINE.

we acquire habits of virtue; and if we choose the other, constantly and deliberately, we acquire habits of vice. Do you admit this?

A. I have already done so.

B. Well, then, will you not further admit that, until virtuous habits are formed, a being created sinless may fall into sin?

A. I do not follow your argument.

B. Every time an object is presented to our mind, which is naturally desirable, but cannot be lawfully obtained, there is a natural inclination towards it which is restrained in the virtuous by their principles. Still the emotion is felt. Every time that it is allowed to dwell in the mind, there is so far a dereliction from what is right, and a tendency to sin. Such a tendency seems to inhere in the very idea of inclination. Do you now understand my meaning?

A. I do.

B. So, then, even for a sinless being, a field of discipline is required, in which he may practise virtuous acts, acquire virtuous habits, and gain for himself that character of mind which alone is suitable for a future life, such as we have contemplated. He cannot afford to do without such a state of discipline as may teach him what are the essentials of a perfectly peaceful and holy society. His virtuous principles would require to be improved, his inclinations to be educated and taught restraint. And such a creature, though he had never sinned, would be in a higher state of perfection, than he would be, were it possible for him to remain in that sinless condition with which he began.

A. Plainly that is so; for in the one case he would only not have done wrong; in the other he would be, in a manner, *unable* to do wrong; and this would certainly be an improvement.

B. Well, then, even for a perfectly uncorrupt nature, such a discipline, as this life affords, would be beneficial. But take men as they really are, with a greater inclination to vice than virtue, the slaves of their passions, and prone ever to pursue the first inclination which seizes them, without an attempt to consider its consequences or resist its influence, of such would you not say that they required discipline to wear out vicious habits, to recover their primitive state of self-government, which indulgence has weakened, to repair the moral sentiments within them in order that they may at length arrive at a secure state of virtuous happiness?

A. I consider, that you exaggerate the evil

tendencies of human nature; nevertheless, I am bound to confess that men do fall very far short of absolute virtue; that vice and selfishness are very powerful in the world. But if this life is, as you imply, eminently suited for a state of moral discipline, why does it not serve its purpose more effectually? for men do not use it for a sphere of improvement.

B. It would not be a state of moral discipline if men were *compelled* to improve under it. The very idea of moral discipline implies that men may or may not make use of it for their improvement. The whole notion of free agency, upon which virtue depends, would be done away with if every man were obliged to act virtuously.

A. But are you so sure that this life does afford such opportunities for improvement?

B. No man can walk about the world with his eyes open, and see the miseries men bring upon themselves for want of self-restraint, by following their inclinations, and giving the reins to ungoverned passion, without knowing that these things are evil, and that self-discipline is essential to happiness.

A. But self-discipline surely will not be required in a world where there are no temptations?

B. Even if it be not, which may perhaps be not altogether certain, the temper of mind which self-discipline creates may be necessary.

A. What! can anything unpleasant be necessary in a state of happiness?

B. Self-discipline may be painful in the acquisition: it may require much watchfulness, care, and trouble. But the whole tendency of our argument is to show that things, painful at first by reason of the stress of attention which they demand, lose their painfulness as they grow into habits, and may even become pleasurable. This certainly is the case in all mental energies; for they who have toiled to gain proficiency feel a pleasure in the exercise of their improved faculties. And if observation can prove anything in these matters, the virtuous feel a pleasure in their self-restraint.

A. But, after all, your argument amounts to this: that men are virtuous and pious from fear and selfish motives, and hence your idea of discipline degrades religion.

B. Pardon me; if I do what God commands, because He commands it, my act is obedience, whether I obey Him through hope or fear; and a continuance of such actions will produce a habit of *obedience*. And if I speak the truth and do what is just and charitable, however much I may begin from lower motives, I shall end by acquiring habits of truth, justice, and veracity. No mistake is greater, no reasoning more distinctly sophistical, than that which refuses to see higher motives, because the action of lower motives may be discerned as well. If it is the case that obedience, love of truth and justice, and charitable conduct are coincident with our own chief interest, that is only a proof of the wisdom and goodness of God, who has made all things to combine for our improvement.

A. Certainly that is a new idea to me, and a very valuable one.

B. And now let us return to that with which we commenced—your idea of a future state. The discipline of the present life is such that all the faculties of our souls may be taught to work in harmony. They may be reduced to order and regularity; undisciplined, they may be compared to the discord produced by the ignorant combination of sweet sounds. They are like the strumming of a child upon an organ. Disciplined and restrained, they resemble the harmonious measure of a great musician, in which each note attains to just the fulness which the master wills. There is no discord, there are no unseemly risings and fallings, but all works together as a finished whole. Such is evidently the condition of a well-disciplined soul, which has learned by long experience the harmony of its existence.

A. In all this I am inclined to acquiesce: and yet there is one point in your argument which does not seem to be clearly made out.

B. What is it, may I ask?

A. It is this. Granting that this life is a suitable sphere for calling our faculties into play, for restraining them in their exercise, and giving to each its proper strength and activity, there is still one quality, or rather one aggregate of qualities, which is proclaimed to be of the very essence of religion, for which we can have no possible use in a future life of happiness. I mean resignation.

B. To put it otherwise, you are of opinion that there will be no *opportunity* for the exercise of this quality in another life?

A. That is precisely my meaning.

B. Do you think that prosperity or adversity is the best discipline for resignation?

A. Adversity, to be sure. Prosperity is no discipline for this quality.

B. Now, to me, it seems that prosperity is, or might be, almost as good a discipline for it as adversity. The rich, the prosperous, and the fortunate, are met by quite as many obstacles as the poor; and I question very much whether, as a rule, those obstacles are not more painful to them, than the hardships of the others are to them. This, you will justly observe, is because prosperity is no discipline to them. But it proves the need of resignation, and points out how that, for the acquisition of happiness, all men must make this life a means of self-discipline.

A. But how will that resignation serve them in another life?

B. Is it not possible that, though there will be no trials to such as have learned self-discipline, the frame of mind which the exercise of resignation creates may be absolutely essential to happiness? I will hazard an illustration on this subject which, perhaps, may make my meaning clearer. Do you expect that men in a future life will know all things?

A. No; for if so, they would be equal to God.

B. But is it not natural to desire fresh knowledge?

A. Assuredly.

B. And is it not certain that some limitation must be placed to our knowledge?

A. Undoubtedly.

B. But how will it be possible to restrain this craving without the exercise of resignation to the Divine decree?

A. But how, then, will the future life be one of absolute happiness?

B. Because men will have learned a habit of mind, which will prevent them from repining, or desiring what they cannot attain. *Without* this, I do not hesitate to affirm that the future life might become miserable.

A. And you think that temptation can reach us in a future life?

B. Certainly not; but the reason is, not that the occasions of failure are absent, but that, to perfectly disciplined souls, they cease to be temptations; they present no allurements or inducements to transgress. Temptation implies *external objects* acting upon emotions existing *within* us; and it matters not whether the objects are actually removed, or the emotions cease to be aroused by them inordinately and beyond measure: in either case they cease to be temptations.

A. In this, indeed, you have certainly met my difficulty, and I thank you for your suggestions.

B. And now, let me ask, have I removed any of your difficulties, in regarding this world as a state of discipline?

A. When I commenced this conversation, I began without much idea of what you meant by moral discipline. You have shown me that this life may be employed for something beyond a mere following of inclination, and that we are able, by habit, to change ourselves to a very great extent from our original condition in childhood. In fact, our condition is such that we have it in our own power, to a very great extent, to make our own character. Nature indicates the way, but does not compel us to follow it. And you have led me to infer that, by a similar education, we are preparing through life for another stage of existence, in which those faculties which we have been educating here may find their proper sphere of exercise. I have, therefore, being gaining new ideas, rather than having previous difficulties dispelled. And without committing myself rashly, I will add, that your arguments seem to dispose of some of the difficulties which beset most theories of human life. However, I will not profess myself convinced or converted, until I have well considered the whole matter again. As I am about to be away for some days, I shall hope to visit you in a week, and report to you the result of my reflections. Good-bye.

B. Till next week then, I wish you "*Farewell*."

DIALOGUE VI.

ON THE DOCTRINE OF NECESSITY.

B. Good morning, my friend! As you have deserted me lately, I have taken advantage of the bright weather to call upon you. I began to fear that you were ill.

A. Oh, no! I am very well. During the last few days I have been devoting much of my time to my favourite occupations, chemistry and geology. I fancy you do not take much interest in them.

B. Indeed I do; though the opportunity of pursuing the study practically has been rarely offered to me. I have lived the greater part of my time in a part of the country where comparatively few interesting phenomena of geology offer themselves, and I have never had the opportunity of using a good laboratory; so that my acquaintance with these subjects is limited. But I feel the keenest interest in both. Both appear to me to reveal the wisdom and forethought of nature's Author: the one exhibiting the minuteness, the other the vastness, of His operations.

A. But I thought that geology and chemistry were supposed to be the most dangerous opponents of religion?

B. Some people, indeed, consider them as such. For my own part, I have always felt that the Book of nature is as much God's work as the Book of Scripture; and I am not afraid that the two will eventually be found contradicting each other, however much difficulties may be found on the surface. But I fear you are occupied, as I see you have visitors in the house.

A. I have a friend staying with me, who is giving me the benefit of his researches in science; and if you will stay with us, I should much like to introduce you. You will find him utterly opposed to you in opinions; and as I have been speaking to him of our late conversations, I should be glad if you would hear what he has to say.

B. I will willingly stay. The opportunity of conversing with a scientific man is a real treat. I am always struck with their clear systematic modes of thinking and speaking; and I am quite sure no one can hear such men reason without great profit.

A. Shall we, then, walk into the library, where my friend is at present?

B. By all means.

A. My dear C., this is the friend of whom I have been speaking to you. Allow me to introduce you to one another.

C. I am happy to make your acquaintance.

B. And I am grateful for the chance which brought me here to-day.

A. I have been telling B. that you and he will not agree.

C. You make us out to be very quarrelsome people, then. I suppose you are tired of the purely peaceful and dispassionate inquiries in which we have been occupied, and want a little excitement for a change? For my own part I prefer to be regarded as a rational animal, and not to be viewed in the light of a gladiator or a bull-dog.

A. It is all very well for you to assume this pacific deportment; but I am not going to let you off for saying that our friend here has been the means of spoiling me as a student of science.

C. I did not say quite that. I only said, that since you have devoted yourself to talking with this gentleman, you have lost something of your practical turn of mind. You are constantly starting off from scientific conclusions, because you are afraid of their tendency; that is, you reject or refuse to see facts, because you are perplexed with words.

A. I cannot allow that the facts of our mental constitution are mere words. I cannot, indeed, put them into a crucible and melt them down. But they are realities to me; and if I find the conclusions of science and the facts of the mental constitution at variance, I still assert that we have no right to let the palpable override the ideal, simply because I can handle the elements of the one and not of the other.

B. May I ask what is the question in dispute? At present, I confess that I have no ideas on the subject of your discussion.

C. Well, sir, our friend told me that you had been proving to him that we are in a state of moral discipline in this life, and that our conduct here deserves and receives reward and blame according to its character.

B. We have certainly been arguing in that direction. And do you find any objection to such a conclusion?

C. Any objection! Why, the thing is absurd upon the face of it.

B. In what way?

C. How can a being who is compelled to act

in a certain way, be a subject of reward or blame?

B. Do you think all our actions are compulsory?

C. Unquestionably. The whole tenor of scientific discovery is to show that everything is the result of certain antecedent circumstances. If you put two chemical elements together, and subject them to certain conditions, a result necessarily follows. No amount of will on your part can prevent it.

B. But suppose I prevent their coming together?

C. You cannot do so; if they do not come together in one place, they will come together at another.

B. However, I can prevent them coming together sometimes, and then the result does not follow in those cases.

C. Possibly; but that does not do away with the necessity of their nature.

B. No; but it shows that my will may modify necessary conditions, and so alter the course of nature.

C. But your will is the result of antecedent circumstances. It is an effect just as much as everything else is an effect. And thus you only push the difficulty a step farther back.

B. I understand you to say, that human action is a result of human motives, and that if a motive is presented to the will it must obey it.

C. That is exactly what I do say, and it at once abolishes all freedom of the will.

B. Would it not be more correct to say that it abolishes freedom of action?

C. I do not perceive any difference between the two.

B. There appears to me to be a very material difference. I will allow that if a motive is present, there is an obligation on the will to obey it; or, if there is a variety of motives, the will is compelled to obey that which preponderates. Now, suppose I am about to act in a certain way under the influence of my motives, have I not the power to say, "I will not act in this way"?

C. Yes; and in so doing you will be obeying another motive stronger than the others.

B. But still it is a motive which originates in myself, and which is simply an assertion that I can act in a certain way, if I choose; and, if I choose, I can refrain from so acting.

C. Still you are obeying a motive.

B. Yes; and that motive is essentially an

assertion of freedom; it is a declaration that I may choose between my actions.

C. But such an act of will may be the result of antecedent conditions of which you are unaware.

B. Let it be so. It does not alter the fact, that I know I am free to choose.

C. And yet if, after all, my choice is the result of antecedent conditions, my consciousness of freedom is a mistake. I think that I am free, while I am really constrained in my actions.

B. I should be ready to admit your argument, if my consciousness of freedom could be imagined to resolve itself into the simple notion that there was nothing to prevent me acting in a particular way; but it implies much more than this. This consciousness, when analyzed, is not only that I am free to act in a particular way, but that I can act in a way directly the reverse. If on a journey I came to two paths, and felt that I was free to choose the one but not the other, I should be conscious of a freedom in one direction, of a constraint in the other. But the two cases are not analogous. When I am under the influence of any motive, I know perfectly well that it is in my power to obey it or not.

THE DOCTRINE OF NECESSITY. 181

C. But you ignore the very point in dispute: that determination is the result of an additional motive.

B. But that additional motive is brought into operation, not *ab extra*, but from within. Even if my actions are the result of antecedent motives, your argument implies that I can originate a fresh motive to counterbalance others; and such origination on my part is the very essence of the idea of liberty.

C. Obviously we shall get no farther by reasoning thus. The fact is that you profess to admire physical science, but know nothing whatever of its method. You talk about origination as if it were a simple notion; whereas science knows nothing of creative acts.

B. Do you mean that, in your reasonings, you have not discovered any point at which creation or origination begins, or that you have proved that it is impossible?

C. It does not greatly matter which way you state the question. That which no experiment can detect may safely be inferred to be non-existent; and as the tendency of science is to show that in nature there is no gain or loss, simply a commixture of previously-existing elements, or a dissolution of compound bodies into their constituents, we may safely infer that as there has been no growth or decay, in any sense, of the increase or decrease of the original elements, so there can be no origination or creation in the usual sense of the words.

B. Would you object to explain in what manner you will apply this assertion, supposing it substantiated, to the case of free-will?

C. Why, obviously, if all phenomena are but the consequences of antecedent phenomena, the idea of an independent and self-originating will must be discarded.

B. You are prepared to carry out this argument?

C. Thoroughly in all its details.

B. You will therefore deny not only a power of origination in our will, but also a Creator of the universe?

C. I shall not stick at that, if it is involved in my assertion. You must not think to frighten me by putting awkward cases.

B. Certainly not; I am not absurd enough to expect that, if you deny freedom and a God, you will be alarmed at anything so unsubstantial as a mere opinion. But my difficulty begins where yours ends. You solve everything by the denial of a First Cause. I cannot imagine the absence of a First Cause.

C. What is the use of entertaining so unscientific an idea as that matter, which only changes its chemical conditions, but never diminishes or increases, should at some time have grown out of nothing?

B. But surely the idea of eternally existing matter is quite unscientific?

C. Not at all. When science cannot detect any traces of a beginning, it is quite scientific to assume that there was no beginning.

B. I thought science assumed nothing.

C. I will change the word; it is scientific to infer the eternity of matter.

B. But I was under the impression that, in order to infer, you must have premisses from which to infer. The induction of eternity from the facts of sense is not possible. Experience has only to do with time, and directly you talk of eternity you have got out of the range of time. And as for a deductive argument for the eternity of matter, you will soon find yourself reasoning in a vicious circle if you attempt it.

C. Ah! now you are trying the old absurd dialectics with me.

B. Well, but will you give me a specimen of your argument for the eternity of matter?

C. Willingly. I will take the instance of a full-grown and highly-developed organism. I analyze it and trace back its connexion with simpler forms of life; those simpler forms I trace back to still simpler ones; till finally I arrive at the earliest condition of life, a simple cell. In all this process I can find no sign of a commencement. It is an infinite retrogression through countless ages.

B. So that, to explain the idea of eternity, you introduce the idea of infinity. You must pardon me if I introduce another piece of antiquated dialectics, and say that you are explaining *ignotum per ignotius.* Infinity is only another name for Eternity. However, you use the words " countless ages," and in so doing you seem to imply that, at some period of the progress, so long ago that you cannot calculate it, the simple cell began to gather to itself the elements of a more complex structure. If so, there was a time when it had not developed; and then it must have had a beginning.

C. You misunderstand the line of argument entirely. These simple cells must be conceived of, as existing at some time without a tendency to development; but they had existed from Eternity before they began to develope.

B. Let us go back to the time before they began to develope. What atom of proof have you adduced that they never were created?

C. I must answer that question by asking what proof have you that they were created?

B. My proof is simply that, having followed the scientific process back to the time at which development commenced, I find myself deserted by science and reduced to pure reason; and that seems to assert that, when the process which is supposed to explain everything had not begun, there must have been an agency at work different from that with which science is competent to deal. This much, however, is plain: we have got rid of the idea of an Eternal development, because there is a time when development did not exist. Infinity and Eternity at once disappear in the crucible of scientific thought.

C. That is mere assertion.

B. We are then reduced to a dead lock. You declare that you *cannot* imagine a beginning; and I, that I *cannot but* imagine it. However, let us look at this from another point of view. Suppose we could observe these germ-cells at the immediate moment, when they commenced to germinate. At one instant there is no movement discernible; at the next there is. Do you not see that a new factor has been introduced—the power of germination? What is it which causes the activity then commencing?

C. The conditions under which they are placed.

B. So, then, a change of condition has taken place; and what causes that change?

C. An alteration in the state of surrounding matter.

B. And what is the cause of that alteration?

C. I am unable to say.

A. I must confess, after listening to your argument, that such a change looks very like a creative act. It introduces us to the idea of a power, impressing upon matter a tendency to change. Such an idea is not, perhaps, exactly what we understand by creation. It is also, perhaps, no real proof of a Personal God. Nevertheless, it points to something different from matter acting upon matter. For, commencing with the idea of self-development, as a reasonable hypothesis, we are gradually brought back to the time when self-development began; and the Power, which gave to matter that capacity for self-development, is inconceivable, except as a distinct existence, external to that on which it operates.

C. Well, as I see I have no chance of convincing you that matter has an inherent power of action, I will leave the subject, only hoping that some day your minds will become a little more scientific. After all, you have wrapped yourselves round with verbal subtleties, but are not a step nearer to an answer to the first difficulty. You have not made it clear that freedom is possible.

B. Perhaps not. But we have proved that it is not impossible; and this *is* a step.

C. But I cannot see that you have even proved this.

B. The idea of necessity is based upon the theory of an infinite chain of cause and effect. Did you not say so?

C. I did say something of the kind.

B. We have shown the impossibility of demonstrating or even of conceiving such a theory, and as the first axiom has been removed, the subsequent conclusion is destroyed.

C. Stay one moment. Suppose that there was a beginning, it is quite possible that the law impressed upon nature, then, was one of necessity, and not of freedom.

B. That point we have already disposed of, or rather we have, at your suggestion, passed off from it to this, which we are now quitting, in the hope that we should obtain fresh light from the discussion; and at the end we are just where we were. We find ourselves able to argue to a certain point, and then comes in the difficulty, that the next step involves an act of imagination, which you think that you *can* perform and I think that I *cannot*. Can you hit upon no more substantial ground on which to build?

C. Not I; I am hopeless of persuading a man weighted with a foregone conclusion.

B. Then the task must fall to me. But I shall be glad of the aid of your scientific mind to help me in my reflections. I am going to take a very long step downwards from the high metaphysics in which we have been involved, and to come to very plain and simple facts. Let us see what would be the practical effect of believing that human beings act under necessity, and not freely. Do you think that society could exist under such conditions?

C. Certainly; for we know that there are some people who believe that they are not free agents, and yet society exists.

B. Yes, but you must remember that, for the most part, these people are unconsciously influenced by the traditions, the practices, and the laws of others, who believe that they are free. And this affects them greatly, though unconsciously, and robs their principle of half its power.

C. In other words, you confess that, in so far as they are influenced by the sentiments of others, they are not free agents; for if they are *unconsciously* influenced, they act by *necessity.*

B. I will give you the full benefit of your argument. These people are *necessarily* influenced by those who deny *necessity.* However, let me proceed. Imagine a society constituted upon the principle that all actions were necessary. Could such men have any idea of justice?

C. Why not?

B. If every motive were of necessity obeyed, it is difficult to see what should cause such an idea to arise, as that certain actions are just and others unjust.

C. Not at all. Men find by experience that certain actions are advantageous and others disadvantageous. To the former they give the name *just*, and the latter they call *unjust.*

B. So that mankind attach no idea of blame to the one or praise to the other.

C. Yes: but they do.

B. Upon what principle?

C. Why, that injury to society merits punishment, and benefits deserve reward.

B. Merits! deserve! Why, what language is this? A *necessary* action *deserving* praise or blame! If it were voluntary, you could not use stronger language about it. If there is no freedom, there is no merit or demerit. And equally we must give up any idea of virtue and vice: our actions have no character about them: they are quite indifferent as far as all moral relations go.

A. I have always felt this difficulty about the doctrine of necessity, that it annihilates morality and condemns the general consent of mankind as utterly fallacious, and their attempts to restrain cruelty, crime, and malice, as wrong. It appears to me that we must give up the idea of keeping order, and consent to utter and complete anarchy in society, because we have no right to punish those who disturb the peace, destroy the property, or injure the persons of others.

B. Set your mind at rest on this point. The same necessity, which compels the robber and the murderer to act as he does, compels the judge to punish him. The whole thing is a matter of necessity, and in no sense a work of choice: at least, such is the conclusion which we are bound to adopt, if this hypothesis be true. However, perhaps our friend here will be able to give some explanation, or suggest something to modify this conclusion.

C. It appears to me that you assume that, if our actions are the result of necessary agencies, we must all the while be conscious of our obligation. But this is incorrect. We may be necessary agents, and yet all the while appear to ourselves to be free. No doubt, if the rest of nature possessed a power of reflection, it would conceive of itself as acting freely, though obviously it is perpetually under restraint. Brute animals, possessed of partial reason, are obviously necessary agents: generation after generation comes and passes away, and they live in the same way, and perform the same necessary actions; and even masses of men obviously act according to fixed laws, because the law of average is in the main correct, when applied to the actions of large bodies of men.

B. This is a fresh argument, or rather series of arguments. It is not a simple statement, and requires to be taken to pieces, before we can see its force. However, if I rightly understand, you assert that, even if men are necessary agents, they will probably believe themselves to be free. And you adduce as a proof, that if Nature could think, she would believe herself to be a free agent.

C. That is partly my argument.

B. Well, applying your argument of expediency, it seems plain that Nature does not possess thought, because it has no need to think or choose. If there were any possibility of the course of Nature being changed by her own agency, then, perhaps, thought would be expedient. But it is just because there is no freedom apparent in the action of dead nature, that we find there no traces of consciousness.

C. Oh! this is an argument based upon the idea of design, and I cannot accept it.

B. Pardon me: it is the very argument of which science makes so much use, that, given the requirement, the means for its fulfilment will be developed. If consciousness had been necessary in nature as a whole, it would have developed in the course of ages.

C. But you have not met my other instances. The instincts of animals are surely a species of reason; and yet animals obviously follow them by necessity.

B. I see you have forgotten part of your instance, which I will supply: "Generation after generation comes and passes away, and they live in the same way, and perform the same necessary actions." This is just the difference between men and animals: in any species of animals you will find comparatively small differences in the power of thought:

their reason is purely mechanical: there is no power of self-development: each one does the same thing in the same way. This looks like acting under necessity. But with men all this is different: there is a variety of intellects, absolutely incalculable: one man chooses one road, another chooses quite a different one: and though the possession of a common nature, and the fact that all are placed in very similar circumstances, causes a general resemblance of character, and a considerable similarity in the actions of men, nevertheless, if you look more closely, you will find that the varieties of character and of action are enormous: whereas in animals of the same species these differences are very slight. But in the actions of men there is nothing which you can compare with the instinct of the beaver, for instance, which *must* build a dam, and whose whole existence is concentrated upon that work. No man, unless he had a theory to uphold, which requires facts to be adapted to it, would see any resemblance between the instinctive habits of animals and the strange varieties of tastes, occupations, and modes of action of men born under the same roof, and nurtured in almost identical circumstances. You may indeed say that the circumstances, though apparently alike, are really vastly different, as different as the characters developed. But any theory of necessity is found to be quite insufficient to account for the vast difference existing between the characters of members of the same family.

C. But will the notion of freedom help us to explain it?

B. It helps us at least thus far, that it does not present a difficulty: whereas the doctrine of necessity has to be pressed far into the region of the unseen; it has to make all manner of assumptions to account for the variety; and these assumptions cannot be substantiated by any proofs: so that the doctrine of necessity is found ultimately to be no more reducible to the evidence of the senses than the doctrine of freedom.

However, this is a digression. Let us return to the point of the practical effect of the doctrine of necessity. Suppose a child to be educated by a necessarian in his principles. He is taught that for none of his actions is he accountable. The consequence is, that when he goes into the world he believes that every course of action which he pursues, of whatever character, is right, or rather, since that word implies responsibility, we will say that he feels himself compelled to follow the present motive. Would such a creature be tolerable in society, seeking his own pleasure, regardless of the convenience and the welfare of others? Would he not soon either annihilate society, or fall a victim to its just displeasure?

C. Yes: it is all very well to state it so; but he soon finds that he is compelled to yield to the convenience of others, and so adapts himself to the necessity of his situation.

B. Do all men so act?

C. No: they do not.

B. Then there is no necessity in the case. If they may or may not follow their inclinations, then your doctrine of necessity is scattered to the winds. If they may choose they are free to choose, and this is the point at issue.

C. But I speak of a moral necessity.

B. A moral necessity implies that it is not absolute, but dependent on a moral character; and a moral character implies a fitness in actions; and a fitness in actions implies a regulating principle within; and that regulating principle, argue it as you will, at length leads you back to a moral Governor of the universe.

C. I cannot permit you to assume so much.

B. Well, you must at least permit me to assume this, that the doctrine of necessity applied to practice, invariably leads to an absurdity.

C. How so?

B. Let us take an instance. Let a man suppose that he is fated to live a certain time, and that no effort on his own part will enable him to escape his fate, no rashness will precipitate it: is such an opinion practically reasonable?

C. I should think any man a madman who acted upon it.

B. Yet it is strictly in accord with the principle of necessity. But if the man who so acts is justly accounted mad, he who acts on the opposite principle is a reasonable man. The result is, that, whether the principle of necessity or of freedom be speculatively true, the former is practically false. Hence, if we apply the same principle to religion, and imagine that, act how we will, we shall not suffer for it, it is only in accordance with experience to suppose that we may find ourselves grievously mistaken. If, therefore, the doctrine of necessity is true, we must not conclude that it relieves us from the obligation of obeying the law impressed upon nature by its Author.

C. Now you are assuming that there is a God, and the doctrine of necessity destroys your proof.

B. Pardon me : it no more destroys the proof than it destroys the proof that our happiness and misery here are dependent upon our mode of action. Necessity, if true, is consistent with things to which it appears opposed, as we have shown. Hence it is no sign that there is no Author of nature, because the idea of absolute necessity appears opposed to the idea of a moral Governor. Here, then, we have a point to begin upon. Whether necessity be a true or false notion, it does not destroy the fact that we are possessed of a moral consciousness. This needs not to be reasoned out. We have this consciousness, as a fact. From it we judge some actions to be right and others to be wrong. Experience further shows that certain actions are rewarded in this life, others punished. Experience of this kind forces itself upon us ; and, unless we have a theory to uphold, compels us to believe that there is a *purpose* in this regularity. However, leaving that point, it is quite plain that, somehow or other, we have a sense of right and wrong implanted in us, and equally plain that our behaviour influences our condition in this life. If there be a God Who governs the universe, and has impressed upon our minds certain ineradicable ideas of justice and benevolence, in accordance with His own nature, then the existence of a sense of moral responsibility becomes intelligible. If there be no God, then why goodness, benevolence, and justice should be so generally respected, and vice, cruelty, and injustice abhorred, and not the reverse, is a thing utterly unintelligible. And that there is a preponderance of opinion on the side of goodness, however little that opinion may be carried out into practice, is too plain to need proof.

C. Well, but you are all this while assuming that there is a God, and that He is a Being with a particular character. What if I say that you are simply personifying your own ideas of what is perfect?

B. You are at liberty, of course, to assert this. Only, if you do, you will be at a loss to give any explanation how those ideas came into our minds.

C. I should say that the ideas of morality were the offspring of enlightened self-interest.

B. Be it so. And how will you explain the reverence felt for self-denial among a large portion of mankind?

C. Easily enough. Men naturally respect that which does them good, and when men are self-denying, others profit by it.

B. I congratulate you on your explanation of the way in which self-denial arises, and am so satisfied with your manner of proof, viz., that men admire self-denial because they may possibly profit by it, that I shall not pursue this part of our subject any farther.

A. I am quite sure that C. does not really mean that this is the sole explanation either of this virtue itself, or of the respect felt for it by mankind. But can you not bring for religion arguments more cogent and which are independent of the doctrine of necessity?

B. Undoubtedly there are many; but if you deal with them as this last has been dealt with, it is superfluous to mention them. First, it is assumed that there is no God; thence it follows that, however natural any explanation of facts may be on the assumption that there is a God, it must be false, because there is no God. Then we are led on to accept any explanation as more correct than that which appears natural. And so you end by proving that there is no God, by *assuming* that there is none; and you explain instances of complete unselfishness, by saying that they *must* be selfish, only you cannot see the selfishness: a mode of argument which *may* be scientific, if only we could see the cogency.

C. I think you are rather hard upon me. I only suggested that, as the arguments which prove the existence of a God can be met by counter-arguments which point the other way, such an explanation as this which offends you might be the right one, as it implies no assumptions, except the very obvious one that self-interest is the strongest passion in man. However, I will patiently hear what you have to say, always premising that you must not take silence for consent.

B. I think the fairest way to attempt to deal with the additional arguments, which are independent of the doctrine of necessity, is to consider what influence they would have upon a man who had reasoned himself fairly into the belief that there is a God, without any knowledge of the historic facts connected with that belief. There are such cases, and so it is not an unfair mode of arguing. Suppose such a man came to view the historic side of this question, how would it present itself to him?

C. Nay, I am a listener. You must not appeal to me.

A. To me, then, falls the duty of answering this question. Well, I suppose he would ask himself the question, "Does the opinion that there is a God show traces of being reasoned out at any particular period in the world's history?" And he would find that it is as old as history. The earliest records which we possess bear testimony to this belief, and their testimony goes to show that the belief in one God was purer and less alloyed with superstitious practices in the earliest times than in subsequent ages.

B. And what would you infer from that?

A. Apparently we must infer, that the belief in a God is a primary instinct of mankind. It is not a late development of reason, because subsequent systems have ended rather to obscure it than to make it plain. Hence in religion, we speak rather of revival than of development.

B. Is there nothing further that would strike the mind of the inquirer?

A. Certainly. He would observe that the testimony of the earliest records declares that this belief was the result of an original revelation.

B. And how would such an announcement affect him?

A. Probably he would see whether any other explanation would serve.

B. And what would be the result?

A. In the presence of C., I am apprehensive of exciting laughter by my reply. Still it seems to me that, as history does not point out any traces of the origination of this doctrine, but rather the reverse, and as the minds of rude and uncultivated men are by no means qualified to evolve elaborate or abstract ideas, but are rather engaged with what is visible, the notion of such a doctrine being revealed is not utterly incredible. All this, I allow, is not demonstration, but it is at least as probable as any other explanation which science gives.

B. I think so too, but our friend here does not agree.

C. I tell you I am a listener. You two flatter one another by making concessions, and talking about reason and demonstration, while all the while you are dreaming. You do not seem to see, that all this fine reasoning is null and void in the face of the fact that all things are by necessity. It is preposterous to talk of the moral government of God by rewards and punishments, and to describe actions as virtuous and vicious, when all the while they can be possessed of no such quality.

B. Here, then, is the point. You say that it is absurd to believe in future rewards and punishments, because no man can be responsible. Apply the same to the present life, and no man can be punished or rewarded for anything that he does. Still, if you act in a certain way, you suffer; if in another way, you are a gainer. You refuse to call them rewards or punishments, and the majority of mankind disagree with you. If they are actually retributions, designed by the Author of nature, they would not be altered in character. In spite of necessity, men *will* feel the sentiments of gratitude for kindnesses, of resentment for injuries. The whole world conspires together to be unreasonable, according to your theory; and your theory, in the world's estimation, leads to all kind of practical absurdities. Right or wrong, the doctrine of necessity would throw all nature out of gear, and bring human affairs to a stand-still. And the whole matter resolves into this:—If the doctrine of freedom is true, then the appearance of design and of moral government, the ideas of right and wrong, and the whole constitution of human society are reasonable: if necessity governs all things, then the whole of the facts, upon which human society is based, at once fall to the ground. And, moreover, as this doctrine, practically applied, would end in the probable destruction of the person acting upon it, so it is possible that it may end in the total ruin of his nature, the annihilation of his capacities for happiness, and all the possible results to which natural analogy points. In short, it is the part of a prudent man not to lean upon such a broken reed, but to allow the experience of his life to weigh down the inferences which he has drawn from a one-sided and incomplete view of the course of nature.

A. Such a conclusion has long appeared inevitable to me; and I confess that it seems less unreasonable to act upon that which leads into no absurdities, however speculatively improbable, than, by following out my reasonings to their extreme limit, to land myself in a position which experience tells me is utterly untenable.

DIALOGUE VII.

THE GOVERNMENT OF GOD: A SCHEME BEYOND OUR COMPREHENSION.

A. Greatly as I was interested in your discussion of yesterday, I must be permitted to observe that it was, on the whole, unsatisfactory. Hitherto our inquiries have been conducted on the understanding that we are both of us in search for one and the same truth, and desirous of discovering it in the scheme of religion, if that scheme is not contradictory to reason. But the discussion of yesterday resembled a tournament with sharp spears. There was an *animus* in the argument, which could not be concealed. And, after all, the aspect in which the entire discussion presented itself to me, was that the two principal disputants were simply seeking to rebut one another's arguments.

B. I am quite aware that it was so. But I do not see how it could be otherwise. Your friend C. took up a ground which is simply destructive of the possibility of religion. His argument, as he confessed, fairly pressed home, leads to the negation of God and of all moral action; and the only way to meet him was to refute his premisses by showing that they led to absurdities, and contradicted the results of consciousness as well as of experience. Such a discussion is essentially unsatisfactory. If you appeal to universal experience, it may be answered that your experience contradicts that of the person with whom you argue; and the same reply may be made to the argument from consciousness. Of what avail is it to say "I know that my will is free, because I feel it to be so," when the upholder of the opinion of necessity can reply, "I know the reverse"? And if you add, that "All men feel that they are free"; he may reply, "I am a man, and feel that I am not free." In such a case, no satisfactory result can, by any possibility, be attained.

A. Notwithstanding, I think we ought to allow the opinion of the vast majority to outweigh the opinion of the few. I wonder you did not press this argument more.

B. Of what avail would it have been? He would have replied that this was a matter of reasoning, and that the reasoning of the majority of men is utterly valueless: it is the few, whose opinions upon refined and abstruse questions are alone of value.

A. Perhaps you acted wisely in leaving the question as you did. For my own part, I think that the instincts or natural opinions of men are of value; and I should consider it very unfair not to allow weight to them, both in the matter of free will and of religion in general.

B. Do you mean that if you found a large portion, say the majority, of mankind agreed upon a certain religion, you would confess that that must have come from God?

A. No, no; I should only allow that that form of religion had, *à priori*, a first claim to our consideration. Religion must be tested by moral ideas; it must show indications of containing in it the essentials of the idea of the Deity: justice, judgment, and truth. What I intended to convey was, that if all men, in all ages, however much disagreeing in details, coincided in paying reverence to the Unseen, this must be taken as a presumption in favour of the real existence of an unseen world. But this, I think, has been implied, if not expressed in all our inquiries.

B. Certainly: I think it has.

A. But I am come here to-day with a new

thought in my mind. Hitherto all your arguments have been about facts. You have said in effect, " There are two worlds standing side by side: the material universe, and the moral universe. Religion asserts certain facts about the latter. In order to judge whether these assertions are correct, let us look to the material universe. In it I find such and such things, corresponding to what religion asserts about the moral world. Therefore religion speaks truly." Is not this a fair representation of the argument?

B. Certainly.

A. But now comes the moral consideration. Granting the force of the argument in establishing the *fact*, it proves nothing whatever as to the justice or injustice, the right or wrong, in short, the morality or immorality of the matters in question. Analogy is useless there; and this, after all, is the great point at issue.

B. You are quite right. *Directly*, analogy gives us no help here; it can only certify to matters of fact. But *indirectly* it can help us very much.

A. How so? How can you argue from the material universe to the justice of the moral government of the world?

B. Observe now what is the objection to

which you refer. You suppose a man to find fault with the moral of government of the universe, on the ground that he cannot see the justice of it. How far do you suppose this objection will be carried by a fair mind?

A. I do not understand what you mean.

B. Will it be said that there are no signs whatever of distributive justice in the government of the world, or will the objection only extend so far as this: that there are great inequalities in the moral government of the universe, which cannot easily be reconciled with ideas of infinite goodness?

A. Oh, I should say that a fair mind would not go farther than the latter objection; but surely that is enough.

B. Perhaps so. But as you concede this, which I confess I cannot imagine you refusing to concede, you will find analogy will aid you considerably.

A. How?

B. No man can look upon the material universe with a thoughtful eye, without being conscious how vast and inexhaustible a field of contemplation it presents. He cannot ponder upon the wonderful works in the fair world, without acknowledging that there is truth in the idea of Socrates, that man's highest knowledge is the knowledge of his ignorance. He will call to mind that the greatest thinkers have confessed, that all their investigations have but sufficed to show them how utterly insignificant all their efforts are to grapple with the infinite extent of the universe. At most they have learned to regard the material world as a grand organic whole, subject to laws and influences, of which the life of man, however laboriously directed to the research, suffices only to disclose a minute portion. They have learned, however, to regard the universe as an organized whole; but how the various forces to which it is subject mutually affect each other, what are the various relations and interdependence of one upon the other, what would be the effect of a cessation of any special force; whether it is possible for any one single minute agency to change without affecting the whole to an indefinite extent—these are questions upon which the most scientific minds are the least ready to express an opinion. That man may fairly be said to know nothing of the universe, who is not aware how every investigation serves to disclose fresh correlations between the forces of the universe, and to open up fresh channels of inquiry, which it is impossible even in imagination to exhaust. The more a man inquires, the wider is the range of subjects upon which he discovers his own ignorance. Without entering into the discussion of any scientific questions, we may fairly assume that the material universe presents itself to the investigator as a system, of which he has but a crude and imperfect knowledge; a system, the details of which are inexhaustible. In such a case, it is quite possible that every individual circumstance may have a relation to the whole, which the keenest eye cannot detect. Do you not agree with this?

A. Most assuredly. It is an ascertained fact that the material world bears every trace of being a system, of which the parts are connected in their operations, by links of various degrees of strength: some obvious to the senses; some requiring deep research and reflection to trace them; some so obscure that we have merely a glimpse of their existence, and infer it from our knowledge in cases more clear to the mental vision. But what has this to do with the point in question?

B. Let us first summarily state the conclusion at which we have arrived. It is very useful to have our premisses succinctly stated.

A. Assuredly; and our present conclusions amount to this, that the material universe is a system or aggregate of connected parts; and that this connexion is clear in some cases, obscure in others.

B. In other words, we have an imperfect knowledge of the universe; but we see enough to infer that it is not a mere casual aggregation of disconnected forces and activities. Now, are there any difficulties connected with the problem of the material universe with regard, for instance, to the law of gravitation, or the action of electricity?

A. Certainly; there are at present very great difficulties.

B. And do these difficulties arise from the nature of the things, or from our ignorance in these matters?

A. From our ignorance, I should say.

B. Now, then, let us apply analogy, and see what is the result. The moral facts of the world are regarded as a system of which we have a partial, and only a partial, knowledge. They present certain indications of the operation of *righteousness, love,* and *justice* in the administration of rewards and punishments; but they have also their difficulties. Instances occur wherein we fail to perceive the operation of those forces, which, from our own observation, the general tradition of mankind, or from their natural instincts, we assign to the Creator as His attributes.

A. But am I not to say, if a thing appears to be unjust, and I can conceive no way in which it can be just, that it *is* unjust?

B. You are stating the matter very strongly. When you say that you can conceive no way in which a certain course of action can be just, you mean, I presume, that, *so far as your opportunities of judging extend,* you cannot see how the ends of justice will be furthered. But suppose you have only a partial, a very partial, knowledge of the action, and are entirely unacquainted with other important circumstances bearing upon it, would you feel justified in pronouncing a verdict of injustice?

A. Will you make your meaning a little clearer?

B. Let us take an instance. Are there not many cases in which, on the first view of a course of action, you would unhesitatingly pronounce it unjust; whereas, when you are more fully acquainted with the circumstances, you are constrained to modify your opinion, if not to alter your verdict entirely?

A. Assuredly that is the case every day.

B. Now consider if the same line of argument may not fairly be applied to difficulties in religion? Is it not obvious that, in the vast scheme of an Infinite mind, it is impossible for any human being to understand the relations of any single act, except in the most imperfect manner? May not the apparent inequalities in the Divine government be such only in appearance? May they not be in reality, when viewed in their completeness, supreme acts of justice and righteousness?

A. They may certainly be so; but it is poor comfort to a struggling soul, tossed between good and evil, to be told that vice may be virtue, only in a different guise. And it seems a strange mode on the part of a good God, of impressing lessons of virtue on His creatures, to assure them that after all wickedness may be goodness, if only we could see it from the right point of view.

B. Stay; that is a misrepresentation of what I said. No argument which we have ever employed will bear that construction.

A. Why, have you not said that the inequalities in the government of the universe may possibly be resolved into acts of pure justice?

B. Yes, I have; and I maintain it. But I have never said that there can be any confusion between vice and virtue.

A. What then is your argument?

B. Simply this: there are general indications of the government of the universe on principles of virtue and goodness. From this, in accordance with reason, we might be led to infer that it was the intention of the Creator, that virtue should be the law of His creatures. To this it is replied that there are many instances, which appear to conflict with the proofs of this; instances of goodness being trampled upon and despised; instances of vice being successful, and gaining advantages for its followers. Now the argument from analogy assists us in this way. The physical universe is regulated by general laws, to which there are apparent exceptions. These exceptions in many cases resolve themselves into instances of the laws, or, perhaps more correctly, are the result of a combined action of various laws. Would you say that the laws have been altered?

A. Certainly not.

B. And yet your judgment as to the consequences of the laws has been modified. What has produced this change?

A. Additional knowledge on my part.

B. Very true. Now turn to the moral world. Certain inequalities present themselves. Are they necessarily instances of injustice on the part of the Creator?

A. They appear so.

B. May not additional knowledge show you reasons and purposes, to which these inequalities serve? And if so, might you not have reason to change your opinion about them?

A. But is not that what I have just said? Your argument would confound all principles of virtue and justice, and abolish moral judgment altogether.

B. Pray consider this. Here is a man in a bad state of health, gradually settling down into a confirmed valetudinarian. A fever seizes him; all the unhealthy humours in his body are concentrated to feed the fever; but he recovers from it, and is once more restored to health. Such cases occur, do they not?

A. Undoubtedly.

B. Is it therefore certain that fever is better than health?

A. It is certain that it is not.

B. And yet the man may be said to have recovered health by means of his fever?

A. Undoubtedly.

B. Here then is a case, in the physical world, of an unmixed evil resulting in good.

A. But physical and moral evil are such very different things. Whoever heard of vice improving a man?

B. Well, I have heard of a man, who had

gone through a course of vice, becoming penitent and avoiding sin the more earnestly for his former experience. Remember, however, that this forms no reason for excusing men for vicious courses. You would not recommend a man in weak health to put himself in the way of infection, although there are instances in which a fever or other sickness has proved beneficial. All that we have to show is that apparent evils may be, when viewed in relation to all their effects, the means of good.

A. How then can we make any distinction between vice and virtue?

B. Surely there can be no difficulty, any more than there is in distinguishing between sickness and health. Vice still remains vice, and is essentially evil, although by the directing hand of God, it may become the instrument of good. As it affects the nature of the man who is subject to it, it is always an awful soul-destroying disease.

A. Why, then, does the Creator permit it to exist?

B. Now you are approaching the question from a different side. What if I reply that I cannot tell?

A. Then I should say we may as well cease talking on the subject.

B. I doubt if you fully understand the force

of my reply. If the universe is a system, of which this earth and all that happens upon it is but a fragment, may I not fairly argue that, assuming the existence of an Infinite Creator, we must look for difficulties which no powers of ours can thoroughly unravel; and that, if there is a general indication of wisdom and goodness in the moral government of the world, we ought to infer that, if we understood the whole, we should find it in accordance with that which we do comprehend? Do you agree with this?

A. It looks like fair reasoning, but the conclusion is somehow repugnant to my mind. Why should not the Creator, for instance, have so arranged the world that evil should not exist, or should be corrected immediately upon its appearance?

B. That I think we can partially answer. In the first place the world is governed by general laws; and if they are to remain general, perpetual interpositions are not to be expected.

A. I do not like the reason, and I think it leads to some uncomfortable inferences. Give me another.

B. Perpetual interpositions would produce bad effects.

A. How?

B. They would encourage idleness and negligence; for if every evil act could be immediately remedied, who would be at the pains to guard against it?

A. That is indeed a reason of value.

B. Then, consider, morality would not exist.

A. What do you mean?

B. Human morality consists in the voluntary regulation of the passions and affections in accordance with a certain fixed law. That law is determined, partially at least, by reflecting upon the tendency of actions. Now if actions never produce any consequences; if the evil is at once, and without any agency of our own, corrected, every inducement to self-restraint, and to all that constitutes our idea of virtue, is removed. In a very short time human beings would cease to be moral or accountable agents. What the result of this upon the universe would be, it is impossible to tell. It is very obvious, however, that all which ennobles and elevates man would soon cease to exist.

A. In this, again, you seem to argue with reason.

B. Then, again, recurring to our ignorance; might not the result of such interpositions have further effects far beyond our knowledge, and entirely subvert the whole course of nature.

In short, we *see* that some evils would certainly arise from constant Divine interpositions. For aught we know, the remedy which we so readily propose, might produce evils tenfold greater than those which they are expected to redress.

A. You have now been arguing, that in those things which appear to us to contradict Divine goodness, our ignorance is a sufficient reason for assuming that they may be found eventually to be instances of it. What will you say if I reverse the process, and say, that perhaps our ignorance blinds us to the eventual results of what appears to be good? I merely put it by way of argument. Why may we not infer that what appears to be good may, in truth, appear to be so only in consequence of our ignorance?

B. The answer is not difficult to discover. We have no reason whatever to infer that evil and vice are the moral law of the universe. We have many reasons for supposing they are not. There is reason, therefore, for assuming that virtue *may* be the law under which man has been created. Arguments from our ignorance of the eventual tendencies of things do in no way invalidate this positive proof. On the other hand, there is *no* positive proof that *vice* can be the law of the universe. Our ignorance is not, and ought not to be, adduced as an objection to what we may infer from analogy or from other sources. But if difficulties are started in opposition to these inferences, then our ignorance of the ultimate tendencies and relations of things is a fair reply to such objections. Do I make this clear?

A. I fear not.

B. Let us take an instance. From our observations of a certain man's actions, we form a judgment of his character; we gain impressions as to the general course of action which he will pursue. In certain cases we do not perceive his drift; but from what we know, we are justified in assuming that he will be true to his character. From our knowledge, we are justified in supposing that he will remain what we have reason to suppose him to be, even in cases where we do not see his drift. But we have no right to assume that, as soon as his motives pass beyond our comprehension, he will change his character.

A. That is true.

B. In the same way, our ignorance may be adduced as a reply to objections against God's goodness, because we have at least some reason to believe in His goodness; but it ought not to be brought to disprove His goodness, because what we know does not lead us to regard Him as evil?

A. I understand.

B. Then once more. The moral sentiments of mankind *on the whole* condemn cruelty, injustice, selfishness, and vice. Experience shews that *on the whole* these conditions of mind do not conduce to happiness. Religion asserts that they are hateful to God, and will be punished. Is it reasonable to say, "I really do not know whether they will or not, and therefore I shall pay no heed to what religion says about them, but, in virtue of my ignorance, intend to run counter to the moral judgments of humanity." Is this reasonable?

A. It appears not.

B. This, then, is a practical reply to arguments against religion, drawn from our ignorance. And once more. Though we are said to be arguing from human ignorance, we are not arguing simply from it, but from something which analogy suggests from the consideration of it. We have seen that, in the physical universe, we often argue wrongly in consequence of *incomplete* knowledge; and now we say that in the moral universe, if we arrive at results inconsistent with the Divine goodness, to which positive arguments point, we have a right to assume, that a clearer and wider knowledge would lead us to conclusions in accordance with those which analogy has presented concerning the wisdom, justice, and goodness of God.

A. In this, again, I feel constrained to concur.

B. And now let us sum up the results of our conversations. We have shown, first, that all arguments on moral and religious questions are based upon probable arguments.' We have seen that there is a probability that we ourselves do not cease to exist when our bodies return to dust; then, that the present life is a condition in which some actions are rewarded and others punished; from which we infer that what religion states about a future condition of rewards and punishments is not unreasonable. After this, we found reason to hold that those punishments and rewards were apportioned according to a moral law; we saw that this life was well adapted to be, and was actually, a condition of moral discipline, as preparing the soul for a higher state of existence. All these things we found to be reasonable, on the supposition that human action was free and not constrained by necessity; and we saw that the doctrine of necessity was involved in insuperable difficulties. Finally, we have proved that any objections which might arise in the course of our reasonings, received an answer from the incompleteness of our knowledge; and that this ignorance cannot fairly be applied to invalidate any of the proofs of religion, although it is an answer to objections to those proofs. And thus we are fairly in a condition to deal with the important questions which now arise with reference to the doctrines of revealed religion.

Part II.

DIALOGUE I.

THE IMPORTANCE OF CHRISTIANITY.

A. In our last conversation, you concluded by saying, that we might fairly approach the subject of revealed religion. Discussions on that subject will consist, if I mistake not, very much in an examination of testimony. We shall have, I suppose, to inquire whether witnesses, who ground their claims to our belief on miracles, are to receive any attention at all; whether any explanation can be given to account for their belief, or professed belief, and there will, doubtless, be other questions springing out of these. But before we commit ourselves to such inquiries, let me ask you whether you consider such an inquiry of importance?

B. Assuredly I do, of vital importance. It cannot but be so, if there be any truth in Christianity at all; and if there be not, it is equally important that mankind should no longer commit themselves to what is false. If I did not *know* that you were serious, I should imagine that your question was a rather unaccountable jest.

A. Well, I am not in jest. But still as I have heard this point seriously mooted, I should like to know your answer to it. The fact is that, personally, I feel that we ought to trace out, as far as possible, what explanation can be given of that transcendent fact in history, the growth of Christianity. The ordinary explanation of the school of Gibbon and Hume, that the credulity of the people and the rapacity of the priests together gave birth to it, seems insufficient to account for the origin of such a power as Christianity, whether its influence has been good or bad. And there seems to be something too tangible, definite, and real, in the supposed facts upon which Christianity is based, to be accounted for in the off-hand way, which men usually adopt, of saying that mankind found an element of truth in the fundamental idea of Christianity, that of incarnate goodness, and so built an ideal superstructure, and propped it up with fictitious stories of the actions of a perfectly good man, and then founded a theory that that good man could only be God in human flesh; and to support this wrote a book, in which he is represented as calling himself God. However, I am anticipating. What I say, then, is this, how will you answer the man, who, believing in a God of nature, says, " And that God is sufficient" ?

B. I should ask him whether he means sufficient for himself, or sufficient for mankind.

A. And if he said " Sufficient for me " ?

B. I don't know that I could answer anything. If a man were to tell me that the notions of God, which he might have reasoned out for himself, without any aid direct or indirect from Moses or the Prophets, or the New Testament, were sufficient for him, I really think I must be silent; or perhaps I might venture to suggest, that among the notions which had sprung up in the world, was one which at least had received material impulse from the New Testament, " No man liveth for himself." Suppose, then, I should say, " You have learned your present faith, religion, doctrine, or opinion, from the light of nature; you have learned that the general good is to be considered before the individual good. Natural religion is enough for you, but you ought not to be satisfied with that. Is it enough for the world in general ?"

A. And what if he replied, "It is."

B. Then I should say, "How is it that by far the greatest number of men do not find it enough? Why are they always running into all kinds of superstitions, inventing all kinds of religions, gross, sensual, or ridiculous? The whole history of mankind is a proof that natural religion is *not* enough for them; either they do not find it out for themselves, or if they seem to have discovered some traces of it, they overlay it with so much that has not the remotest connexion with it, that they are scarcely in a better condition than if they had no religion at all."

A. But what if he reply, "This is to some extent true. So far as Christianity makes clearer the moral law and our relation to the Creator, it is beneficial. All that it professes to contain beyond this is superfluous and unimportant." To this what should you reply?

B. I should say that his words were ambiguous.

A. In what way?

B. He might mean either that the doctrine of the Trinity was superfluous, or that by it the moral law and our relation to the Creator were made clearer. If he meant the latter, then we should be in agreement; if the former, I should say that, in my opinion, his notions of Christianity were entirely inadequate.

A. In what way?

B. Perhaps if you will state, what you conceive to be the idea formed of Christianity by such a man, I shall be able to explain myself more distinctly.

A. Being in that condition, at least partially, myself, I can very fairly do so. Now I conceive that Christianity was intended by its founder, to be a religion to reform the moral darkness of the human mind. Its object was to set before men the consequences of sinful and vicious lives, and to give them a supreme motive to virtue, by presenting to them the idea of God, under the form of Infinite Love. God being their Creator, and His essence being Love, the immediate consequence is that love must be the actuating principle of human life. To love God and love our neighbour, is the whole duty of man; and this I take to be a full account of the importance of Christianity.

B. You have, indeed, stated a very essential, perhaps I may say the *most* essential moral element in the Christian religion; but in so doing you have omitted some very important points. In the first place, will you tell me in what way this clearer notion of Divine goodness was conveyed to mankind?

A. As far as we can see, it was impressed upon mankind by Christ, Who, as it is related, went about doing good, and calling all men to the love of God.

B. Observe, then, the founder of the Christian religion practically taught the doctrine of love to God by works of mercy and healing. Those works were, or at least appeared to be, beyond the power of human skill. The healing of paralytics, of the blind, the deaf, the dumb, and the insane, was effected, or at least supposed to be effected, by the founder of Christianity; and He Himself professed to act as He did, in accordance with predictions uttered hundreds of years before. See, then, the Christian religion is held up to us, as being founded by miracles and in accordance with prophecy; and thus it must be regarded as an *authoritative republication* of natural religion. Hence your view of it is not quite so simple, obvious, and reasonable as you supposed. You are already, in a measure, committed to miracles and prophecy; at first blush, then, you must either throw over the whole early history of the religion as a mere fabrication, or give up the preacher of love and righteousness as an impostor, or prepare to consider the question of miracles and prophecy. You will find it very difficult, indeed to an unbiassed mind pretty nearly impossible, to accept either the first or second alternative; most men who accept either, do so because they think it impossible to accept the third.

A. And yet I see, if I accept either of the former, I must resign my idea of Christianity having any foundation in fact, and believing, as I do, in a moral governor of the universe, I must content myself with the notion, that He leaves His creatures to blind themselves to moral laws by all manner of cruel superstitions.

B. This, then, which you estimate as the essential part of Christianity, that it is a republication of the law of nature, implies many other notions, not quite so easily disposed of as is frequently supposed. It is quite possible to assert, that the founder of Christianity really had a clearer insight into moral questions than other teachers who preceded Him. Whatever else be thought of Christ, the morality which He inculcated will probably be allowed to be in advance of His generation.

A. Few will be found to deny that.

B. Did He not also act so as to impress upon

His disciples, that He was endued with supernatural powers?

A. Assuredly this cannot be doubted.

B. And if He did not possess them, would not His life be an entire deceit?

A. May He not have thought it right to produce an impression upon men by the appearance of miracles, in order to influence them more strongly by His moral teaching?

B. In that case, His actions would have been an entire contradiction to His teaching; for the spirit of His doctrine certainly was, that it is immoral to do evil that good may come. However, let me ask you to reserve this point for the present, as we shall probably consider it more fully afterwards.

A. Certainly, if you desire it. But you will pardon me for suggesting, that you are addressing yourself to a question not greatly concerned with the difficulties of Christianity. They who hold the doctrines of natural religion do not impugn the morality of Christ's teaching. They allow that it set before men a high standard both of action and worship. It inculcated pure and high-minded lives, and a spiritual worship of one God. The real objection to it lies in this: it professed to announce new truths, and enjoined fresh beliefs in accordance with those supposed truths. It spoke not only of a Father, but of a Son and a Holy Spirit, and announced the necessity of a belief in this triple Godhead.

B. It did so. And if it announced fresh truths, what possible reason can you assign for not believing them?

A. Pardon me. The great truth of the existence of a God, though announced by Christ, was discoverable by reason—at least reason made it probable. But here are new dogmas, of which reason knew nothing; therefore they could have no real claim upon mankind.

B. Do you mean that no truth, of which our own reason has not apprised us, is to be believed?

A. No: but that no truth, which reason might not possibly discover, is binding upon the conscience.

B. But can you certainly know that reason could not possibly ascertain these truths? You do not know how far reason, pure and unassisted, could have discovered the existence of a God. Indeed, some men assert that their reason fails entirely to ascertain this primary truth. After sifting away all that human intellect has done in this respect, you will find that you must supply something, in the nature of a primary instinct or a revelation, to account for the existence of the belief.

A. I believe that I have acknowledged the necessity of this before.

B. Very well. Now that primary truth, however the knowledge of it has been derived, demands our assent as being true. That our reason corroborates the impressions derived from our instincts is indeed an additional obligation to believe it. When primary ideas are supported by proof, the intensity of the conviction is increased. Still truths, however ascertained, demand assent from us.

A. Certainly.

B. Now Christianity gives expression to certain facts unknown before: it tells us of the existence of God the Father, which had before been known; it informs us also of new truths, viz. of the triple nature of the Godhead, and of the relation of God the Son and God the Holy Ghost to man. If these are truths, and if there is such a Trinity in the Godhead, we are bound to act upon the belief, just as much as we are bound to act upon the belief that there is a Creator.

A. But surely there is not the same obligation to believe in the Trinity or Triplicity of God, as there is to believe in a Creator. The latter is attested by evidence of all kinds: the former rests only upon assertions unsupported by proof.

B. As for the exact and precise mode in which God is to be conceived as a Trinity, it may perhaps be impossible to define or understand it; but the point at issue is, whether we have a right to believe, upon the assertion of the Founder of Christianity, that God stands to us in a three-fold relation, as Creator, as Redeemer, and as Sanctifier. You say that the first is, for the most part, an inference of the reason: the two last relations are unattested by any proof, and only came into existence with the introduction of Christianity. Suppose this to be the case, yet, *if it be a truth*, it makes little difference how we become acquainted with it, so long as we actually do know it. Once made known, it is at our own peril that we reject it and the moral obligations connected with it.

A. What do you mean? Do you mean that it is no more perilous not to believe in a God at all, than to refuse to believe in the redemption and sanctification of mankind?

B. I intend to say, that if salvation has been offered to men by God the Son, and if the means of acquiring a greater state of holiness is offered to us through God the Holy Ghost, and if these facts have been made known to us, it is at our own peril that we reject them. Directly they become known to us as facts, they lay us under an obligation to act in accordance with them.

A. The inference would seem to be, that we are bound to believe anything which professes to be a Divine revelation.

B. No; by no means. But if it be announced by one Who professes to have a Divine revelation, and in Whose career no signs of hallucination are to be found; by one Whose life in purity, beauty, and completeness stands unrivalled among mankind; Who wrought miracles, raised the dead, cured the blind, the dumb, and the leper; Who died, but rose from the dead; Who appeared after His resurrection to many; Who was seen by several to leave the earth in a condition of glory:— if such a man proclaims a revelation, it merits our best attention; and if the revelation, though it cannot be proved by reason, contains nothing repugnant to reason, and falls in with the moral facts of human nature, then I say that we reject such a revelation at our peril.

A. Yes; but see how much you are assuming.

B. I am aware of it; but at present we are only seeing what is the importance of Christianity, supposing it to be true. The question with which we started was "Is it worth while to spend our time in investigating the evidence for Christianity?" And now you see that, even if Christianity were only natural religion in a new guise, it would be important, because it comes attested by authoritative evidence. And if it professes to be more than natural religion, we have no right to reject its claims, unless we also reject that part of it which attests natural religion.

A. I cannot in the least see that we are bound to accept its claims as a revelation of new truths, because it bears witness to old ones.

B. At all events, if you reject the supposed new truths, you do so because they are not true. Now suppose a man related to you certain events, some of which were familiar to you and others quite new, would it not be reasonable to believe what was new, if you found that the account of the old was perfectly accurate?

A. I suppose so.

B. But you propose to act quite differently with regard to Christianity. You will accept its testimony to natural religion as valuable, but will repudiate its claims in any other respect.

A. But is the testimony of Christianity even to natural religion perfectly unimpeachable? It seems to me that many of the principles of the Christian faith are incompatible with the truths of natural religion.

B. Will you mention an instance?

A. Natural religion inculcates obedience to parents, for example, as essential to a good life. The reasons of this we can partly comprehend. But Christianity lays down certain positive injunctions founded simply upon the *ipse dixit* of its Founder, or even upon inferences from His word, and requires men to obey them, even when they contravene the duty of obedience to parents. The law of the Christian Church appears to be, to set obedience to *ordinances* before obedience to *natural laws*.

B. Surely this is a misconception of the Christian religion. The Founder of Christianity rebukes the Scribes and Pharisees for the very things you instance. He is very severe in His rebuke of those who plead the service of God as an excuse for neglecting their duty to their parents. And the same is true of the whole course of His teaching. He always sets moral duties above positive enactments.

A. But surely it is no misrepresentation to say that in most cases, when a moral duty and one of positive enactment come into collision, the greater number of Christians would consider it less dangerous to neglect the former than the latter.

B. I do not think they would. But supposing that they would, what would it amount to? A proof that they had misunderstood their Lord, but not an atom of proof that He ever encouraged or countenanced such conduct.

A. But I thought the voice of the Church was sufficient reason for the obedience of her children.

B. Not as against the commands of our Lord. And if anything can be plain, it is that He was utterly opposed to those who made religion consist in outward observances. You have only to read His controversy with the Pharisees respecting eating with unwashed hands, or plucking the ears of corn on the Sabbath, to see how entirely He repudiates anything like a mere formal obedience.

A. It seems to me that you may be a very reasonable man, but you are scarcely loyal to your religion, in thus giving up all its positive enactments; and I really do not see, after all, that you ought to complain much of those who regard Christianity as only one of a number of partial glimpses of truth.

B. I am at a loss to understand you. I have never said that *positive* commands are not to be obeyed. I said indeed, that, if *positive* and *moral* laws conflicted, the latter must be considered pre-eminent, because they are enjoined by our religion and sanctioned by our conscience. But then you should remember that if positive and moral commands appear to conflict, I hold that the antagonism arises from a misconception of the scope and meaning of the former; and I have not acknowledged the point which you assume, that direct injunctions, of which we do not see the ground, are not binding. Moreover, all the commands of Christ have the value of moral precepts.

A. How do you establish that? Where is the moral obligation to believe in the Trinity?

B. That point has already been made clear. Christ proclaims Himself the Saviour of men. If He be so, there is a moral obligation of love, reverence, and worship, arising from a sense of gratitude for the unspeakable benefit conferred upon us. Again, if the Holy Spirit be the agent of our sanctification, there is a similar moral obligation of love, reverence, and worship to Him.

A. But what will you say to the question

of baptism, for example? There is no moral obligation there.

B. Oh yes, there is, to those who believe that baptism is a means of grace.

A. Now you are involving us in the metaphysics of theologians.

B. It is all very well for you to put aside the argument. I am simply stating the grounds upon which the majority of Christians consider themselves bound to obey Christ's behest in this respect. I firmly believe that all Christ's commands have a moral basis. That basis is, that by obeying them, we obtain the assistance which is requisite to enable us to attain to moral purity, and to fit ourselves for a future life in the society of those who are supremely holy. I am quite aware, that these questions belong more to the domain of what we call Christian ethics than to the investigation of the truth of Christianity. But as you have challenged me to assign moral grounds for our obedience, I am compelled to step aside from the more general considerations in which we are involved, and to specify our particular reasons for obedience to individual commands.

A. Do I understand you to mean that every Christian doctrine has a moral basis?

B. Most emphatically.

A. What is the moral basis for the doctrine of an infallible Church?

B. I know of no such doctrine.

A. Surely it is of the very essence of Christianity.

B. I do not think so. The Scripture doctrine of the Church is not correctly described in that way.

A. What is the Scripture doctrine of the Church?

B. It is this. The Christian Church is a society founded by Jesus Christ for the purpose of preserving and bearing witness to the truths which He proclaimed. Without such a society, those truths could only have had a precarious and temporary existence upon earth. They would have been confined to a few persons, and after their death would have gradually passed out of remembrance. The principal duty of the Church is to maintain and teach those doctrines. So long as they are the basis of its teaching, the Church will stand; it has Christ's promise to that effect; but if she fails to teach the doctrines of Christ, both those which are purely *moral* and those which are *positive*, the Church has no ground for expecting a prolonged existence. If by *infallible* you mean a Church which teaches indefectible truth, then her infallibility rests upon the infallibility of her Lord: and so the evidence of it is identical with the evidence of Christ's Divinity. If you mean, that whatever the Church teaches must be true, because she is the Church, then I say that no such doctrine is obligatory upon men.

A. Well, if you could show me that all the doctrines of Christianity had a moral basis, I think I should be ready to believe them. At all events I should feel bound to try. The real difficulty which meets me and many others at the outset is, that there are a vast number of minute and intricate questions which I am required to accept, before I can be counted a Christian at all.

B. Even there I think you are greatly mistaken. There are some truths, not self-evident, which a Christian is required to believe. But I cannot find that they are numerous or minute. They are practically comprised in the Apostles' Creed.

A. Surely, surely, you are understating the case. Every Church requires of its members much more than that. Your own Church demands assent to Thirty-nine Articles, upon every kind of subject.

B. But not as essential to salvation. A distinction is always drawn between saving truth and matters of opinion. Now what the Church of England says about the Thirty-nine Articles is, that when questions arise respecting the meaning of the teaching of Christ and His apostles, these articles express the view commonly known as that of the Church of England. They are a kind of test, by which a man may judge whether his opinions accord with those of the Church of England. But it is not supposed that they are all of equal value or importance. The condition of membership of the Church is contained in the doctrines of the Apostles' Creed, or even in less than that.

A. But would the Church of England justify a clergyman for admitting an adult who professed only a belief in the Trinity?

B. Most assuredly.

A. You make the essentials of Christianity very few.

B. It was the intention of its Founder to embrace within the range of His society as many members as possible.

A. In fact it seems to me that you will scarcely exclude anybody.

B. I could wish that none were excluded. But I fear that you do not see that those essentials are as fatal a stumbling-block to many as if they were ten thousand. The doctrine of the

Divinity of Christ, which is essential, is a point so difficult to human reason to comprehend, that hundreds or rather thousands declare that they cannot accept it. And it includes in it a vast number of other questions. There is, it must not be forgotten, a definite demand for belief in certain fixed truths of revelation. This I say by way of caution, lest you should erroneously conclude that every one who confesses the high morality inculcated by Christianity to be admirable is thereby a member of the Christian Church.

A. Once more the difficulties begin to close me in. Your last observations had opened out to me a hope, that I might at once call myself a Christian. I see now that you still shut me out in the cold.

B. Do not say so. Perhaps on further investigation you will find, that many of the difficulties to which you allude may find a parallel in the order of nature. And so, upon the principles which have guided us throughout, you may be led to allow that the demands which the religion of Christ makes upon you, are not greater than those to which you yield, when accepting the moral government of the universe as a demonstrated truth.

A. Make that clear to me and I will render

you my thanks by conforming to the faith which you uphold so strongly.

B. That indeed will be the most acceptable reward that it is possible for me to receive.

DIALOGUE II.

ON MIRACLES.

A. In the course of our conversation the other day, I said that your argument would lead to the conclusion that everything, which asserted itself to be of Divine origin, would claim our undeviating and complete obedience. Such a result would evidently be an evil; for every impostor and marvel-monger would at once be invested with a halo of sanctity, and be at liberty to trade upon the credulity of mankind. To this you replied, that no such danger was to be apprehended from Christianity; its claims are such as to preclude the suspicion of imposture, and its evidences are such as to give a Divine sanction to all the words of its Founder. Supposing that I allow, for the present, that no imposture was possible, that Christ lived a life of exemplary purity and simplicity, I have yet to meet the difficulty that He might be an enthusiast, and therefore in His speculative theology unreliable. To this you reply, by anticipation, that being supplied with Divine authority over the forces of nature, the words which came from His lips touching Divine truths must be unimpeachable. Such reasoning would appear valid were it not for one fatal flaw. A miracle is simply incredible; no evidence could prove it.

B. Why do you consider that a miracle is incredible?

A. Because it is a contradiction of the laws of nature.

B. What do you understand by a law of nature?

A. I understand those fixed undeviating principles, by which the Deity has ordained that the course of nature shall be conducted.

B. Pardon me, if I say that you speak rather boldly as to the mind of the Deity; but not to observe upon that, I should like you to tell me how you know the laws of nature?

A. By experience and observation.

B. Do experience and observation inform you that nature is governed by laws which cannot change?

A. Certainly.

B. Let us take an instance and examine, shall we say, the law of gravitation?

A. If you please.

B. As I understand that law, it asserts that certain matter upon this earth, when unimpeded, tends to fall towards the centre of the earth; this, no doubt, is an instance of a still more general law respecting the properties of matter. Now how have we learned this property of matter?

A. Simply by observing that within the experience of all persons such has been the case.

B. In this case, then, a law of nature may be defined to be the result of the united observations of men?

A. Yes; it is a generalization from experience.

B. You consider that there is no assumption, no particle of imagination, involved in the notion of a law of nature?

A. No; that is the beauty of science, that the laws which it establishes are the results of observation and experiment.

B. Let us take another instance, the rising of the sun. You will say, I presume, that the daily appearance of the sun above the horizon is an instance of the operation of a law of nature?

A. Undoubtedly; it is one of the commonest and best established facts in nature; the whole world bears testimony to it.

B. To what?

A. That the sun will rise regularly every morning.

B. What! does the whole world bear testimony to what has never happened?

A. I fail to understand you. What can be plainer than the whole life of man is regulated by this universal conviction, that the sun will rise to morrow?

B. But you said just now, that the whole world bears testimony to it.

A. Well, does it not?

B. How can it testify to the rising of the sun *to-morrow?* testimony is of the past.

A. But the invariable rising of the sun up to this day, is a proof that it will rise to-morrow, is it not?

B. A presumption, I grant you, quite sufficient to act upon, but no irrefragable proof.

A. But the regularity of nature is a thing proved beyond doubt.

B. And how do you know that nature is uniform?

A. All experience proves it.

B. Experience can only properly apply to the present and the past. A thing has happened regularly in time past; it happened to-day. So far experience can go. Directly, however, that you proceed a step beyond this, and assert that it will happen to-morrow, you imply something more than experience; you imply the principle " that the course of nature is uniform."

A. But you will not deny that principle?

B. Probably not; but I am now pointing out on what ground that general law is assumed. You argue that the sun will rise to-morrow, because it has risen hitherto; that is, you imply a belief in the uniformity of nature; this uniformity of nature you prove by observing that the sun has risen uniformly. Now consider; you prove your general principle by a number of observations. If the sun did not rise to-morrow, your principle would be proved false and be no principle. You know nothing about the future, but you assert unhesitatingly that the sun will rise to-morrow. And so you *prove* the uniformity of nature, by *assuming* that it is uniform.

A. I do not quite understand this. Have I not a right to assume that, if the past has been of a certain character, the future will be like it?

B. Undoubtedly, you could not live or act without so doing; but the point is, that you do *assume* it. You argue from the past to the future upon the principle of their *likeness or resemblance.* And this is an assumption.

A. Say rather a self-evident principle.

B. That would not be correct: that only is *self-evident* of which the contradictory is *impossible.* But to say that the future will *not* be like the past, whatever else it may be, is not the assertion of an impossibility.

A. But if the same thing recurs over and over again, this surely is a proof that there is some permanent underlying cause which produces it.

B. Softly; grant that there is a cause, all that we know of it is from its effect. As far as the effect goes we know of the cause, but not a step farther. If we say that the cause is permanent, that is just the same assumption as to say that the effect will recur. We know absolutely nothing more of the cause than of the effect; in fact we know less, for we only know it through its effect. And to assert that the cause *will* produce its effect, is to assume the principle that the future will be like the past.

A. But is it not true that we argue from experience, that the future will be like the past?

B. No, we assume it; we do not argue from

experience. Experience has only to do with the past, and the sole ground upon which we trust experience, is the principle in question which we *assume*, that the future will resemble the past.

A. But you do not mean to say that the whole progress of science has depended upon a precarious assumption? Do you think that inductive philosophy depends upon a principle which it cannot prove? Your opinion on this matter would destroy confidence in science.

B. Not so; it ought only to destroy your confidence in some of those excessive claims which scientific men advance. If they say that the sun will rise to-morrow, I assent, because I understand that statement with the implied proviso of probability; but if they intend to assert that it is *impossible* that the sun should not rise to-morrow, then I demur, because a principle is assumed which, however generally true, is incapable of rigid demonstration.

A. Ah! now I detect the fallacy of your reasoning. Of course it is possible that the sun may not rise to-morrow, because a new cause or influence may be brought to bear, neutralizing those forces which cause the sun to appear over the horizon.

B. I do not think your criticism affects the question. We might take any other instance, the most scientific induction you please, and, after all, the arguments will be found to amount to this. A certain phenomenon is to be accounted for; observation and strict investigation are brought to bear upon it; all the antecedent circumstances are carefully inspected; if possible, observations are made of the phenomenon under all kinds of aspects; and in the end the result of this part of the process is, that it is ascertained that the phenomenon A is preceded uniformly by the phenomenon B. Hence is inferred what is called *a law of nature;* but in the inference there enters in just that assumption of which I have spoken: because in all cases which I have observed, A is preceded by B; therefore in all cases which I have not observed, and in all future time when B occurs, A must follow. Do you not see that in this there is a plain assumption of the principle that the future will be like the past, and here the process ceases to be scientific? Up to that point the inquiry has been conducted on strictly logical grounds; but here comes an assumption which you cannot prove, and which, state it how you will, is resolved at last into the simple reiteration of the principle, that the course of nature *must* be uniform.

A. But to deny it, would be to contradict all experience.

B. Do you mean all *your* experience, or universal experience?

A. Universal experience, of which mine is a type.

B. In that, again, you are not arguing, but assuming. You fancy that all men's experience must resemble yours; but you do so on the ground, that the course of nature is uniform, that is, you reiterate the old assumption.

A. Yet, if it be not so, it would be impossible to act at all.

B. Perfectly so; but in so speaking you are quitting the high ground which you have assumed, that it is *impossible* for the laws of nature to be suspended or contravened; as for the uniformity of nature, I cordially confess it: what I object to is the *assumption,* that that uniformity cannot possibly be suspended for any purpose. As a practical principle, the uniformity of nature is invaluable; but when you require me to give up all miracles, on the ground that the observed laws of nature cannot be contradicted, then I examine into this principle itself, and find that, however certain it may appear, it involves an assumption quite incapable of proof; an assumption not self-evident, but an absolute *universal*, evolved from *individual* observations, and incapable of being proved by the laws of nature, because it is itself employed to substantiate those laws.

A. But what if I say that miracles are impossible, because they are contrary to all experience?

B. You have stated that already, and I have shown it to be an assumption.

A. But how is it an assumption?

B. Because it begs the whole question. No one believes in miracles, except on the ground that *in some one's experience* they have occurred. We say that the testimony which we have to miracles is strong and credible, and if you say that nothing which does not come within your experience can be believed, you will find such an assertion extremely embarrassing, and likely to limit the progress of knowledge; for if your neighbour has had experiences which you have not had, on this principle you will have to reject his testimony utterly. You will find such a principle impossible to work.

A. Yes; but there is a difference. When his experience contradicts the laws of nature, then I shall say it is impossible to receive it; so long as it keeps within the bounds of known law, I shall believe or not, according to my estimate of his character. But no testimony can prove what is beyond all experience and therefore impossible.

B. I confess I can only repeat what I have said before. If we are not to consider the statements of our witnesses as part of the experience of mankind, you can of course get rid of any miracle by at once denying the truth of the testimony. But, even then, you have only shown, by the help of a very remarkable assumption, that this, that, or the other miracle has not taken place.

A. A very small thing this, I presume!

B. Small or great, it is unimportant when compared with the points with which you started.

A. How so?

B. You commenced by stating nakedly, that miracles are impossible; you end by saying, that you will not believe any one who bears witness to a miracle.

A. Where is the difference?

B. Little, perhaps, in your intention, but still this. We have seen that there is no *à priori* argument against a miracle. A miracle, then, is not impossible. But you will not believe that one ever occurred; and why not?

No longer, because it *cannot* have taken place: but because it *has* not taken place. The *incredulity* remains: the original ground of it is gone. You will not believe that any experience can contradict *your* experience.

A. Add, also, the experience of all other men.

B. The experience of all other men, with the exception of those whose experience bears witness to the miracles. If you persist in asserting that their evidence, however otherwise unimpeachable, must go for nothing, because it contravenes general experience, I can only reiterate that you are arguing in a circle. "All things must happen in the way that we see them happen; there can be no variation, because any variation would imply that they have not always happened according to a regular law." Such is your argument; and turn it how you will, it *depends upon itself* for its validity.

A. I begin to see that there really is a difficulty, and that I have been too hasty in assuming the *impossibility* of a miracle. Yet still the *improbability* is so great, that I should require the very best of evidence to prove it.

B. Certainly, that is but reasonable.

A. Now, as in the ordinary course of nature

no miracle has ever taken place, it seems to me, that we ought to view with the utmost suspicion any evidence which professes to assert a miracle.

B. If you mean by *suspicion* careful scrutiny, I agree with you; if, however, you mean a determination not to believe, and a grave prejudice against the witnesses before they have been heard, then I must remark that you will be misled by scientific imagination.

A. Scientific imagination! My good friend, you might as well speak of irrational reasoning.

B. Pardon me. If when science shows you perpetual instances of uniformity, you assume, by help of the principle just discussed, a *necessary* uniformity in nature, then you are the victim of scientific imagination. Your mind is influenced by what Bacon calls an *idol*, an image, which has usurped the place of the logical understanding, and distorts the faculty of perception; I say, then, that you must not begin with a prejudice *that a miracle is impossible*, but must suppose that, *being not impossible*, it may be proved by sufficient evidence.

A. It is very difficult to abolish this notion from the mind.

B. Doubtless; and therefore in all fairness

you ought to scrutinize your objections very closely. However, it may assist you to know, that a miracle has already taken place, upon evidence which cannot be refused.

A. Pray what is that?

B. Creation.

A. Do you mean the Creation in the first chapter of Genesis?

B. No, I am speaking of a beginning of things.

A. But what if things had no beginning?

B. To imagine that, is to imagine a greater marvel than any Creation; or rather, I should say, you cannot imagine it; it is incredible in fact, and impossible in thought. You may imagine a portent which never occurred, or a monster which never existed; but to imagine the eternity of matter is impossible; science will not permit you to do so. Scientific investigations lead you back from the more complex to the simpler; but go as far back as you will, you come at last to a stage when absolute simplicity is reached. Call it what you will, a germ or a protoplasm, there is at least an end to the series.

A. But if I say that the original germ has existed from all eternity?

B. In so doing you deny the protoplasm; for if there is no beginning of germination, there is no protoplasm.

A. But the protoplasm may have existed, and yet not begun to germinate.

B. Then, in the beginning of the process, a new force has come in, and there is a change in nature: something has begun to operate which a moment ago did not operate. Here, at once, is the outline of a Creative act, and a refutation of the uniformity of nature, for the new force has produced *change*.

A. But what you regard as a *new* force, should more properly be stated to be a *latent* force suddenly introduced into the sphere of the germ in question.

B. Immediately that you use the word "*suddenly*," you acknowledge an infraction of the uniformity of nature.

A. Still, may we not imagine that there are *unknown* forces, to which all these results may be ultimately reduced?

B. Once more, when you suppose unknown forces to operate, you surrender the position you have assumed. If unknown law is to be brought in to explain difficulties, I cannot see the difficulty of believing that the Creator may have caused those unknown laws to operate on occasions which His Infinite wisdom has appointed.

A. But by unknown law, I mean permanent operating agencies, not occasional and capricious ones.

B. In short you prefer to accept on *faith* hidden causes of which you know nothing, rather than the will of the Creator, of which the vast majority of mankind consider themselves to have at least an indistinct impression.

A. Pardon me, it is you now who are arguing in a circle. You wish to prove the existence of God by the evidence of miracles; now you are assuming His existence to prove miracles.

B. No; you are mistaken. I do not imagine that men will be persuaded by miracles of God's existence; nor did the Founder of Christianity hold any such opinion. "If they hear not Moses and the Prophets, neither will they be persuaded though one rose to them from the dead." Such is His language. Miracles imply some sort of a belief in God previously to their being used as evidence. They imply a personal God, One Who has power to act on nature. Without this belief, they are of no effect; for a man whose mind is firmly persuaded that religion is a delusion, must necessarily view all its evidences through a different medium. He must resort to any explanation, however violent, to remove the evidences. Such a man cannot accept miracles as evidence, because his first principle is that, there being no *active God*, no interference with nature is possible. But the force of miracles, as evidence, is to serve as Divine credentials, and to prove the introduction of a distinctive change in moral and religious knowledge.

A. Do you not then regard the Christian miracles as intended to convert the heathen?

B. Certainly; but not as adequate to *convince the Atheist*. The scope of a miracle appears to be this. At certain periods of the world's history, great changes in the moral atmosphere, as well as in the religious belief of mankind, have been effected. On certain of these occasions, but especially at that time, when One appeared to revolutionize the religions of the world and to preach a doctrine—which required, as its primary element, personal reverence to the Teacher, as to One far above the sons of men—strong attesting proofs were needed that the doctrines inculcated were of Divine origin. The highest human virtue was no sufficient proof of this. Nothing but a superhuman power over nature could give adequate proof of the truth of the claims urged by such a Teacher. But if He were such as He declared himself to be, then His miracles would be the most natural result of His life, and the only sufficient proof of His Divine mission. It is no exaggeration to say, that if such a person as Christ ever did appear upon this world's scene, so far from it being extraordinary for Him to work miracles, it would be extraordinary if He did not.

A. How so? His doctrines, if true, would win their way by their intrinsic truth.

B. Not necessarily so, if they are the revelation of truths not discernible by reason. When a person professes to instruct us in new truth, our first natural question is, "What proof do you give, that we should believe you?" The only possible reply in such matter as this is, "The works that I do, they bear witness of Me." For of the secrets of the spiritual world, and of our relation to them, our own knowledge, acquired chiefly from sensible objects, cannot be sufficient evidence. If a person of eminent excellence and integrity asserts a knowledge of Divine things not possessed by others, we have a right to demand a proof of his spiritual insight. No proof of this could be so convincing as a palpable exhibition of power over the hidden forces of nature. I do not mean to say that *power* is all that can be discerned in the works of Jesus Christ, nor would I have you to suppose that I think no other form of evidence of value; but such evidence, if afforded, would plainly demand our assent more powerfully than any other.

A. But, as I read history, great reformers of religion and morals have succeeded without miracles. Mahomet, for instance, and Luther, required no miracles to support them.

B. Luther, you must remember, appealed to previous miracles. He endeavoured to restore the religion, which Christ had founded, to its original purity; he professed to make no revelation. Mahomet did profess to make a revelation, but if you will compare the position occupied by Christ, with reference to the social forms around Him, with that occupied by Mahomet, you will see a good reason, why miracles should be essential to the one and not to the other.

A. How will you convince me of that?

B. The system of Mahomet, though in many ways novel, cannot be considered greatly different in its moral tone from the ordinary Oriental religions. It did, in fact, in the majority of cases, adapt itself to the people among whom it arose. In the hands of Mahomet religion was drawn down to the level of ordinary morals: the special forms of self-indulgence, to which Eastern nations are prone were allowed, or only lightly condemned; and thus there was no special difficulty to prevent such a system taking root. But it was very different with Christianity. It presented an ideal of life elevated, but not alluring. It set itself directly in antagonism to the leading ideas of the world, and boldly required the surrender of all that men hold valuable, the acquisition of an entirely new moral code, and that of such a nature, that the opposition of all classes might be expected to its development. It is of course easy to assert that this system, if true, would have made its way without assistance; but one must confess that, according to universal experience (which has occupied us so much in this conversation), such an event would be incredible, and scarcely less a marvel than any special miracle objected to.

A. Still, it appears to me some ground of objection against the Christian miracles, that they do so evidently fit in with Divine claims. They are just the events, that in those days would catch the ignorant and superstitious, who would not care to inquire into the validity of what was reported.

B. But you must observe it as a remarkable fact that the early Christian writers, though they had the record of the miracles before them, refer to them as evidence with comparative reserve. They knew of the miracles, as reported in the Gospels, and yet they dwelt upon other points as of more importance.

A. Is that in truth so?

B. I think, if you will examine, you will not long be in doubt.

A. And how do you account for it?

B. Because of the constant claims of sorcerers and magicians to divine power. Hence it would seem that, so far from inventing these miracles for purposes of evidence, the early Christian writers, while believing in them, appealed to other evidences on behalf of their faith. This may be taken as an argument in favour of the miracles, because it proves that the early Christians did not invent them, in order to have a miraculous basis for their story.

But the question of the nature of the testimony upon which we believe the Christian miracles, is entirely independent. What we are really discussing is whether a miracle is *possible*. We have seen then that in the nature of things there is no necessary absurdity in the occurrence of a miracle. *Absolute uniformity* in nature is really an assumption, based upon individual observations, and cannot be taken as in itself a disproof of all miraculous agency. The idea of a *beginning* seems to be necessary to the human mind: we cannot divest ourselves of it. Even were matter eternal, the development of matter involves an idea of commencement. The idea of a personal God removes any difficulty against miraculous agency; but that idea is antecedent to a belief in miracles, and is not and cannot be proved by them. We have also seen that, if a revelation of new Divine truths were to take place, the best credentials of the agent in the revelation would be a power, delegated from God, to suspend the ordinary course of nature. Still it is necessary to remind you, that you must not regard miracles as the *sole* evidence of Christianity, but must take them in conjunction with many other things. These evidences have a correlative value: they tend to prove and to throw light upon each other; and therefore, though no part of our evidence can be regarded as, in itself, absolutely demonstrative, yet the whole taken together may be found to command an assent of a very marked and decided character. This however is plain, that whatever be the value of the assumption that the course of nature is uniform (and no doubt it is most valuable), yet it *is* an assumption based more or less on probable evidence, and has no claim to be regarded as of such *à priori* value, that the testimony of sane, serious, and truthful witnesses is at once to be rejected, because their testimony and this principle are found to be in conflict.

DIALOGUE III.

OBJECTIONS TO THE SCHEME OF CHRISTIANITY CONSIDERED.

A. You must not suppose that your argument of yesterday has obviated all the difficulties which occur to me in reviewing the Christian religion. A miracle, viewed as a suspension of the general laws of nature, may be possible. I mean that, as an abstract question, the possibility of the suspension of God's laws may be conceded, and yet the particular miracle, or series of miraculous events, called the Christian religion, may still be objected to.

B. I never thought that my arguments yesterday were a full answer to all objections. All that I was concerned to prove was, that the rejection of Christianity because it professes to have been established by miracles was unreasonable. It is quite open for you to object against the particular miracles in question. You may say that the proof of their having taken place is unsatisfactory, and this is a distinct question. Or you may assert that, so far as a claim to miracles establishes the proof of a religion, my last arguments may be held to prove the truth of any religion which lays claim to special miracles.

A. May I not also say that the internal difficulties of the Christian religion are so great as to amount to a disproof of its truth?

B. You may, of course, say this; but you will have to substantiate your objections by details.

A. That I proceed to do.

B. In what manner?

A. Thus. I say at once, that the so-called Christian revelation seems to fail from its own inherent weakness. It professes to be a declaration, on God's part, of certain new truths, and a republication of others known before. If it comes from God, it ought to be more complete than it is. But, as is confessed on all hands, its doctrines are beset with difficulties. Many things are left in great uncertainty: some of its doctrines are absurd and inconceivable: large portions of it, notably those which treat of the position of the clergy, of the nature of the Lord's Supper, of the gift of the Holy Ghost, have tended to foster tyranny and superstition. What can be more monstrous than the doctrine of Transubstantiation, or of the Infallibility of the Pope, or of the power of men to forgive sins? And yet all these doctrines are deduced, with how much justice I do not say, from the words of Scripture.

B. Pardon me for interrupting. You surely will not say, that if men choose to imagine that they can deduce conclusions which cannot properly be drawn from the Scripture revelation, this is an argument against the revelation?

A. Why, yes. If it came from God, such things would not be possible. My objection here is that the supposed revelation is utterly uncertain, and therefore not a revelation at all.

B. Well, let that pass for the present: we will revert to it. I should like to hear a continuation of your objections. Possibly we may find general considerations sufficient to answer your difficulties, when the whole tenour of them is stated.

A. Then, again; here is a revelation intended for all mankind, which was really given only to a few, and even now has only penetrated to a small portion of mankind. That is a grave objection. The Revelation is only partial at best. And even what is given is based upon such uncertain arguments, that it ought not to be reckoned compulsory on men to believe.

B. And now tell me what you expect in a Divine revelation?

A. I expect that it should bear such evident traces of the Divine intention, that no one should be able to dispute it; that it should immediately commend itself to all men; that it should have no uncertainties, no possibility of being misinterpreted, or of being applied to selfish purposes of individual aggrandisement; that it should not be subject to capricious alteration by the agency of fraud or time; that every man should have it in its perfection and entirety.

B. And on what grounds do you found such an expectation?

A. On my ideas of what is to be expected from God's goodness and providence.

B. Let us turn from revelation to the natural world. Do you find all things there just as you would expect? Are there no difficulties in it?

A. Certainly there are. But then, in discerning the Divine agency there, I have been left to my own experience and reason to trace out the laws.

B. So then, confessing that *on the whole* there are signs of God's providence in the world, you are still constrained to admit that there are many things contrary to your expectations?

A. I have frequently confessed it to you.

B. And yet you will not admit that a particular revelation is Divine, because it does not accord with your preconceived expectations of what it ought to be. Let me put the matter in this way. Surely you would not hold to this opinion in the following circumstances. Suppose you lived under a code of laws, which in the main were just and upright, but yet contained some things, the drift and tenour of which you found it difficult to comprehend; and that on a certain occasion the governing body (supposed to be the same which made the first code) suspended the laws and introduced others, would you consider it a proof that the new laws did not come from the same source, because there were also difficulties in them? If you knew yourself to be an incompetent judge in the former case, you would also expect to be at fault in estimating the latter. Is not that so?

A. I do not like this *general* way of arguing, because my objections are *particular* rather than general.

B. Still, I must ask you to state, whether the confessed difficulties in the natural government of the universe ought to prepare us for difficulties in revelation, or not?

A. As far as this general proposition goes, I do not object to it.

B. Without, then, entering farther into the general view, let us attend to the particulars which you enumerate. Shall you object to specify one special objection which you think insurmountable?

A. By no means. I think that by far the best plan. If the revelation is from God, then they who conveyed the revelation must be inspired; but the doctrine of the inspiration of Scripture is quite untenable.

B. That is a very broad charge.

A. But not more broad than just. How can that be inspired which is full of errors and contradictions?

B. Why, truly, if you could show that the narrative in the Bible is so contradictory, that no possible explanation can reconcile the difficulties: this would go far to shake the doctrine of its inspiration. Still, even if this were so (which I do not grant), you must remember that the account at least of the Christian revelation contained in the Gospels does not depend upon the inspiration of the writers. The only question is, whether what they relate is credible and true; because, if their narrative is a faithful account of the life of Christ, of His actions and His teaching, a few inaccuracies in the narrative would not alter the general facts. They might indeed shake the general theory of inspiration. Some extreme theories, such as that of *plenary verbal* inspiration, are indeed refuted by the narrative, because it is plainly impossible that Christ could have spoken different words at the same time; and plenary verbal inspiration implies that every single word was dictated directly by God, and thus God would be made to dictate inaccuracies as pure truth. This I will concede, but I cannot think that this is all which you mean.

A. By no means. Is it not strange that God should dictate inaccurate grammar, for the Evangelists and St. Paul wrote very strange Greek? And is it not also strange that He should permit various readings to perplex the believer?

B. My good friend, you are not surely going to insist upon this as an objection!

A. Why not?

B. Who ever told you, or how have you gathered that God has promised that the Jews of Capernaum, or Nazareth, or Jerusalem should write Attic Greek, or that He has led us to expect that He would preserve the record from the effects of time or the errors of copyists?

A. Why, I cannot see how the revelation can

come from Him, unless He extends this protection to it.

B. In other words, you return to your old argument. You evolve an idea from your own mind as to what God ought to do, and when you find it not done, you at once assume that the hand of God is not traceable in the work. Surely in a revelation you ought not to erect your own fancies into absolute canons.

A. But if not, I do not see how we are to judge at all of the matter.

B. I wish I could get you to see this, that we must be very incompetent judges of a revelation, because we have no experience, except that of nature, to judge from.

A. Well, then, I will change my ground, and will revert to the argument that revelation, instead of conveying certain knowledge to us, leaves us involved in as much obscurity as before. How can that be a revelation which is capable of being interpreted in a thousand different ways? It is impossible to believe that God would intend to supply us with knowledge, and, instead of so doing, involve us in difficulty.

B. Do I understand you to mean that the language of Scripture ought to be more clear?

A. Yes; and more than that, it ought not to be capable of being misunderstood.

B. Now let us take a parallel instance. How does God give us information in the natural world?

A. By reason.

B. And is reason a certain and infallible guide? Do all men, from the same premisses, arrive at the same conclusions? Do they not, according to their preconceptions and associations, diverge asunder as widely as possible? And yet they have the same facts to argue from. This does not indeed show that there is not one right way; but it does show that the guide to knowledge which we possess is by no means a certain one. And so revelation, though it has but one right meaning, may be interpreted a thousand different ways, according to the idiosyncrasies of the reader.

A. Yet you would think that only one way of reading it should be possible, when it is conveyed in language dictated by Almighty God.

B. Let me again say that we have no proof that the *language,* as distinguished from the *matter,* was dictated by Him. But, besides this, just consider what so frequently occurs with language in ordinary matters. Is any thing more uncertain or capricious? However precisely any document is worded, an acute lawyer will find a flaw, or at least raise a doubt as to its meaning. A subtle casuist will so employ words, that all his hearers will believe him to mean one thing, while he means something quite different. And yet language is God's appointed means of conveying knowledge. Why should we expect that these difficulties should not arise, when information is conveyed to us through the medium of revelation?

A. But then you must remember that if Christianity is true, errors as to its truths are incomparably more important than in other things.

B. Be it so. And yet there are things vitally affecting men's temporal welfare, in which the uncertainty of language grievously misleads them.

A. But in addition to the uncertainty of the Christian revelation, I find an objection in its evident incompleteness. Instead of telling us the whole of that which we desire to know, it leaves us in great darkness upon many of the most interesting and essential points. Some things are enlarged upon at great length, which are of small importance and only of temporary interest: others, which we crave to know with all the longing of which our nature is capable, are passed over with a word.

B. And do you think this a fair objection to the Christian revelation?

A. Clearly it is. Revelation professes to instruct men in vital truths. If it does not, it ceases to deserve the name.

B. Let me be sure that I comprehend the scope of your objection.

A. What does revelation tell us of the *origin of good and evil,* and their essential relations to one another? How does it explain the introduction of evil into the universe? You will say, perhaps, in the narrative of the Fall. But that is not so; for, even in that account, the author of evil is already existent; and theology has been compelled to indulge in all sorts of fantastic dreams to explain this great fact. Then what does revelation tell us of the *nature of the soul?* Nothing at all. All the most difficult problems are left untouched.

B. I think, if you study the Christian revelation carefully, you will find that it tells us very much about the soul. It does not indeed explain how the soul and body become united (speaking popularly); nor does it explicitly propound a theory of psychology; but of the facts of the soul's life it tells us very much, and of the effects of evil upon it. These are surely interesting matters, of no less importance than the speculative questions to which you refer.

A. Still we ought to hear more of those psychological questions.

B. That is, you are of opinion that we ought. Now let us turn to nature, and see what is the case with the information which we derive from her. Do we find that the lines of knowledge which nature opens to us, are exactly proportioned to our expectation? Are the matters which are of most vital importance, always the readiest to our hand? *Astronomy* is a glorious and interesting science; but, as far as we can see, neither so important nor so vitally interesting as the *laws of human life.* The remedies for disease are, one would think, matters of universal interest; and yet perhaps nothing is more uncertain than the mode of treatment of disease, the influence of remedies upon the human organism, and all the details of medical science. What can be stranger than that men have traced the laws of the heavenly bodies, have been able to predict the exact hour at which flights of asteroids made their appearance, while the knowledge of what is serviceable to relieve pain and disease remains most uncertain and rudimentary, even in the present day?

A. But is that so?

B. You have only to observe the fluctuations in the theory of medicine, in the course of a generation, to be assured of it. At the present day the acknowledged theory is, that you can only assist nature to cure herself. Compare that with the theories of a few years ago, and how uncertain does the science seem! And yet nothing can be more shallow, than the sneer of some thoughtless people at physicians, as if they were ignorant and stupid, for they number among them some of the brightest and most acute intellects of our time; and the higher the intellect, the more readily will it confess the uncertainty of its knowledge.

A. But how does this serve your argument?

B. In this way. If you argue about the sciences *à priori*, you would expect to find the science of *healing* much *easier* to acquire, much more *certain* in its application than the science of *astronomy*. If you look to the facts you find the reverse to be the case; and, therefore, if in revelation you find some things made clear, which appear to be of less importance, while others of deeper interest are left uncertain, you ought to acknowledge that the laws of natural information and of supernatural instruction are analogous in this respect.

A. Well; but if it be reasonable to expect

a degree of uncertainty, of ambiguity, and of apparent disproportion in a revealed account of things not hitherto known, surely it is not reasonable to expect that the language shall lead to inevitable tyranny or superstition.

B. Tyranny and superstition are very great evils, but they are both the abuse of something in itself not evil but good. Tyranny arises from the possession of superior knowledge or power by bad men: superstition springs from an ignorant and blind adhesion to a distorted idea. You would not condemn knowledge or science, because men make use of them for their own ends: you would not call a law evil, because ignorant men, urged on by designing men, misunderstood it. You would say that the remedy for both was increased knowledge and higher principles.

A. Exactly so; and this is what Christianity denies, that there can be increased knowledge or higher principles than exist among Christians.

B. That some Christians say this, I readily acknowledge; but that it is the correct view of revelation, or that the Christian Church as a whole has countenanced it, I emphatically deny. Indeed the Christian Church is often condemned for the opposite fault. It is said that they are not content with revelation as it stands, but found additional truths upon it; and that even Christian *morality* is *progressive*, is undoubted. That we can improve upon the knowledge or the morals of our Founder, we deny; but that the early Christians comprehended the whole breadth and depth of His teaching, we do not maintain for a moment. They were subject to the opinions of their own times, and acquiesced in many things which the spread of Christian principles has rooted out.

A. Nevertheless, superstition and tyranny have flourished in the Christian Church, and that, by virtue of the language of the so-called revelation.

B. This is unquestionable; but that it should be so, is only analogous to the course of events in the world. If this had been impossible, if every error of opinion had been at once extirpated, and every moral delinquency punished, the system might have been more ideally complete, but it would have contradicted the doctrines which it contains; for it would have allowed no scope for self-renovation and discipline, which is of the very essence of the revelation; and so far from demonstrating that it came from the Author of nature, it would have been subject to the objection of setting the God of nature and of revelation at variance with Himself.

A. How so?

B. Because, if we reason from nature to revelation, as more or less we do and must, we should find no analogy between the two; and then men might easily say either that nature was evil or revelation false, because they did not accord with one another.

A. Well, if we must expect these difficulties in a revelation, surely we might anticipate that it would be entrusted to proper men to administer it. I do not speak of the ordinary administration of church affairs, but of the strange story of miraculous gifts of language, of interpretation, of healing, and the like, being given to the early Christians, not in any sort of order, but broadcast and indiscriminately; so that the possessors of them misused and abused them, and had no sound judgment in the employment of them, but played with them like children, seemingly unconscious that they were a trust from God for the salvation of mankind.

B. I will not stop to complain of your highly-coloured picture of these disorders, but will simply call your attention to a plain fact. These gifts or graces were supposed to be, and were,

God's gifts. The possessors of them were conscious of their powers, and were able to employ them as men employ gifts of memory and genius. They had a certain control over them, depending upon their will; for these gifts were not, like the *possessions* of which we read, energies acting within them *against* their will. If they had been thought to be such, the writer of the Epistle to the Corinthians could not have enjoined them to exercise a *control* over their gifts. Such being the case, these special gifts have a certain analogy to gifts of genius and memory. Have they not?

A. Perhaps so.

B. Now let me ask you, do men possessing these gifts always employ them with discretion? Do they not frequently misapply them and abuse them?

A. It is proverbial of them, I confess.

B. Why then should you find such a difficulty in the indiscretions, and it may be absurdities, into which these men ran? You have a parallel in the natural world, and there it does not startle you. You do not find *genius* of necessity united with *discretion;* you do not find the best men always possessed of the greatest powers, or the men of greatest power always the best men.

A. I shall not press this objection any further, because I acknowledge a certain justice in your reply. There can be no doubt that men of genius frequently act with great indiscretion, and cause their own great gifts to be thought lightly of. It does seem quite possible, that moral excellence and discretion may be wanting even in those who seem born to improve mankind. But I have not exhausted my list of difficulties. Perhaps the one which I have now to urge, is the strongest of all. It is a question upon which Christians themselves seem utterly undecided, and yet, before any man can embrace Christianity, he may fairly demand to have it answered.

B. Pardon me for interrupting you; but I must interpose to say, that when you speak of accepting Christianity as an intellectual system, you are forgetting that its primary object is not to satisfy the intellect, but to improve the heart; and to speak of demanding a proof of every portion before you accept anything, is like refusing to act virtuously, because systems of ethics are not logically consistent.

A. Well, now, you have unintentionally anticipated my objection. I was going to say that, if Christianity is a rule of life, it ought to be simple and easy to comprehend; instead of which it is abstruse, and comprises all manner of metaphysical questions, which are unintelligible to the vast majority of men, and certainly of little use for practical purposes.

B. And if it be so, how does Christianity differ from the ordinary practice of human life? In each, the general principles are clearly defined; plain people can walk by them; but if the reasons and causes of these principles are to be sifted, the most acute intellects are baffled in the inquiry. Examine any system of ethics, and apply it to practice; you will find that difficulties present themselves at every turn. Take, for example, the ordinary doctrine, that the prime law of moral action is the *greatest good of the greatest number*, which is undoubtedly true. Apply it to practice, and you will see how immense are the difficulties which present themselves. Individual interest is to give way to general interest. Some are to suffer that the whole may prosper; but every one feels that his own suffering, if inflicted without consciousness of ill-desert, is an injustice; and thus, *practically*, individual interest, if it do not appear inconsistent with the general interest, asserts itself even in very excellent men; and yet, perhaps, these individual interests are seen to be, *in the long-run*, injurious to the well-being of the whole. I only instance this, to show how hard it is to ascertain great principles, even when the general rules of action are clear enough.

A. But the especial object of Christianity is to supply an unerring rule of right action.

B. Yes; but you forget that the reasons for the rule lie deep in the constitution of things. To discern them requires deep and mature study; it involves subtle questions as to the nature of right and wrong. Any system, which professed to abolish these investigations, would stand condemned by being inadequate to human nature. The Christian revelation does profess to give rules of action, and to supply additional knowledge upon the deepest truths; but it never professes to make men more than men; it never tells them that they can measure the universe in the hollow of the hand, or that they can comprehend the whole of God's nature. If it did, it would abrogate the very idea of an Infinite Being, because that which is infinite cannot be measured.

A. So then the end of the Christian revelation is to tell, us that reason is given us to no purpose?

B. Certainly not. Reason is not deposed by

T

the Christian faith, but her sphere is defined with greater clearness.

A. And, pray, what is left for her, if she can neither determine absolutely what is right or wrong, nor judge whether the revelation to which she is to bow, is good or evil? And how can she distinguish between the Mohammedan and the Christian faith, if she is not allowed to discriminate between what is true and what is false?

B. But have I said that she is not allowed thus to discriminate? Surely she can discern whether the principles involved in these are good or evil; and she can judge of the evidence for either, whether it is sufficient to establish its object or not.

A. But how is this possible, if we are not allowed to say, "This or that cannot have come from God"?

B. But you *are* allowed to say so. If the Christian revelation contains any plain *immoralities*, any contradictions of the grand *principles* of justice, then you can say at once that your reason refuses to accept it.

A. I could supply you with a list of cruelties practised in the name of God, and even of direct commands, attributed to Him, to inflict punishments, which, if you adhere to your concession, would justify me in rejecting the revelation at once.

B. In so doing, you would of course bear in mind, that a contradiction to a moral law implies an injunction to practise immoral *habits*. Individual commands, *in themselves*, are not proof sufficient of an abrogation of moral laws.

A. Now you are withdrawing your concession.

B. Not so; but, for particular exceptions to the law of mercy, there may be sufficient reasons; whereas an *injunction* to be unmerciful would at once condemn a religion.

A. Are there not abundant instances of the encouragement of an unmerciful temper in the Jewish Bible?

B. I do not think that the tenour of the Old Testament can be fairly reckoned to be unmerciful. Certainly there are severe injunctions contained in it, on the strength of which the Jews may have encouraged a cruel disposition in themselves. But it is by no means the same thing, to be called upon to execute sentence upon the wicked, and to be yourself cruel. Otherwise judges must be accounted the most cruel of all men, which is plainly not the case. The execution of an established law by no means implies harshness or vindictiveness in those who execute it; and so the Israelites were instructed by God to be the means of punishing atrocious criminals, yet they themselves were commanded to practise mercy in a very high degree, a degree far exceeding that in which these virtues were practised by contemporary nations. It is, indeed, impossible here to discuss all the questions connected with objections to the Old Testament. But the essential point can be succinctly stated. No proof can be adduced of the encouragement of a cruel, vindictive, or unjust *disposition:* many proofs can be given of the contrary. And the Christian revelation (applying that word to the Scriptures of the New Testament) pre-eminently enforces lessons of love, justice, and mercy.

A. This I confess; but still it has not of necessity produced a corresponding result. Christians have been as unmerciful as heathens, when the power of exercising severity has been placed in their hands.

B. Possibly; but in so doing, they have gone against not only the *spirit,* but also the *letter* of their law; and in so doing they have proved themselves unworthy disciples of Christ: they have not shown that the revelation enjoins, or even permits, such acts.

A. But if the Christian revelation does not countenance immoralities, it does not therefore follow that it is Divine. We may be too hasty in this respect. It may be a very high-toned and useful code of morality; and in consequence of that, men may have too readily accepted its declaration as to its Divine origin. In fact the evidence upon which rests its claim to be reckoned Divine seems to be insufficient; and on this point at least our reason may employ itself.

B. Undoubtedly; but as this is quite a distinct question, and as our conversation has extended over a very wide range of subjects, I think it will be better to take this by itself, as a matter for separate consideration.

A. I quite agree with you, and shall hope to resume the question another time.

DIALOGUE IV.

ON CHRISTIANITY AS A SCHEME IMPERFECTLY COMPREHENDED.

A. You will remember that there was a point on which we did not touch in discussing the general objections to the Christian revelation, or shall I recall to your mind the conclusion of our last conversation?

B. I recollect perfectly that you stated that you thought there were objections to Christianity, which the evidence on which it relied was insufficient to balance or at all events to outbalance. Was not this so?

A. Well, perhaps, that is the form in which I somewhat hastily stated what had occurred to my mind. I was rather perplexed with some of your arguments. But all of them, as it appeared to me, ignored a very essential, indeed a vital, question. You had been labouring to show that it was reasonable to expect, in a Divine revelation, difficulties analogous to those found in the ordinary course of nature. But such arguments in no degree proved that the things objected to were in themselves right. And your own concessions show that, if the things objected to are in themselves wrong, no analogy will alter their moral character and make them right. If religion inculcates the belief in *moral falsehoods* and *intellectual impossibilities*, then religion is false, however many analogies can be adduced to bolster up the falsehoods.

B. As far as we went last time, I only endeavoured to prove that your instances were not, as you seemed to assume, conclusive against the truth of Christianity.

A. But that is very unsatisfactory. What I wish to see is that Christianity is not only not demonstrably *false*, but also that it is demonstrably *true*, *just* in its principles and *complete* in its evidence. If I see a man acting in a manner which appears to me based on unrighteous principles, I may be unable to prove that he is a villain, but that is a very different thing from being convinced of his goodness.

B. Let me recall to your mind a conversation which we had not very long ago upon a kindred subject. You will remember that in speaking of the difficulties connected with the moral government of the universe, we found that

that government was a system of which we knew some parts, but were not adequately acquainted with the whole. It is a system in which means are employed to produce results, and it is regulated by general laws. If we knew the whole intention of this system, we might possibly comprehend every detail; but, inasmuch as we are acquainted with detached portions of it, it is conceivable that the apparent difficulties are the results of our ignorance. The general signs of goodness are an argument that the *whole* is good; and it may perhaps be found, that increased knowledge would enable us to connect the various isolated details, so as to show, that the whole system is completely pervaded by the spirit of goodness, justice, and truth, which apparently regulate a part.

A. I perfectly recollect the conversation, but it seems to me that it is of no assistance to us here.

B. On what grounds do you so conclude?

A. First, I do not know that Christianity is a system such as you describe. I thought that the whole truth was supposed to be therein revealed. At least I am sure that many Christians speak and act, as if they have attained the end of all moral knowledge in Christianity. Secondly, I cannot understand that a dispensation based on exceptional miraculous interpositions can be carried on by general laws. It appears to be grounded on a suspension of general laws. And, thirdly, I am dissatisfied with the assumption, that the salvation of the world requires to be effected by the slow application of means to ends; for if God wills the salvation of men, surely His will might be far more effectually performed, than by a tardy process extending over thousands of years, and attended by all sorts of disturbing circumstances.

B. If you were going to judge a system of philosophy, would you not think it right to begin with an examination of the principles on which it professes to be based?

A. Unquestionably I should.

B. And would it be fair to assume that it is not what it professes to be?

A. It would be most unfair to beg the question thus.

B. And if some who held the system were ignorant of what the system itself professed to contain, would you be content, acting as a philosopher and not as an advocate, to refute their ignorance of their own system?

A. Certainly not.

B. Well, then, let me beg you not to be

misled by any incomplete notions of Christianity, but to accompany me to the fountain-head of the whole, the revelation of the Bible.

A. Pray proceed; I am all attention.

B. Now the Bible does assert that Christianity is a system. It implies that the moral government of God is a system beyond our comprehension, but yet one of which the eventual result is, that all creatures shall receive according to their deserts; and of this general scheme, Christianity is a portion designed for the completion of the providential government of God. It tells us that, among other mysterious purposes of God, He has determined that a Divine Person should come, "Who is to gather together in one the children of God that are scattered abroad" (John xi. 52), and "establish an everlasting kingdom, wherein dwelleth righteousness" (2 Peter iii. 13). It tells us "that the Spirit of Christ, which was in the Prophets, testified beforehand His sufferings, and the glory that should follow; unto whom it was revealed, that not unto themselves, but unto us they did minister the things that are now reported unto us by them that have preached the Gospel: which things the angels desire to look into" (1 Peter i. 11, 12). It thus speaks of a continual preparation for the

Gospel, which should at length be preached. After a certain time, it continues—"In the fulness of time," Eternal Wisdom, "being in the form of God, made Himself of no reputation and took upon Him the form of a servant; and being found in fashion as a man, He humbled Himself and became obedient unto death, even the death of the Cross; wherefore God also hath highly exalted Him, and given Him a name, which is above every name: that at the name of Jesus every knee should bow, of things in Heaven, and things in earth, and things under the earth; and that every tongue shall confess that Jesus Christ is Lord, to the glory of God the Father." Another part of this Divine Economy was the *miraculous* mission of the Holy Ghost, and His *ordinary* assistance to good men. Then we are told of the invisible government of Christ over His Church, and of His return to judge the world in righteousness. "All power is given unto Him in heaven and in earth" (Matt. xxviii. 18). "He must reign till He hath put all things under His feet." "Then cometh the end, when He shall have delivered up the kingdom to God, even the Father; when He shall have put down all rule and all authority and power. And when all things shall be subdued unto Him, then shall the Son also Himself be subject unto Him that put all things under Him, that God may be all in all" (1 Cor. xv. 28). Now I am not concerned to enter into all the details and the meaning of the scheme here portrayed. What I wish to show you is that, whether the system is true or false, it is surely unjust to say that, in the face of all this, Christianity is not a system.

A. Surely, according to your description, it is a most elaborate and perplexing one. The things here spoken of sound like the visions of a dreamer.

B. I forgive you the remark, in virtue of the unwilling concession, that it is beyond our present powers of comprehension. I will only pause to say, that the details here gathered from portions of the Scripture seem to imply much more than is expressed. It *is* incomprehensible, in the sense that we cannot grasp the whole.

A. But how do you employ this for your argument?

B. I think it is a sufficient answer to your first point, that you do not think Christianity to be a system imperfectly comprehended. If you will take the trouble to examine the passages here brought together, you cannot fail to be struck with the number of questions which

CHRISTIANITY IMPERFECTLY COMPREHENDED. 301

are at once opened in all directions. You will see that, like the system of nature, Christianity, if true, involves a vast amount of considerations on subjects beyond the grasp of our faculties. And if our ignorance of nature may be justly adduced as a reply to difficulties in nature, so our ignorance of the whole scope of the Christian dispensation may be fitly produced as a reply to difficulties connected with that dispensation.

A. But how, then, is Christianity a revelation at all, if it leaves so many things unrevealed?

B. In the same sense that anything else is a revelation. It is the *withdrawing of the veil* from certain things, hidden before, but not the opening up of *all* the mysteries of creation.

A. Well, even granting this, it seems to me that your further argument from analogy will be stopped by the consideration, that Christianity does not profess to work by general laws.

B. On what grounds do you assert that?

A. Why, in the first place, it commences by a stoppage of nature's general laws.

B. How do you know that the miraculous interposition is not part of the general system of nature? May it not have been the intention of the Creator, that an *additional* force or forces should be brought into play for a special purpose, at a particular time? How do you know that the whole may not have been foreordained by the Providence of God from eternity?

A. Because then it would not be a miracle.

B. That answer will not serve you, because we have already agreed that what is miraculous to man may be only a portion of the Divine plan. It is as if, once in the course of ages, a planet in its orbit comes in proximity to a comet, which then passes away into space. The effect is produced once for all, but both planet and comet are subject to general laws.

A. But is there one atom of proof of such a fanciful analogy? Is there anything in the natural world to compare with the introduction of Christianity?

B. Possibly not; but there is something which may explain how we come to regard some things as dependent on general laws, which in themselves appear to be utterly capricious.

A. Of what do you speak?

B. Tell me, on what principle do you infer that nature, I mean physical nature, works by general laws?

A. By an induction from experience, to be

sure. I see that the same results follow constantly from the same antecedents, in a vast number of cases, which daily present themselves. We have gained a knowledge of several laws of matter, and we know also that living agents act very much by general laws.

B. Very well; I quite agree with you. Tell me; do storms, earthquakes, famine, and pestilence destroy mankind by general laws?

A. Of course they do.

B. That you haev learned by continued induction.

A. No; we have not yet been able to learn the laws of the progress of these unusual phenomena. But they must be by general laws, otherwise nature would not be uniform.

B. And is it a fixed law, which causes people, born at such and such a date, to be of such and such a temper and capacity: are those laws fixed by which thoughts come into men's mind? Are all the unexpected events upon which the history of the world hinges, also subject to fixed laws?

A. Most assuredly.

B. I quite agree to this, too. There is no such thing as chance or accident. Everything is, however little it appear to us to be so, the result of fixed laws. But what I ask you to observe is, that our belief in this fixity of law is by no means the result of an adequate induction in many cases. Where we cannot trace the appearance of law, we assume it from the apparent uniformity of nature.

A. I admit that.

B. Why, then, may we not assume that God's miraculous interpositions are also by fixed and general laws?

A. I don't understand.

B. Why should we not say that God, for special purposes unknown to us, has so determined that at a certain period fresh forces should be brought into play, and that they should cease to operate as soon as the purposes were accomplished, much in the same way that a great military genius arises for a time, and changes the whole course of history and then disappears, leaving the ordinary laws to operate as before.

A. But what would such a concession prove?

B. It would show that the progress of Christianity was by general laws, and that there was no need to expect a constant and sustained intervention of fresh forces to meet every transient difficulty. And this, you will observe, is the objection which is so often raised against Christianity. Its miracles have ceased, and therefore men refuse to believe that it ever had any to show.

A. But pardon me for saying, that this argument does not meet my original objection, that moral difficulties in Christianity remain such in spite of analogy.

B. That, I thought, was answered already. If Christianity is a scheme beyond our comprehension, if in it means are employed to produce ends, and if it is carried on by general laws, why then it is analogous to the moral government of the universe; and the moral government of the universe contains difficulties and irregularities. What is more reasonable than to expect similar ones in the scheme of Christianity?

A. But you have been speaking of means being employed to produce ends. By this, I suppose, you denote the various preliminary dispensations of which the Christian is supposed to be the culmination. What an intricate and elaborate plan this appears to be, and how utterly injurious is it to the dignity of an all-powerful God, to be compelled to employ means to effect His purposes.

B. That God employs what we call means, is one thing; that He is *compelled* to employ them is quite another. Perhaps the good resulting from the use of means is greater than we are able to judge. But be this as it may, your argument will prove too much. If the use of means is a refutation of the scheme of Christianity, so also is it a refutation of the scheme of nature. Human life is exactly analogous to Christianity in this; so, too, is the vegetable kingdom. The history of the ripening of the fruits, of the opening of a flower, the very changes of the seasons, will answer your objection, or render it fatal to the idea of a God. In nature growth is progressive: the development of reason is progressive; the character of a man is the result of a long series of antecedent circumstances. Infancy is a preparation for childhood; childhood for boyhood; boyhood for mature manhood. Thus everywhere we see the slow, deliberate maturing of a plan in the events of nature. And it is not unreasonable; on the contrary, it is most natural for Christianity to present itself as the mature development of a scheme, which, through progressive stages, has been carried on from the earliest times till now.

A. It is, I acknowledge, something gained in our inquiry to learn that Christianity presents itself as a progressive system. But I wish to learn something concerning the details of that system. Your answers to my difficulties, taken *en masse*, are to some degree convincing. But what I fear is, that the details will be found inconsistent with the analogy of nature. Are you prepared to find a parallel for every minute particular which perplexes the inquirer?

B. It is, perhaps, too bold to say that I can do so; but I think in many cases surprising resemblances may be traced between the principles of the Christian religion and the general phenomena of the moral universe.

A. With that assurance I will ask your permission to close this conversation. Be assured that next time I shall come with an array of questions, which will tax your ingenuity to the uttermost to meet.

B. I will try my best to assist you, for I do not forget your assurance, that you feel no positive dislike to Christianity.

A. Indeed, no; I should only feel too grateful, if a religion which promises such unutterable blessings, should be found such that a man who tries to discover the truth is not compelled, by the weight of the objections, to forego the happiness which Christians profess and appear to enjoy.

DIALOGUE V.

ON THE APPOINTMENT OF A REDEEMER AND MEDIATOR.

A. It appears to me that we have now reached a critical stage in our investigations, upon which much that has gone before, and all that is to follow, must depend. You have shown me that Christianity, as conceived by you, is a system consisting of various mutually-related parts. In this system, we are made acquainted only with certain portions; the scope of the whole is not known to us. As in the system of nature, so in that of Christianity, much is left unrevealed; and in consequence we are compelled to acknowledge, that the existence of difficulties and objections is, if not what we ought to expect, at least not a refutation of the whole. However, there are portions more fully revealed than others, and these we are at liberty to examine by the light of our moral nature. If they are absolutely contradictory to truth and goodness, then we may reject them.

B. I can only take exception to one part of what you have said: we have established our conclusions at present, each on independent grounds. If what you are now going to object to shall prove to be really objectionable, future argument may be precluded; but you ought not to argue backwards, and deny what you have previously assented to, in virtue of a point which we fail to establish on independent grounds.

A. I shall not dispute your position, because you will readily see that the point now at issue is simply the central doctrine of Christianity. If we reject that, all the rest is valueless.

B. What is the matter to which you are referring?

A. The doctrine of a Mediator between God and man. It appears to me to be simply preposterous.

B. What do you understand by a Mediator?

A. I understand the word according to its etymology, one who stands between.

B. You object, then, to the whole idea of any one intervening between God and man, so as to be the means by which God communicates the knowledge of Himself and the possession of His blessings.

A. I do.

B. But surely you have not considered that in nature nothing is more common than this.

A. How do you make that out?

B. Is life one of God's gifts?

A. I apprehend it is so.

B. Do we not receive the gift of life through the instrumentality of others? Are not our parents the means by which we are made? Surely this is a case in point. We know of no other way by which we could exist, except by their intervention.

A. That is quite true.

B. And do we not, as children, have our sustenance, our protection from danger, our education, and the means of attaining manhood by means of others? And when we are men, are we not constantly beholden to others for every kind of blessing? If this is all your difficulty, I think you need scarcely be in haste to reject Christianity.

A. But on reflection, I see it is not all my difficulty. The Christian notion of a Mediator involves much more than this.

B. It certainly does.

A. So far as you have gone, you have spoken only of bodily intervention. But the idea of an intervention between God and the soul is what perplexes me; for the very idea of the soul is that it is a *spiritual* essence, capable of holding communion with God; whereas the body is only animate matter, and incapable *in itself* of communion with its Maker. Now that the physical gifts of God may be ministered to this *material* body by means of *material agents* is one thing, but for the soul to require an intervening agent between it and God is quite another.

B. You must not overlook the fact that our instruction in morality, our knowledge of God, so far as that is aided or increased by the instrumentality of others, is an instance of the intervention of a Spirit between our soul and the God of all spirits. Every *moral* influence which is imparted by others, is distinctly a spiritual agency, and not physical and material.

A. I am bound to confess that my objection was somewhat hasty; but yet you will confess that all these notions are of minor value, when compared with the idea of a Mediator through Whom alone we can have access to God; for in this idea is implied that the Creator has separated Himself from the creatures whom He made to serve Him. To suppose that God has given us a soul to serve Him, and that that soul cannot do that for which it was created, seems very like a contradiction.

B. I think you do not quite realize the Christian idea of a Mediator. That idea is, that through a Mediator we are able to take hold of God's mercy and pardon.

A. But that notion is stranger than all. Why should we not be able to obtain God's forgiveness, when we need it, for ourselves?

B. Let us consider the course of nature. You have admitted, I think, and will not withdraw your admission, that there are signs in the natural world of the assignment of rewards and punishments.

A. I admit it fully.

B. And those rewards and punishments follow, in the way of nature, as consequences of actions. I mean that poverty, sickness, infamy, untimely death from disease, and the like, though they follow by natural consequence upon vicious actions, are still punishments.

A. I think so.

B. Now there is no absurdity in supposing, as indeed you have already conceded, that future punishment follows upon determined vice and wrong-doing *naturally and inevitably*, just as a man who trifles on the edge of a precipice, in the way of natural consequence falls down, breaks his limbs, and, without help, perishes.

A. Indeed, I think that the only rational notion which we can form of future punishment is, that it is not an arbitrary decree of God, but the natural consequence of our actions, arising out of the permanent and complete degradation from virtue, which the *habitual* practice of vice has brought about.

B. This being so, let me point out to you certain facts, which may assist us in the present emergency. According to the course of nature, certain evil consequences will probably, and do generally, follow our misconduct. We are punished for it. This is a general law at all events; but as a matter of fact, all the evil consequences do not always follow. The Author of nature has provided remedies and means of alleviation for the punishments which would otherwise have followed upon our evil actions. These reliefs and remedies are attended often with pains and difficulties. Persons may do a great deal towards remedying the evil which they have done, and towards gaining relief from the sufferings which they undergo. Is not this so?

A. Pardon me for saying, that you have asserted so many things in a brief compass, that I really am quite unable to give or refuse my assent to what you have said. Would you object to stating your assertions separately, so that I may be assured that there is nothing to which I shall afterwards have to except.

B. I ask your pardon for having, even in appearance, mixed up different assertions in one sentence, so as to entrap you into unwary admissions. But to state them distinctly, you are, I think, willing to acknowledge that the idea of future punishment following upon present wickedness, *by way of natural consequence,* is not unreasonable?

A. So far I assent.

B. And if this be the case, we have a basis on which to found an argument with respect to future punishment.

A. At least we have some kind of an analogy.

B. I do not ask you to press it to the utmost limit, but only to observe certain facts, arising from the comparison of natural events with the supposed consequences of deliberate and determined vice. Do you consider that the natural consequences of vice invariably follow, and in a degree proportioned to the amount of vice?

A. Assuredly not; the smallest experience will prove that this is not so.

B. And would you argue from this that such consequences are not natural?

A. No; I should say that they are natural, but in some degree preventible.

B. And I presume you would mean that, if not prevented, they would be sure to follow?

A. Of course; but why do you ask?

B. Because many people assert that the absence of invariable sequence in these matters is a disproof of a universal or general law. I mean, that if, in the majority of cases, certain consequences follow certain actions, but amidst the millions of instances in the world many exceptions are found, it is argued that there can be no general law of sequence.

A. They who draw such an inference, can hardly be aware of the immense appearance of irregularity in inanimate nature. In many departments of physics calculations are baffled by reason of exceptions; and yet to assert that there is no general law regulating the phenomena of meteorology (for example) would be unscientific to the last degree.

B. Then you would not consider exceptions to the general consequences of moral actions as a disproof of the law of connexion between actions and their results?

A. Clearly not.

B. So that we may fairly reckon this first position established, that there is nothing unreasonable in conceiving future punishment attached to present wickedness as a natural consequence.

A. I will concede the supposition.

B. Now consider this. We have said that, in regard to the present life, experience proves that the natural consequences of actions do not invariably follow. How are they prevented?

A. By the intervention of other laws, I suppose.

B. I do not think you would be satisfied with that answer in my mouth. To make the question and reply clear, let us take the instance of a man walking on the edge of a precipice, and slipping or becoming giddy. The consequence, of course, is that he will fall over. But would this invariably follow?

A. Why, no. He might, perhaps, save himself from falling, or another might come opportunely to his aid.

B. And to proceed with the instance; if he fell and broke a limb, would it naturally follow that he would perish?

A. If no one came to his aid, he would. But the ultimate consequence of his temerity might be prevented by timely help.

B. I dare say you think this illustration

somewhat childish, but it has a point in it. You will see, in the first place, that in such a case the consequences of our actions may be prevented wholly or in part; some portion of the evil result may be prevented, either by ourselves or by the aid of others; and, secondly, you will perceive, that there is such a thing as our safety or recovery being effected wholly by the instrumentality of others.

A. But surely this instance is not to the point. You are pressing analogy to a perilous length, when you illustrate the consequences of moral iniquity by purely physical instances. The very essence of vice is *purpose and intention*, and in this case there is no shadow of moral causation.

B. I wish you to regard it only as a parable, if you choose to call it so; it is an illustration of the kind of reasoning which I am employing, not an instance of moral action. But let us now turn to the consequences of moral actions. It is plain that the consequences of vice are such as we have above described them—disease, disgrace, ruin, and sometimes death. In some degree or other, these consequences will follow, unless prevented; nevertheless these consequences are sometimes prevented, partly by our own exertions, partly by the aid of others.

On the whole, when our faults have been light, the rule is that we ourselves may do much towards averting the natural results: in proportion as they increase in intensity, our power to remedy them is less; however, in a greater or less degree the power is put into our hands of extricating ourselves, or employing the aid of others to assist us in extricating ourselves, from the bad consequences of our actions. Does not this appear to be the ordinance of nature?

A. It appears so.

B. There are, then, signs in the natural world of severity and also of compassion, supposing the moral universe to be the work of a personal God?

A. This I acknowledge.

B. Might we not, then, argue that in our highest relations to an eternal life and an all-just God, which constitute the sphere of religion, we might expect to find a similar constitution of things existing? Should we not expect that an escape from the evil consequences of our actions might be offered?

A. Certainly we should; but, in all this, you do not touch upon the question of a Mediator.

B. No; because we have not yet reached that stage in the argument: still we have a kind of foreshadowing of it in the fact that we are dependent on the instrumentality of others for relief from the results of our actions. Up to a certain point we are, at least in a degree, able to rescue ourselves; but it is plain that this is not always possible. Do you not allow so much?

A. I do.

B. But now it is necessary to introduce another element into our calculations. If there is anything at all in religion, it is abundantly plain, that in relation to an all-pure Being our condition is very different from what it is, viewed only in relation to the present life and to our fellow-men. It is not a question peculiar to the Christian religion. All thoughtful men in all ages confess, that they fall very far below their own ideal standard of perfection; but beyond this, they acknowledge that not only are they deficient, they are actually offenders against the moral standard which they are forced to recognize; they have been the cause of confusion and misery in God's universe. Mankind, as a rule, contemn God's authority, and infringe His laws; they are injurious, in a high degree, to their fellow-creatures, who are also God's creatures. In short, the moral fact of the existence of sin in the world is undeniable. I am not now speaking of the Christian representation of the nature of sin, but simply of the appearance which it presented to thoughtful men, before the Christian faith was promulgated. The existence of moral evil among mankind you will not, I presume, dispute.

A. I should be blind to do so; nay more, were it not for a consciousness of it in myself, I know not why I should be engaged in these discussions. No one can live in the world, without perceiving that moral evil is the most potent influence and the most tremendous fact in the whole universe, defying all the best endeavours of mankind to extirpate it.

B. But if this be so, and if, even in the present world, the effects of vice are confessedly extreme misery, irretrievable ruin, and even death, have we not reason to apprehend that, in relation to a future life, its consequences may be infinitely more awful than they are at present?

A. Analogy seems to point that way.

B. And might we not presume that, if the severe laws of nature were intensified in proportion to the enormous increase of the guilt of sin, viewed as an offence against a moral God, nothing that we could do could prevent the punishment of sin? Might we not become hopeless, under the influence of our experience of the ordinary course of nature?

A. Your conclusion, however painful, appears to be only just; so much so, that it has often struck me, that the only safeguard against despair or recklessness is to avoid the question altogether, and to reflect only upon matters of present interest. The relation of man to God, viewed in connexion with the great prevalence of moral evil among mankind, always appears to me a question of so hopeless a character, that no investigation will clear it, and no advantage can come from it. I am sensible that, from an advocate's point of view, such a confession is most imprudent; but I am not pleading a cause, I am seeking for truth. I am quite unable to agree with those who regard moral evil as only a falling short of ideal perfection. The grosser vices which disgrace civilization are to me positive evils, not simply the negation of good; and so also the more refined faults or sins,—to which those who are not gross offenders are exposed (I mean all those faults which lurk under the veil of decent outward behaviour),— appear to me to be positive evils. Without re-echoing hyperbolical expressions about " the whole world lying in wickedness," I cannot close my eyes to the fact, that, viewed in relation to an all-holy Being, the vast majority of mankind are in a lamentable condition.

B. I thank you for your candid admissions, because they are an indication of that love of truth which characterizes all your conduct. Now tell me, do you think that any thing which men could do, would suffice to recover them from their proneness to sin and to make them holy?

A. I consider that sorrow and amendment ought, in all justice, to procure pardon for sin.

B. Let us return to the course of nature. You have, in your experience, known persons who have ruined their fortunes by extravagance, who have brought diseases upon themselves by excess, and have incurred the penalties of the laws of their country by disregard to the well-being of society. Will sorrow and amendment of life always restore them to the condition in which they were before such actions?

A. Not always, I confess.

B. Moreover do not the acts themselves, or the habits from which they spring, tend to impair the natural powers of recovery?

A. I am bound to confess that they do.

B. And are not men compelled to make use of the assistance of *others*, to aid them in repairing the injury done to themselves, whereas, except for their ill conduct, they would have had no need of seeking such assistance?

A. That, too, is true.

B. Now I argue from this, that we are not unreasonable in accepting the teaching of Christianity, that in our higher relation to an eternal existence we have need of something similar. Sin, by its very nature, tends to incapacitate us from recovery by our own *unassisted* efforts: the consequences of sin may follow if unprevented, and the prevention of them may only be possible by the aid of others. Observe, however, that I do not say that repentance and amendment are of no value; but that, *in and by themselves*, they may not be sufficient.

A. Such reasoning does seem to have a show of truth.

B. Moreover the natural instincts of mankind have led them to the conclusion that human repentance is not all-sufficient for forgiveness; for in the heathen world, the idea of propitiatory sacrifices was very prevalent. And though the exact value attached to these sacrifices is not known, nor perhaps could have been declared by the heathens themselves, this is rather an argument in favour of my views, because it points to the existence of a natural belief, that something more than mere repentance was necessary to restore the equipoise of man's moral nature.

A. This seems to me to be a really valuable argument, because it is not based upon *à posteriori* views derived from Christianity. It is very difficult in dealing with arguments, which are drawn from the natural feelings of mankind in these our later days, to distinguish what is *natural and original* from what is the result of Jewish and Christian ideas, which have as it were become ingrained into the nature of all nations who have had acquaintance with those systems of religion. The idea of *propitiation*, whatever else it may signify, seems to point to a natural feeling, that sin is something more than mere *incompleteness:* still I am far from accepting this *alone* as a demonstration that we need a propitiation.

B. It would, indeed, be most absurd to regard it as a demonstration. It is, in fact, only one thing among many which will build up a probable argument; and, so far as I have used it, I have only applied it to show that the idea of *mediation* is not unnatural. It is an evidence that Christianity did not *invent* the notion, that repentance is not enough to atone for sin, but that it existed before Christianity, and so far as we can judge, independently of Jewish influences.

A. Let it, then, stand for what it is worth. I do not like arguing from the infancy of the world to its matured state; but still, if there are any innate propensions or natural inclinations of men, they ought to be allowed to take their place in such an investigation as this.

B. Now to proceed. Suppose that we had arrived at this stage of our argument without revelation, and had seen that the laws of the universe are, though severe, yet not without signs of compassion; that the consequences which should follow from our actions, are sometimes prevented by the intervention of other persons; that repentance or sorrow for our errors, *genuine* sorrow arising from the feeling that we have morally erred, is not always enough to reinstate us in our previous position. Suppose, also, that we had learned to regard, with many of the ancients, our present existence as most imperfect, and not only imperfect, but such as is described by the Latin poet in the words, " I see and approve the better part, but I pursue the worse;" a state in which our passions constantly subdue and hold prisoner the sense of right. And suppose that, at this stage of our inquiry, we came upon the Bible. What should we find its language to be? It represents man in a fallen condition, with capacities for good overlaid and overpowered, it matters not how, by passions and inclinations to evil: it asserts that the consequences of our sins will surely follow, if not prevented; that to repent is indeed necessary to forgiveness; but that we are not able, of our own strength, to feel sorrow in that degree which the nature of our sins demands; that we need Divine assistance and supernatural strengthening to work out our own salvation; and that God must, in some supernatural way, work in us and for us, to enable us to attain to that condition of repentance and that purity of heart which alone He will accept.

A. Are you not softening down some of the features of the Christian revelation, to which you refer? I should like to hear some of the grounds on which you state this as the sum of the Christian revelation.

B. Pardon me, I am only stating, in general terms, the analogy between revelation and nature. I have said that we cannot expect to find particular analogies for every minute detail. If there are some things which seem hard to accept in Christianity, remember that there are things almost equally hard to receive in the moral government of the universe. But in answer to your immediate question, I will adduce the salient and central passage round which almost the whole of the distinctive faith of Christians groups itself; "God so loved the world, that He gave His only begotten Son, to the end that whosoever believeth in Him (in such a way as to do what He enjoins, and to follow His steps), should have everlasting life."

A. I see you introduce a parenthetical explanation of the word *belief* into your account.

B. I do so to obviate your possible difficulty, that my previous account of what is required of Christians scarcely tallies with the condition here introduced. It does not belong to our present inquiry to speak of what Christian faith is, but the whole tenour of the Gospel is to represent it as a *practical* habit of mind.

A. Pardon my interruption. Pray continue your account of what you consider to be the Christian notion of mediation.

B. It appears to me, that the Christian religion falls in with the experience of mankind, at least to this extent, that it represents God as ruling the world by fixed laws of justice, and yet giving evidence of His compassionate tenderness for His creatures. In both spheres man is a free agent; as a free agent he has sinned; by hereditary transmission or otherwise, this tendency to sin has become a general law, drawing men away from goodness and depriving them of much of the power which naturally (using the word to signify by Divine appointment) belongs to them. The consequence should be that men would be punished. But yet God gives to them assistance by which, in conjunction with their own efforts, they may be relieved from the consequences of their sins. For you should observe that Christ represents Himself as sent by the Father. The very name Christ, or Messiah, the Anointed, implies the setting apart by God for a purpose. That purpose is a compassionate one—to enable men to escape misery and acquire happiness. Is there anything to complain of in such an idea of God's government of the world?

A. Why, yes; it represents God as inconsistent with Himself. Surely either He ought to inflict upon men what they deserve, or to pardon them for their transgressions. It seems to be a poor and strange compromise between justice and goodness, that God should interfere with His own decrees.

B. No more strange than that He should enable us to escape the consequences of our actions, by means supplied by Him. Justice and compassion do appear to be conflicting laws; but as they are found in one sphere of existence, we ought not to complain that they are to be traced in another. If His goodness supplies us with friends to assist us in less important matters, why should we find a difficulty in the idea that, in matters infinitely more important, He should send us a Friend, Whose good offices transcend those of any earthly friend as much as the concerns of eternity transcend those of the present time?

A. But surely, according to the Christian idea, the manner in which we receive aid from Christ, is in no degree comparable with that in which we receive it from our fellow-men.

B. Doubtless there are phases of Christ's *mediatorial* office, with which nothing earthly can compare. Still to some extent a comparison may be established.

A. Will you specify the similarity?

B. Have not many epochs in the history of the world been marked by the appearance of teachers who have declared to men, in a new and striking form, their duties? Has not what we call the progress of the world been effected by men who in various ways enounce the truth?

A. Unquestionably.

B. Such men, regarded as exponents of the Divine will, are, in the strict sense of the word, *mediators:* they *stand between* God and His creatures. The Hebrew prophets, many of the ancient philosophers, poets in all ages, men of science, all these are to be reckoned as appointed agents by whom God is made known to us.

A. Yes; but what has this to say to the mediation of Christ?

B. It represents one phase of His office. He was "that Prophet Who should come into the world." He taught mankind "to live soberly, righteously, and godly in this present world," in expectation of an eternal existence. He distinctly instructed men, how to approach God in *worship,* setting before them this mode of intercourse as a preparation for a full communion with God hereafter. He declared the efficacy of *repentance,* and imparted to every one knowledge of the truth, which has proved of inestimable comfort to millions in the hard struggle for existence.

A. But this might have been done without any introduction of the strange and mysterious teaching upon which Christians dwell so fondly.

B. Yes; but He connected this teaching with further instruction which, true or not, has exercised an incalculable influence, and, as we think, has conferred extraordinary benefits upon the human race. To make this clear, let us take the instance of another great teacher, Socrates. Upon how many amongst us has his teaching an influence now?

A. Upon but a few, I fear.

B. And yet he too taught the truth. Why is it that the influence of the one extended to so few, while that of the other is felt up to the present time?

A. I suppose, because the teaching of Christ was more practical and suited to the wants of greater numbers of people.

B. That is one reason, perhaps; but not, I think, the most important. Do you not think that the idea which animated Christ's ministry, *that He was founding a kingdom, into which His followers are called as citizens*—a kingdom over which He was to reign invisibly—is the cause of its wide-spread influence? This kingdom is regulated by a code of laws which He enounced. It consists of those who are still on earth fighting life's battles, to whom the present time is a period of discipline; and of those who are withdrawn from the present scene, and are waiting for the fulfilment of His promises. By the influence which He exerts upon His followers, they are being gradually educated unto a condition of perfection, "unto the measure of the stature of the fulness of Christ." According to this idea, Christ is the Mediator between God and man, by Whom the human race, or at least those who obey His laws, are being made fit for a habitation in the presence of an all-pure God.

A. But there is no shadow of demonstration of this to be derived from nature.

B. Possibly not: it is a state of things which we learn only from His revelation. Yet such a notion of spiritual improvement is not inconsistent with what we observe as the object and work of the great renovators of society at various epochs of the world's history. Towards moral improvement our own efforts are by no means all-sufficient: we need counsel, example, and assistance to effect it; and if the soul be indeed eternal, and its existence progressive, we find nothing subversive of moral ideas in the notion of spiritual development by means of spiritual influences which are not capable of analysis by physical methods. At all events such an idea is not contrary to reason, in the sense of being *contradicted by experience.*

A. But even if I were to concede the possibility of a spiritual kingdom, there is another aspect of Christ's mediation, which is utterly repugnant to moral ideas, and which no analogy can establish. The Christian religion represents Christ as an *atoning sacrifice.* According to this idea, Christ was offered as a *victim to reconcile God to man.* In this are implied several things to which I must take decided exception. First, the idea of expiation represents the future happiness of man as entirely *independent* of himself. Secondly, it makes his salvation a deliverance from God's wrath, to effect which the *innocent* was to suffer for the *guilty.* This is a breach of the law of justice, which is part of the idea of God. These things seem to me unanswerable objections to the Christian doctrine of atonement.

B. In reply to this, I must draw your attention to the fact, that the thing objected against, is just one of those matters on which we are profoundly ignorant. How it comes to pass that men are more inclined to evade than to perform what they know to be right, we cannot say. But the *fact* is one of ordinary experience. Again, we cannot tell why our natural efforts after a higher condition of our moral nature are so weak as they are. However, that they are weak each man's experience will convince him. On these points we are greatly in the dark. Now the question of man's redemption, as revealed in Christianity, is closely connected with these deep questions. When we can solve the one, we may expect to comprehend the other. When we can understand the power and influence of evil; what it is that gives it such strength in the world as it plainly has; what is its effect upon the human constitution, and in what relation its prevalence and power place us to the all-pure God—then, and not till then, shall we fully understand this question, and be able to judge whether an atonement for sin is not requisite. But let me ask you what you mean by an atonement?

A. I mean the death of an innocent person by virtue of which God pardons the sinner.

B. But I understand you to say that this idea did away with human responsibility.

A. Well, and does it not do so? If I am only pardoned by reason of what another person does, it is very like being pardoned without any moral action on my side.

B. But surely if, when you are in great straits and cannot extricate yourself, another gives you assistance, it does not of necessity follow that you do nothing for yourself. If a man is frozen in the snow, and another gives him brandy and enables him to use his limbs, would you say that his safety was procured without any agency of his own?

A. No, assuredly not. But if I read Christianity aright, something more is implied in an atonement than merely rendering assistance. Christ actually suffered for mankind, *the just for the unjust.*

B. I have already said that, in this matter, we are so completely in the dark, that it is unreasonable to expect to see everything distinctly. The efficacy of Christ's death upon our nature is a thing which transcends all our faculties to ascertain. But that the atonement leaves nothing for us to do is plainly not the case. Whatever else it effects, it does not take away man's responsibility, or render his natural powers valueless towards working out his own salvation. But it does nerve him for a contest, to which he is otherwise unequal; it gives him just the strength which he requires. Beyond this it may have other effects: *we* believe that it has; but we believe this, as we believe other mysteries, in virtue of our belief in the dignity and power of Christ, Who has revealed them.

All that I contend for now is, that the objections to the atonement arise from assuming that the whole matter is before us, which it plainly is not.

A. But even in the case of our being ignorant, you have before allowed that moral difficulties are certainly of great importance in these questions; and I think the moral difficulty against the atonement is such, that even *you* will acknowledge it. How can we believe, that a purely innocent person was ordained to suffer for the guilty? It is incredible.

B. Does it seem so incredible to you? What then will you say to the experience of every day, that the innocent suffer through the faults of the guilty?

A. Why; I can hardly believe that they do.

B. Surely you will see it everywhere. It is as much a law of nature as anything else. In the Christian religion we are commanded to suffer for one another, and the opinion of society has adopted this notion as moral. But, besides this, we are often *necessitated* to suffer for others—parents for children, friends for friends, fellow-countrymen for fellow-countrymen. Half the good that happens in the world arises from the voluntary sufferings which people undergo for others; and more than half the evils which are prevented, are prevented by the self-sacrifice of a few on behalf of others. If therefore you object to Christianity, that it demands our acceptance of a belief in benefits procured by vicarious suffering, my answer is that your argument, if strong against Christianity, is far stronger against natural religion.

A. How do you make out that?

B. If you think that the doctrine of the atonement is enough to disprove Christianity, much more will it show that God does not direct the course of nature. In the ordinary course of events the innocent suffer for the guilty, and that of *necessity*. Christianity asserts that Christ *voluntarily* offered Himself: "He gave Himself a ransom for many." According to the Christian account, it is not the forcible offering of a victim, but a voluntary sacrifice of a loving Friend, which forms the centre of the system; so that I am right in saying, that this argument tells with greater force against natural religion than against revelation.

A. But consider how different the degree of suffering and the nature of the sufferer, in the Christian dispensation, are from anything which we know of in nature.

B. Very true. Nevertheless that is no

answer to the fact, that it is so ordered that in the ordinary course of life the innocent do suffer for the guilty.

A. But yet I do not see, that any adequate reason is assigned for so stupendous an event as that to which we are referring.

B. In short, you return to your old argument, that when you do not discern the whole state of the case, you consider that your inability to discover the whole is sufficient reason for rejecting, not only what lies beyond your apprehension, but also that part in which analogy seems to point out similarities. This however has been seen to be an insufficient ground for disbelief, in the case of natural religion: why should it not be so in revealed religion also? The constitution of the world and God's natural government of it is shrouded in mystery. Step by step we reason back, until we are in the region of things beyond experience. Yet, in the natural world, the laws of action are made sufficiently plain for ordinary intelligence; and in revealed religion, enough is made plain for the life of godliness. If there are things which lie beyond our comprehension in the latter, so are there in the former; and if we do not reject all moral action because of the difficulty shrouding the ultimate facts on which morality is based, so we have no valid ground for refusing to allow, that the ultimate mysteries of the Christian faith are of the nature of those things which may one day be made clear. Part of the doctrine of mediation is in accordance with observed facts. The rest, though we cannot reason up to it from experience, is yet seen to be not contrary to it; and if a revelation exist at all, such difficulties may be expected to occur, because we cannot know the whole of the design of God in ordering the world as in fact He has ordered it.

DIALOGUE VI.

ON THE WANT OF UNIVERSALITY IN REVELATION, AND OF THE SUPPOSED DEFICIENCY IN THE PROOF OF IT.

B. Before we proceed to discuss the positive evidence for Christianity, I should like to ask you whether there are any further questions to dispose of? It will be well to ascertain beforehand, if we shall enter upon this inquiry without any concealed points of difference, from which fresh difficulties may arise.

A. It seems to me that we have not yet reached the point, at which we shall profitably undertake the examination of external evidences. Once or twice I have gathered from your observations, that after all I must not expect demonstration. With this I should be content; but Christianity demands such ungrudging assent, it claims such absolute belief, that I must hesitate to give up my reason and will on insufficient evidence.

B. Surely that is but reasonable. If the

evidence is insufficient, you ought not to acknowledge it as sufficient. But then sufficiency is a relative term. Sufficient evidence in the mouth of some will mean absolute demonstrative certainty.

A. Pray consider this. I believe the truths of physical science, because there is no possibility of disbelieving them. Will Christianity afford me such certainty as this?

B. Do you believe with absolute conviction those points in physical science which lie beyond experience? Suppose, for example, a theory is started as to the condition of the earth, based upon observed facts, but extending beyond them; do you feel certain of the truth of the theory?

A. None of the theories of physical science fulfil such a condition; they are only generalizations from experience.

B. But will you not allow that, even in these sciences, there are degrees of certainty?

A. Undoubtedly there are. When opinions are expressed to which facts seem to point, but which are not certainly borne out by the facts, I take them for what they are worth; I suspend conviction upon them. In other cases I accept without reserve what science declares, because the observations made are absolutely certain and convincing.

B. You say that you take some opinions for *what they are worth;* will you explain this somewhat indefinite expression? It may mean that you accept, or it may mean that you reject them.

A. My acceptance or rejection will depend entirely upon the degree of evidence adduced. In some cases I should be *inclined* to receive them as true, although I do not feel wholly convinced of the truth of the opinions: in others I should be *inclined* to reject, although I am not satisfied that truth is entirely wanting.

B. If I understand you aright, you acknowledge that, even in physical science, there are degrees of conviction. Plausible objections may be urged against a theory, and yet, on the whole, the balance of probability may be on its side. Now answer me this: If the particular theory required not only a passive assent, but an exercise of the active powers as well, would this be justly reckoned as an additional objection to it?

A. Certainly not. In the case of health, if I am satisfied that a particular theory has a show of truth, I hold it to be not only wise, but absolutely incumbent upon me, to frame my habits according to the regimen prescribed by the theory. If physiologists assure me that exercise is necessary for health, I not only assent to what they say, but I take exercise. If they tell me that a particular kind of exercise is most beneficial, I feel bound to adopt that kind, if I possibly can.

B. Now I suspect that if you apply this reasoning to religion, you will find that this element of *active exertion in accordance with its doctrines* is one of the principal objections to it. If it were only a question of thinking in this or that way, men would not find such objections to religion. It is because it demands that its doctrines, considered as truth, should be carried into *practice*, that it is charged with irrational dogmatism, and its claims stigmatized as overweening and arrogant.

A. Pardon me; I do not think it is the practical portion of Christianity, which presents a difficulty to most minds. What staggers them is its unpractical and impracticable doctrines.

B. Perhaps it would be an unfair retort to say, that those only who have striven to carry the doctrines of religion into practice, can pronounce whether they are unpractical; but I believe that an ambiguity exists in the word *practice*. It is generally taken to mean our actions with reference to society. But, on the supposition of the existence of a God, our actions in relation to Him, our thoughts and emotions as regards the unseen governor of the universe, are as much to be considered practice, as the commonest acts of our daily intercourse with one another; and certainly, with regard to Him, the thoughts which religion brings before us are truly and thoroughly practical, whether they be founded on reality and truth or on mere imagination and error. But the question which you have raised is, Are not the absolute claims of religion barred by the uncertainty of its evidence? Is it not so?

A. It is. I say that since there is no absolute proof of religion, it ought not to require unconditional acceptance; and further, that, since it has not been given universally and with equal clearness to all, it seems doubtful whether it can have originated from the universal Creator.

B. We have, then, two questions before us. With regard to the first, the unconditional acceptance of Christianity (for we must not forget that it is *that* which we denote by the word religion), you will not, I suppose, object to those accepting it absolutely, to whom it appears absolutely true?

A. No, I should not, if they will allow me the freedom *not* to accept it absolutely. But I hardly see the relevancy of the question.

B. Well, it occurred to me just then, that the unconditional acceptance of Christianity is viewed by some as amounting almost to a moral obliquity; but with regard to the question before us, you say that the uncertainty which attends the evidence for Christianity is a positive argument against its truth. Has it ever occurred to you that the uncertainty of which you speak is, in a great measure, *subjective?* it arises from the circumstances of those who come to the investigation.

A. I hardly understand your meaning.

B. Perhaps if we consider the case of our ordinary actions, you will see what I mean. Suppose we take pleasure and pain, as the standard by which to try whether a certain thing is desirable or not. Now the pleasure or the pain will vary according to the circumstances of the person; to a man in health it may seem pleasurable—to a sick man the reverse; to a lethargic man the pursuit will appear so distasteful as entirely to outweigh the probable pleasure; death may very likely intervene before the end aimed at is attained; or perhaps it may occur to us, that possibly the thing desired will not after all fulfil our expectations. We may argue, that very probably men have exaggerated its value and importance. Notwithstanding, we do every day set aside all these possibilities, and pursue our end, in spite of the various hues which it assumes according to the state of our nerves, and in spite of all the possible drawbacks which from time to time occur to us. Is not this so?

A. Certainly.

B. Now is the evidence for Christianity very much more uncertain than the evidence upon which we are compelled to act every day? are the possibilities attending it more various than those which attach to our ordinary pursuits? are the blessings which it promises very inferior to the pleasures which we think we may gain from ordinary pursuits?

A. Perhaps not.

B. And if so, why should we turn into an argument against Christianity the very facts which, if anything, tell in favour of it by showing that it depends on evidence analogous, in its uncertainty, to that which claims our practical assent every day that we live?

A. But such an answer as this does not meet my other difficulty, that a revelation so partial and variable as this is represented to be cannot be Divine.

B. In other words, you assert that a revelation, of which you know nothing *à priori*, cannot be from God, because it is not given in the manner and degree which you have prescribed for it in your own mind.

A. You may certainly silence me by putting the matter in that light, but you can hardly expect me to be convinced by such an argument.

B. Well, I think you ought to accept it, to employ your own words, for what it is worth. A revelation of God's will implies the unfolding of something concealed from man concerning the Divine nature, attributes, and purposes. If part of those purposes consists in bestowing different degrees of light on different persons and races, you ought not to reject the revelation for being true to what it reveals.

A. I will not pause to argue this point at length, but will state my position somewhat differently. I find that a revelation, professing to be of vital importance to mankind, and exhibiting a condition of things of equal interest to every individual member of the human family, is delivered in a most arbitrary and incomprehensible manner. Some portions, indeed the greater number, of mankind are totally unacquainted with it. Of the rest a very large proportion have but the most fragmentary notion of its contents. To many it is presented encrusted with a vast accumulation of legendary and purely imaginary details. It is confessedly corrupted by superstition, and trammelled with the inventions of designing men, so that the utmost historical acumen is hardly able to discern between the true and the false. Only a very few among the millions of the human race are supposed to possess it in its purity. Now does it not appear to the last degree unlikely, that a benevolent Creator should compel men to risk their eternal happiness upon a system of doctrines so obscured, so corrupted, and perverted as this?

B. The gist of your objection seems to lie in a suppressed premiss that all men, whatever their opportunities, will be judged by the Creator according to the same standard of knowledge; but if you will bear in mind, that men will be judged according to what they *have*, not according to what they *have not*, much of your difficulty will vanish. For example, the heathen, who have no knowledge of Christianity, are in a different condition from the Mohammedans, who have some stray gleams of light. These again are differently situated from those Christian communities who have greater, although an imperfect knowledge; and these are to be reckoned as responsible for less than those who possess the pure light of the Gospel.

A. As regards a final judgment, such an explanation as yours would serve to vindicate the Creator from merciless severity and injustice. So far I acknowledge the force of your reply; indeed I believe that nothing injures the cause of free thought so much as the attempt to represent the God of the Christians as a kind of malevolent demon, gloating over the sufferings which He has the power to inflict. There can really be no question, to a mind free from prejudice, that Christianity does represent God as a loving Father, a benevolent Spirit Who desires that all men should seek the way of happiness, and grieves over the perverse and obstinate sinner. I will not pause to consider the appropriateness of this human imagery to an Infinite Being: suffice it to say, that I acquiesce in the representation as a worthy one, and will not quarrel with the language. But when we come to practical questions, is it not staggering to find that the same God, so full of love and fatherly kindness to mankind, is represented as providing so unequally for them; that the religion which, after long centuries of struggle, has at last obtained from men an acknowledgment that there is no respect of persons with God, but that in His sight all are alike, that this very religion should represent to us, as the work of God, such an unequal distribution of His highest favours as that which I have just described?

B. You think it, then, a disproof of the Divine origin of the Christian revelation, that all men have not alike possessed it?

A. I think it looks awkward for its claims.

B. Has it never occurred to you to compare this inequality with that which is the most striking fact in the whole history of the world? Wherever you turn, you will find persons possessed of most unequal advantages. What account will you give of the reasons, why some are rich and others poor; some are surrounded by estimable friends and acquaintances, others are thrown into the company of the worthless and dissolute? Look at the different advantages afforded by education, by national institutions, by geographical position, by climate and all the thousand influences by which character, either individual or national, is moulded. What explanation will you give of all this?

A. I can give none, I acknowledge.

B. And yet you think all this reconcilable with a beneficent Creator? In fact, the proofs of His existence far outweigh the contrary arguments. But if you will once concede, as you do, that you do not know the reasons of all this diversity of advantages, it is but a part of the same concession to allow, that the different advantages, with regard to Christianity, enjoyed by various ages and by different men, are also compatible with the Divine origin of the revelation.

A. The analogy between the two cases seems to be of some value, I acknowledge.

B. Moreover, let me observe, that if Christianity had been presented equally to all men, it by no means follows, that it would have been equally obvious to all. Differences of character and of mental perception are constituent elements of human nature: they are of the very essence of human freedom. Now the supposition, that all men throughout the whole earth, should, at the same time, have been equally prepared for the revelation, is at least as remarkable as the supposition of the existence of the revelation at all.

A. I do not quite understand you.

B. It would be, I say, a most astounding idea, that the moral and mental condition of the human race should, at a certain time, have been completely and individually uniform.

A. It would indeed!

B. But if your demand were conceded, nothing less than this would be required.

A. How so?

B. Because then the revelation would not have been equally afforded to all.

A. Surely if the same facts were exhibited to all mankind, they would have been equally favoured.

B. Not so. A revelation takes place, in order to effect a moral regeneration: it presupposes a certain moral condition, a degree of mental and moral development, to appreciate it and assimilate it.

A. Stay: you are proving too much. Do you mean to say, that Christianity is not adapted for races in all degrees of development?

B. The Christian revelation, according to my conception of it, comprises, in its range, elements suited to every age and disposition. Nevertheless, I maintain that, had it been published in earlier times, it would not have met with such ready acceptance, nor would its doctrines have spread so rapidly over the world. The proof of this you will perhaps think strange in my mouth. It is this: among the uncivilized heathen Christianity does not, at present, meet with such ready acceptance as ardent missionaries could hope. *One* of the chief causes of this is, that the precepts frequently appeal to a higher condition of mental and moral progress than they have attained. To men, who hold revenge to be a sacred duty and regard bloodshed not only without abhorrence, but with approbation, a long period will have to elapse before they can assimilate the high-toned morality of Christianity. I do not, indeed, consider this a full explanation of the question, which, as you will easily see, naturally runs up into matters involving the most subtle analysis of the moral constitution of man. It will not, for instance, explain the comparative want of success of Christianity among the Hindoos; but it will make clear what I intend by the assertion, that the same facts and doctrines may be suitable to one age or individual, while they are only in part adapted to another.

A. I see that you have anticipated the objection I was about to raise.

B. I think, then, you will be prepared to acknowledge, that a uniform and contemporaneous promulgation of the revelation would not have had the effect which you attribute to it. It would in fact, even in that case, have been of unequal influence upon the various nations of the earth.

A. I confess that your inference seems to be probable.

B. And this, I imagine, will be an answer to a further objection, that Christianity does not present itself with equal force to all dispositions among ourselves.

A. But surely this is a confession of weakness. It ought, if of Divine origin, to be of such power that no one could deny or doubt the value of its testimony.

B. In that case, however, it would have been totally at variance with the rest of nature, for the testimony of all nature to the spiritual world is only probable. Perhaps the only fact which is not of this character is the consciousness of individual existence, the sense that "this is I," and that "I am different from the things about me." If revelation forced itself upon us, we should not of course be able to say that it did not come from God; for, according to the supposition, we should be *compelled* to acknowledge it; but we should be, in a manner, constrained to adopt Manichæan ideas, and say that the rest of our knowledge and that on which it is based, the facts of experience, were *not* from God.

A. Are you not becoming somewhat over-subtle and drifting into metaphysics? Why should the certainty of revelation force us to believe that all other knowledge, not being certain, comes from an evil source?

B. On the ground of the uniformity of the divine activity, or, as it is usually called, the uniformity of the laws of nature. When we find that revelation has a degree of uncertainty in its evidence, we say that it is on a par with the rest of nature; whereas, if the moral revelation were the only certain thing, it might, on the one hand, overshadow all inquiry on other subjects, and so prevent the work of the intellect being carried on; or, on the other, it might, and probably would, fail to effect one of the purposes for which it was promulgated.

A. Pray, what is that?

B. The moral probation of mankind.

A. Do you think that purity of life and piety would be less hard, if men had intellectual certainty of the truth of the revelation? Surely you know, that to be *intellectually* convinced of a thing which is distasteful to us, is a very different thing from practising it. Do you not think, that as far as moral actions are concerned the probation would be equally severe, whether the revelation were intellectually certain or only probable?

B. I can hardly say. I believe there are persons who, being in their hearts convinced of its truth, do yet act in defiance of it. But I was thinking rather of another class of persons.

A. To whom do you refer?

B. I was thinking of that not inconsiderable class, on whom vulgar temptations have no effect. I mean the men who have their passions under control, or are not greatly affected by them; who do not care for the ordinary prizes of ambition, for the praise of men, for wealth, or luxury, or ease, men of pure lives and earnest hearts, who, content with little, give themselves up to reflection and contemplation.

A. But how can the uncertainty of the evidence of Christianity be of advantage to them? These, you know, are the very men who most commonly find a stumbling-block in the uncertainty of revelation. Is not the want of certainty the greatest possible *disadvantage* to such men, supposing that belief in the revelation is really necessary to the completion of our moral training?

B. When I say that the deficiency in the proof of Christianity is profitable to them, I mean, that the investigation of doubtful evidence, and the acceptance of the necessity to act upon a preponderance, however small, may be the very training of which such men stand in need. It may possibly be needed to remind them of their spiritual nature; it may be advantageous in recalling to mind the ultimate obscurity in which the end of the most careful analysis is shrouded. So long as a man is engaged on questions over which he has to a great extent obtained a mastery, so as to possess an almost intuitive appreciation of the tendency and nature of the facts submitted to his mind, he is in danger of forgetting the immense uncertainty in which other problems, beyond the range of his inquiries, are involved. One advantage, then, or at least one element of discipline which the uncertainty of the evidence of Christianity affords, is the constant check it presents against intellectual arrogance. It may be reasonable to say that religion, in its external presentation, is obscure and uncertain; but to say that it is false because it is obscure, is not reasonable. Yet this is the danger, to which very many men in these days are exposed.

A. Yet, surely, if a king were laying down laws for his subjects to obey, it is only reasonable to expect, that he would make those laws so clear that they could not be misapprehended, and would provide an evident proof that they were *his* laws and expressed *his* will.

B. That depends entirely upon the object which he has in view in the promulgation of them.

A. If he meant the laws to be obeyed, any other proceeding would be ridiculous.

B. Not necessarily so. A king might have either of two objects in view. The first might be simply to *have his will performed:* in that case his instructions would be as clear and explicit as possible. But he might also wish to *test the fidelity of his followers:* in that case he would probably lay down general rules for their guidance, but he would leave room for the exercise of their discretion, their attention, and their honesty. To exercise the first, he would take care that they were placed in positions of some difficulty, where the exercise of a nice discrimination would be necessary: to evoke the second, he might leave the rules of conduct partially obscure, so that thought and care would be necessary to comprehend them, and to carry them into operation: and to try the third, he would leave them with such circumstances of temptation around them, that their principles would be tested in the performance of their functions. Can you not imagine that such might be the object of a king, and that his subjects might possibly be placed in such circumstances for a definite object?

A. Certainly I can.

B. Now revelation asserts, that such is the government which God exercises over the world. The Founder of Christianity compares the condition of men in this world to such a state. "The kingdom of heaven is like unto a certain king, who went into a far country to receive for himself a kingdom and to return." He is represented as entrusting his treasure, in various degrees, to his subjects; and, on his return, as inquiring into the manner in which they had employed their trust.

A. But in such a comparison He is speaking of moral qualities, not of theological speculations.

B. If you will reflect, you will see that the King is represented as giving treasure of various worth to the several servants. Now intellectual powers are to be considered as one of the possessions—shall I say the most valuable of all?—entrusted to men. Accordingly men are responsible for the use they make of them. There is nothing unreasonable in the supposition that they may be misapplied. When therefore you imply, as you do in the above assertion, that no responsibility attaches to the abuse of powers of intellect, you are practically denying them to be the gift of God.

A. Well; I did not intend to deny our responsibility for the exercise of our reason; but it appears to me, that you will find it very difficult to decide *what* is an abuse of our reason. It is obviously a function of the reason to ascertain what is the *criterion* of correct and incorrect reasoning, where the use ends and the abuse begins. It is easy enough to assert that there must be a limit to our speculations, and that any attempt to pass beyond it will be unavailing. But then who shall decide when that limit is reached? The reason itself alone can do this; so that, although there probably may be a limit to the investigations of a finite intelligence, it is impossible to say when that limit is attained, and preposterous to condemn, as a moral obliquity, its transgression. Besides, you must confess that in every age the supposed limit has varied. The cry of "impious and atheistical" has been raised over and over again, where you would acknowledge it to be undeserved; and so, even though we acknowledge a theoretical limit, we can never practically determine it, and must be content to let men speculate and think without imposing a restraint upon them, which *may* be wrong and *must* be unavailing.

B. I think you have gone beyond the mark at which we are aiming. With much that you have said, I agree. I do not believe that any external compulsion or denunciation will prevent men from speculating on religious questions. Any limit which is imposed on human investigation, must be voluntary, the result of an inward consciousness that such inquiries do not lead to any further knowledge, or, at least, to any greater certainty upon the points in question. But you should bear in mind, that the assertion of the abstract impossibility of our revelation very much resembles an attempt to limit human thought; for the arguments employed reduce themselves to one of two principles: either the nature of the revelation is impossible, or the whole is self-contradictory. We need not pause to argue the latter question. It is no doubt interesting to investigate particular difficulties in the narrative, but it need hardly be stated, that most of these difficulties are such as will be found in any history of events, however assuredly true. The real question always is, whether or not a revelation, viewed in the abstract, is possible. Every system which attacks Christianity has this for its central principle. But to assume that it is impossible, is to limit the human intellect; it is to say that the only principle we have to go upon is material experience; it is to assert that the necessities of human thought, which assert themselves beyond all contradiction, the uncontrollable aspiration of the human heart after a moral standard, higher than any of which it has experience, the intense desire to receive a solution of those mysteries of existence, the happiness and misery of human life, and above all the deep-seated consciousness of a spiritual being which, after materialistic physiology has done its worst, and dreams that it has crushed it, springs hydra-headed from the mutilated carcase, or soars again ever-new from its ashes; it is, I say, to assert that all these things are mere imaginations, childish dreams as they are called, and to forbid men to harbour such ideas, because there is no logical or material basis open to the senses, on which to found an argument.

A. But tell me, how is it limiting human thought to forbid it to wander into dreamland?

B. Because the argument against revelation is based on observations upon the material side of nature. It practically denies all that may not be hammered out of flints or resolved into primary elements of matter. To say that, because such observations carry certainty with them, it is unreasonable to accept anything not *formally certain* as a ground of action, is, as I have shown, to deny or to ignore the whole of the moral side of nature, in which such physical and absolute regularity is never to be found. In fact, I do not hesitate to say, that they who reject revelation on the ground of the uncertainty of its proofs, ought logically to go farther, and to refuse social life, because of the difficulties which perplex it. I will commend to you this reflection, as a thing well worth consideration in judging of this part of our subject. But there are some further points to which, if you are willing, I should be glad to direct your attention.

A. I am quite ready to listen to them.

B. Do you consider that a person who has no doubts, and one who is perplexed with doubts, upon a given question, stand in the same position?

A. Pray explain your meaning.

B. Imagine that you had received a benefit, and that it might possibly have come to you from a certain person, would you be in the same relation to that person as if you knew certainly that you owed nothing to him?

A. Assuredly not.

B. Would you not say, that any one with any sense of gratitude and prudence, would consider his relation to that person altered by the possibility of which we speak? Even if he did not feel actual gratitude, he ought at least to have a *tendency* to gratitude.

A. I think so.

B. In the same way, even if all that the evidence of religion amounts to in the mind of a man is, that the system of Christianity may *possibly* be true, he ought to acknowledge that his position is not the same as if no such possibility had occurred to him.

A. I think that such an inference is inevitable.

B. The possibility, then, of the truth of Christianity ought to have such an effect upon a reasonable man, that he should live as if the things therein declared may possibly be true.

A. But Buddhism and Mahometanism or even Polytheism may possibly be true. Ought men to live as if *their* doctrines were obligatory?

B. Pardon me; I did not assert that a man, who sees in Christianity only the possible germs of truth, would be compelled by his reason to conform to its whole system. Besides, I think you are confounding in thought the accidents of a system with its essential principles. Now the essential principles of Christianity are, we have seen, comparatively few. They are not contradictory to experience, so far as experience will guide us; they are not opposed to the dictates of morality or to the order of the universe. If any one will show me, that the other systems are equally free from grave objections, I will acknowledge the justice of your remark. But if you had heard me to the end, perhaps you would not have found it necessary to ask the question.

A. I beg your pardon for interrupting you, and in return I will acknowledge the justice of your distinction between the principles and accidents of a religion. If I comprehend your meaning, you intend me to infer that a man, who acknowledges the possibility of a revelation, of a redemption from sin by a Mediator, and of distinct duties towards God, ought at least so to live as not to contradict any of the practical requirements of such a belief.

B. More than that, such a doubting apprehension ought to lead men to inquire further into the question of religious duties; it ought to prevent them from rashly and inconsiderately rejecting evidence; it ought to induce them to seek eagerly for every new light. If religion assures them that there are modes of acquiring an insight into Christianity other than reasoning and argumentation, they should be *disposed* to adopt them. If it inculcates, over and above common virtues, the practice of certain peculiar qualities, humility of mind, gentleness of temper, a disposition not to resent injuries, self-denial rather than self-assertion, self-distrust rather than assurance, they should be ready to turn a willing ear to its suggestions.

A. In fact, you think that the *possibility* of religion ought to influence men as strongly as its *certainty.*

B. No: I do not say so. Though in the two cases the hopes, and fears, and obligations will be in different *degrees*, yet these hopes, fears, and duties will all have reference to the same subject; and the question, what men are bound to do and what to refrain from, will not be very different in the two cases.

A. No doubt, there is a kind of prudence in avoiding what may perhaps end in injury to ourselves; but it is possible to consider this a low and unworthy motive for doing violence to our freedom of thought. I am inclined to think that religion is actually rendered repulsive to some men by the prominence given to such reasonings.

B. You must not assume that, in setting out this side of the question, I am producing these lower motives as the only or the most valid grounds for piety and religion. It should be borne in mind, that I am showing cause why men should not be irreligious. The higher motives are to those, if there are any such, who have never felt them, like scientific problems to the uninstructed, simply unintelligible; for you must bear in mind that the practical way in which the negation of religion is supported, is very much on a system of *profit and loss*—" Is it worth while to put restraint upon oneself, to adopt a constrained system of life, on the mere possibility of advantage?" To those who employ this mode of argument under any shape, my reply is, that as wise men they are bound to mould their life in accordance with this contingency. But, even on prudential grounds, there are higher motives than this.

A. And what may they be?

B. By the rejection of religion, however doubtful, they may do more injury than by acquiescing in its teaching.

A. How will you convince them of that?

B. Whether I shall convince them or not is a question; but the ground of my assertion is simple. Religion does at least profess to uphold the cause of virtue; its principles *appear*, to say the least, to be uniform with those which maintain the coherence of society. The rejection of the one may not of necessity involve the dissolution of the other; but, from the very nature of association, men will class religion and social order together, as mutually related.

A. Do you mean to imply that they who are instrumental in effecting change, are necessarily irreligious?

B. Far from it: nothing can be less true. What I say is, that if the cause of religion and of social order are thought to be related, men who reject religion on the ground of its uncertainty, and refuse to act upon its precepts, will encourage and countenance those who repudiate virtue and desire the dissolution of society. They themselves may have no such thoughts; nevertheless, such a possibility ought to be a warning to all men not rashly to accept religious difficulties as conclusive arguments against religion. Social anarchy and religious disbelief are often found to go hand in hand, though possibly the advocates of the one have really no sympathy with the promoters of the other.

A. I think I could find good arguments against your position, or, at least, I could show that you have generalized too rapidly in this matter. Revolutions are not always irreligious. Our own Great Rebellion certainly was not, but, on the contrary, was brought about by the most severely and fanatically religious of men. But to argue this question would take us into general history and away from the field of our inquiry, and I shall content myself, unless you wish to enter upon an historical investigation, with recording my protest.

B. I thank you for so limiting the matter. In what I said, I was referring to revolutions in nations, where the question between *belief and unbelief* had assumed prominence, and not to the seventeenth century, when the idea of the rejection of Christianity was hardly entertained by any large number. With this reservation, you will scarcely dispute my assertion that the uprooting of the social fabric and the rejection of Christianity go hand in hand; at least, they who desire the overthrow of all law and government regard Christianity as their most detested enemy; and the point which I would press upon your attention is, that an active disregard of religion brings with it possible evils, the consideration of which ought at least to have *some* weight with men who account themselves responsible for the consequences of their actions.

A. It appears to me, that it is essentially an immoral proceeding which you are advocating; and I can scarcely imagine one more likely to subvert the cause which you espouse. It is Hobbes' doctrine in a grosser form, " The State must have a religion ; therefore, whatever religion the State establishes, the subject must adopt." However pernicious in its ultimate tendencies, however opposed to advance in knowledge, if it only professes to fall in with established principles, it must be accepted.

B. You are not serious in what you are saying, I perceive; so it is scarcely worth while to reply to such a curious misrepresentation.

A. I am quite serious, I assure you, and fail to see how I have misstated your position.

B. By omitting the whole of the ground upon which it is based.

A. How?

B. I said, that in a case where the reasons for and against a course of action were nicely balanced, such considerations as those above stated ought to have their weight in influencing our conduct; but such a statement in no way implies that, in cases where the arguments preponderate on one side, any considerations of utility ought to prevent us from accepting and acting upon them. The whole force of the arguments rests upon the alleged uncertainty and doubtfulness of the proofs of religion. The line of reasoning would only be immoral upon the assumption that the truth of Christianity is *practically disproved.*

A. I confess that my attack did overlook this point.

B. And yet it is, you must remember, the nucleus round which all our conversation to-day centres: and lest it should again elude us, let me state simply that to which my remarks have tended. The proof of religion is acknowledged to be doubtful, to be made up of a series of arguments, each of which is only probable; nevertheless, doubt implies some kind of proof, it denotes that there is some probability in favour of religion. Thus, if a certain number of ideas were to come into your mind at random, you would have *no doubt* about them; you would say that their relation and connexion was incredible, for that there were no grounds for supposing them to have taken place. This is not a case of *doubt,* you only can doubt when you see reasons for and against facts. Do you acknowledge this?

A. Certainly it is quite clear that I do not *doubt* the *truth* of what I *know* to be *false.*

B. Religion then is, you will confess, a matter of doubt?

A. I do.

B. And if true, a matter of vital interest?

A. Undeniably.

B. Since then it has evidence in its favour, and is vastly important: can you deny that, *practically*, men ought to have a dutiful regard to it, because it may be true, and, *speculatively*, they ought to be doubly careful, lest they reject it on insufficient grounds? Such, in short, is the line of thought which I have endeavoured to draw out.

A. I cannot deny that it sounds reasonable. However unsatisfactory it may be to doubt about anything; still, if probability is all that we are to expect, we ought not to treat that probability as if it had no existence.

B. And now let us take another step. You have complained of the doubtfulness of religion, and speaking of it as a speculative subject, I argued that the very difficulty of its proof was a means of discipline to contemplative minds. I now say that it is a discipline and a probation to the careless.

A. In what way?

B. Just as difficulties in the practice of virtue are a source of discipline to the moral faculties.

A. I must ask you to explain more fully.

B. Let us take the case of a thoroughly careless man, who heard it said, that the proof of religion is involved in difficulties. It is probable that he would reject it without consideration. Should you consider such conduct morally justifiable?

A. Certainly not.

B. So that here at once is a mode of discipline arising plainly from the uncertainty of the proof. And to carry this a step farther, there are men who, after entering upon the inquiry, find it perplexing; and being very willing that it should not be true, readily explain away what tells for religion, conceal from themselves much evidence which they might see, and act altogether as *they* do, who, being desirous of following wicked courses, shut their eyes wilfully to what, in the natural world, is to be regarded as sufficient evidence of the tendency of actions. Now, as in that case we saw that the natural world afforded clear opportunities of discipline to those who will accept them, so in the case of religion the very doubtfulness of its evidence has this at least of good, that it requires men to keep a careful watch over their thoughts, lest they blind themselves to what lies before them, lest they immorally explain away arguments, and reject evidence which they ought to accept.

A. But you do not mean to assert, that ignorance of the laws of evidence is to be regarded as of the same nature as neglect of the plain laws of morality?

B. I cannot see why, amid such a variety of dispositions as we meet with, there may not be many to whom the regulation of their mental constitution is the work set them to do, just as in the majority of cases the regulation of the moral faculties is the special discipline assigned. And you must remember, that even in cases of moral action, the discipline assigned is often not to exercise self-restraint, but rather to guard against false appearances, undue influence, and deception on the part of those about them; and, in numberless cases, the principal difficulty is to exert attention, in order to know what is the reasonable and prudent part to act.

A. Will not this line of reasoning make out that an oversight is as bad as a deliberate wilful wrong?

B. Not necessarily. It is only said, that there are men who, having the power of testing evidence and omitting to exercise it, are responsible for their omission. If they have not the power of testing evidence, the arguments employed above will apply to them with double force; they have no right to profess certainty, where they are incapable of ascertaining it for themselves.

A. But may not some minds be so constituted as to feel the force of one kind of evidence much more than of another? For example, the evidence of physical phenomena seems to many men infinitely more convincing than moral evidence or inward consciousness, as it certainly is less fallacious. Now if a man says that one *physical* fact must outweigh any amount of *moral* evidence, are we to consider that man sinful for his assertion?

B. I have shown that, so long as moral action exists, its evidence is purely probable, and if a man asserts that nothing but physical proof will convince him that he is a responsible being, he must be held accountable for the consequences of that belief. And to put the matter very plainly, the physical proof of a God is impossible; for physical facts result only in facts resembling themselves, sensible and palpable: yet if a God there is, we are in some relation to Him. If we deny Him, we deny of course the relation; but our denial does not destroy the relation; it makes no change in it; and it is self-contradictory to assert, that if we are eternal existences, we can be annihilated. Yet that is the only solution which, on the theory just started, that men are not responsible for errors in their conclusions, it is possible to imagine.

A. According to this argument, ignorance is no excuse for us; and you will require from an uninstructed heathen the same degree of belief as from the most enlightened philosopher of the most civilized races.

B. By no means; to be ignorant, not having had the means of gaining knowledge, is a widely different condition from careless or wilful blindness; the one is culpable, the other is inevitable, and the opportunities of knowledge do certainly affect the relation of man to God, as revealed in the Christian Scriptures.

A. Can you not, however, find it within the limits of possibility that a man, after honestly and carefully weighing all the evidence on one side and on the other, may at last find the difficulties in the Christian doctrine so great, that he cannot give his full assent thereto?

B. Such a condition is possible, without doubt, and not by any means uncommon. Education, association, and the tone of the age, frequently spread difficulties in the way of the acceptance of the Christian faith. But yet the main argument of this conversation remains untouched—that such doubts do not justify rejection or hostility to the Christian scheme—at most they justify suspense of judgment. Let a man have ever so many difficulties, there are points in the Christian scheme to which we may claim his assent. If there are others on which he must suspend his judgment, let him at least not proclaim bitter hostility; let him not war with sneer and sarcasm; let him not confound in one common reprobation, or treat with supercilious disdain, all who can accept more than he. Let him only acknowledge, that where he finds doubts, there must be reasons on the other side; let him apply to moral problems the reasonings which he would acknowledge valid in the ordinary concerns of life; and I make bold to say, that he will end by not considering the absence of universality and the presence of uncertainty in the Christian scheme as decisive reasons for casting it aside.

DIALOGUE VII.

ON THE POSITIVE EVIDENCE FOR CHRISTIANITY.

A. Of all the conversations which we have had on these matters, that of yesterday has seemed to me the least satisfactory. Not only did we seem to be making no way, but the ground which you took, appeared to me to be lower than that which you have hitherto assumed, and, indeed, than the dignity of the subject required. If the Christian religion is to supply matter for the whole of the thinking part of man; if it is to elevate his soul above sordid aims and sensual desires, it ought not to rest for its support on mere appeals to hope and fear, to profit and loss. It ought not to say to a man, "If you accept not me, take heed lest you fall into something worse;" but it ought boldly to take its stand upon the highest ground, and to be able to say, "There is no pursuit so dignified, so refined, and so elevating, as the practice and the theory of the Christian religion." It ought to assert and make good its claim to be "*Ars artium et scientia scientiarum,*" the most beautiful of arts, the science which gathers all others to it, as handmaidens and attendants, to set off its excellence.

B. My good friend, it is quite possible for religion to assert and make good this claim, and yet to employ the arguments made use of yesterday. Let me explain how. You are, I know, not only a practical and a scientific man; you have also a great love and admiration for genuine poetry. Now in the course of your experience, you have met with men in whose idea poetry is but "prose run mad;" or at best, a musical way of expressing fanciful and half-formed thoughts. You and I do not think so: we believe that many sound and genuine thoughts are to be found in poetry, which real life conceals; we believe that poets stir up in men great principles, which the actual wear and tear of practice would hardly allow them to perceive. But if you were to employ to the despisers of poetry, the mode of argument which to us is full of weight, you would be wasting labour, because such thoughts are impossible to them. In the same way, if you argue with men to whom the principles of religion are not familiar, who deny the beauty of holiness, and demand a reason why they may not reject religion, you have to fall back upon a different line of argument. The real question yesterday was, what advantages can religion claim for itself over irreligion? Such a question, however it sounds, means in effect what *material* advantages; and in reply to such a mode of interrogation, we were compelled to employ a utilitarian method.

A. But surely you might have argued differently with me. I am not disinclined to listen to any rational arguments in favour of religion.

B. No, but you made yourself the mouthpiece of objectors who *are* disinclined, and it was to your words, not to your impressions, that I addressed myself.

A. Well, I will forgive you, if you will deal more candidly with me to-day. I wish to know how you will sum up the positive evidence for Christianity.

B. Let me ask you, how far you intend to go into the question. Will you indicate the line of thought which you wish to follow?

A. I wish, of course, to hear all that can be stated as a direct proof of Christianity.

B. Such a statement would be almost interminable. If all the minute questions and difficulties which may have occurred to every student of Christian evidences are to be discussed, we shall have to institute an elaborate investigation of manuscripts, various readings, disputed passages, questions of authorship, chronology, the meaning of words, the degree of information possessed by various writers; we shall have to make minute inquiries into historical facts; we shall be compelled to discuss inscriptions in various languages—Assyrian, Egyptian, Greek, and Latin—for all these things form part of the evidences of Christianity. Besides this, we shall have to decide questions of evidence, whether witnesses are reliable, whether, if truthful in intention, they are competent; every chapter, almost every verse of the New Testament, and very much of the Old, will have to be minutely analyzed; a knowledge of Hebrew, as well as Greek, must be presupposed; not a mere cursory acquaintance, such as will suffice to decide whether a certain passage will bear the meaning usually assigned, but a deeply critical knowledge to ascertain what is the true and certain meaning of the writer. Besides this—

A. Stay, stay; I acknowledge, that upon such an inquiry I am incompetent to enter. I had looked only for certain general arguments, upon which an ordinary man might pass a judgment; but to perform the functions which you have enumerated, a man need be a complete encyclopædia of science. Yet answer me one thing. How can you expect to convince ordinary people of the truth of Christianity, if the proof is beset with such amazing investigations? Not one man in ten thousand has the leisure or the faculties for it.

B. If I were to answer you in my own way, I should reply, that the spiritual nature of man bears witness to the spiritual truth of Christianity, and his moral nature to the moral facts; and, therefore, they who accept it on these grounds, will find sufficient proof of it in those evidences which lie level to their faculties.

A. You mean to acknowledge, what Hume asserts, that the greatest miracle in Christianity lies in the acceptance of it by reasonable men.

B. I forgive you for repeating the well-known remark, because in the way you have just stated it, it is capable of bearing a true interpretation. Jesus Christ has said, that they that do the works shall know of the doctrine; and I firmly believe, that a man who adopts the moral system of Christ, on the principles and for the motives which He sets forth, will not find any great difficulty in the evidences for

Christianity. But let me ask you this question. Do you not think that they who reject Christianity, act for the most part more strangely than they who accept it?

A. My impression is, that on purely rational grounds, I must answer your question in the negative.

B. Pray consider this: the evidences of Christianity form a long train of arguments, many of them independent of one another. It is a well-known principle, that the probability of an event is to be considered as the result, not of the *addition*, but of the *multiplication* of the independent probabilities in its favour. Now what men frequently do is this; they seize upon some argument which strikes them as uncertain, and on the basis of this reject all the other evidence as worthless. Every age has a special bias; men adopt the objection peculiar to their generation, and neglect the consideration of all other modes of proof favourable to Christianity. This is illogical to the last degree. Then, again, many of their difficulties are not only suggested by others, but are actually adopted from others. Thus men accept, as demonstrated facts, various critical theories of the origin of the Gospel Narratives, of the authorship of the Epistles; they accept the conclusions, without examining carefully and judicially the processes by which those conclusions were inferred; in short, in order to refuse credit to the Scriptures, they repose credit in men whose writings frequently they do not study deeply, which they do not attempt to sift, which very often they only know at second hand, and which they estimate according to the judgment of some one whom they respect. Very many men reject Christianity upon grounds which are utterly insufficient. Their science is imperfect, their criticism inadequate; they accept an argument or an assertion, backed by a great name; they have neither the opportunity nor the acquirements necessary for a strict investigation. Surely in a matter of such moment, such hasty and inconsiderate behaviour is the part neither of a philosopher nor a practical man.

A. In what you have said there is much truth. No one can justify the hasty way in which objections are snatched up and passed on from man to man. Every man who can read and write thinks himself competent to decide questions which have occupied thoughtful men for generations, and the due discussion of which implies frequently a life-long study of a special subject-matter. Nevertheless, the main proofs of Christianity must lie open to the capacity of ordinary men, otherwise there could be no pretence of conviction on the part of such.

B. If I were to ask you to assign the historical basis of the Christian religion, to what would you point?

A. To the collection of books called the New Testament, no doubt.

B. And should you object to receive the testimony which they afford to the founding of the religion?

A. I should say, that those books represent a current tradition and system of doctrine, which had gathered round the name of one central figure; and that it was probable that, in the course of time, an accretion of the marvellous had been added, partly through the fervour, partly through the pious frauds, of the earliest propagators of that religion.

B. Let us examine your view. You will, I suppose, acknowledge that such a person as Christ did once live and teach in Judea—that He was born of humble parentage, somewhere about the time usually assigned? Heathen writers, as you probably know, can be brought to attest this much.

A. Yes; I think that upon this point I need

not delay you: that a person, who claimed to be the Christus or Messiah, did appear about this time is, I think, a well-ascertained fact. I cannot think it possible that such a person, so definitely and circumstantially described, can be the offspring of a mere religious imagination. Moreover, I consider that the passage in Suetonius, referring to "One Christus," sufficiently establishes the fact of His existence. Beyond this, there are other passages in Roman writers, which forbid the denial of it.

B. We need not, then, pause to argue the mythical theory, that such a person is a mere ideal, without any reality of existence beyond the imaginative brains of some poor fishermen, converted tax-gatherers or tent-makers, or the hysterical visions of some Jewish women? You will allow that the existence of Jesus Christ is a fact, which we have every reason to acknowledge?

A. I will grant this, but let me caution you as to the nature of the admission. All that it amounts to is, that a certain person once lived Who gathered round Him a body of admirers, principally poor men like Himself. I have conceded nothing as to the description given of Him in the Gospels. The question, how far, in the lapse of years, His actions were distorted, His words magnified into lessons of Divine wisdom, and all the circumstances of His life invested with a halo of mysterious romance, in no degree enters into my concession.

B. I quite understand; however, I wish to draw your attention to two expressions which you have just used, in order to know whether you employed them advisedly. You spoke of Christ's admirers being *poor men like Himself*, and you ascribed the miraculous accounts of the Gospels to *the lapse of years*. Have you any wish to modify either of those expressions?

A. By no means. I think they correctly express my meaning.

B. It is plain, then, that the authors of the narratives called the Gospels, to take the most unfavourable case, must have derived their information, directly or indirectly, from these same poor followers of Jesus Christ.

A. I suppose a portion of the facts must have been handed down from their narratives.

B. And you wish to imply, I presume, that the story, so handed down, grew gradually into the dimensions in which it has reached us.

A. Yes; I imagine it possible that, in the hands of later disciples, embellishments were added to grace the narrative and make it palatable, and that, by these means, the miracles were introduced, and the history made attractive.

B. This is, you think, a more natural account of the matter, than that the narratives were the composition of the persons to whom they are attributed?

A. Well, it appears to me a possible explanation, and it frees us from several difficulties; it would explain how discrepancies have arisen, according as the tradition varied, and it would very fairly account for the introduction of the miraculous element into the history.

B. Ah! now I see your reason for adhering to this hypothesis; you still consider the miracles a difficulty, and so you will adopt a theory, which allows of the miracles being later interpolations. Your argument, or rather I should perhaps say the argument of those whom you are following, is simply this: "Miracles are impossible, therefore any hypothesis which gets rid of them is reasonable." Of course you are aware that there is no ground, in the world, for accepting this hypothesis, beyond the fact that it is not impossible. The first three Gospels were accepted by the Christians early in the second century (that is, within a hundred years of the death of Christ), as the undoubted production of His contemporaries; one of them, at least, bears traces of being written for men well acquainted with Jewish customs and traditions; another, to all appearance, was written by a contemporary and fellow-traveller of St. Paul; it is dedicated to the same person to whom a treatise, which has the strongest internal marks of being written by one of his followers and personal friends, is addressed. If it were not for the miracles, no one would find any difficulty in assigning the Gospel of St. Luke and the Acts of the Apostles to the same author. Now you should remember, that the destruction of Jerusalem and the annihilation of the Jews as a nation, took place within fifty years of the death of Christ, and that, therefore, there is a presumption that a writer, who presupposes an intimate knowledge of Jewish customs, wrote his narrative before the destruction of Jerusalem. And if the Acts of the Apostles is the work of a contemporary of St. Paul, it is almost impossible not to accept the Gospel of St. Luke as of equally early date.

A. But all your supposed proofs go upon the supposition that the facts alleged are not interpolations, designed to give proof of the genuineness of the narratives. What is more likely than that they should be interpolations?

B. It would be impossible now to enter upon the discussion of this question, but I may be allowed to say, that the theory of interpolation as applied to the Acts of the Apostles, will be found to be almost untenable; however, as I may have to speak of this hereafter, I will not press the matter, but let me ask you to attend to this. Numbers of sects and heresies arose in the second century. Now the Gnostics and the Marcionites knew of the Gospels. Marcion flourished about A.D. 138; he wrote a Gospel probably about 130, adapting what previously existed so as to suit his particular views. Recent writers have established that the Gospel of Marcion was an adaptation of St. Luke; at all events, it is fairly shown that such a Gospel existed before A.D. 120. The idea, then, that this Gospel was composed in the middle of the second century is utterly arbitrary; and surely the testimony of the whole Christian Church, that this and other Gospels were the work of contemporaries of the Apostles, ought to be of weight, when there is nothing but surmise to be set on the other side.

A. I confess that this argument has much weight with me; but still you will only thus bring evidence for their origin as early as the first half of the second century.

B. Still if, in the second century, we find that the Gospels, as they now are, did exist and were spoken of as the work of those whose names they now bear, this is strong evidence. If the genuineness of the Gospels had been doubted, there were surely men among the heretics who would have made use of the doubt; and we should have heard among the defenders of Christianity of replies to these objections. But the fact is, that the Christian writers assume as a point undisputed the genuineness of the Gospels. And more than this. It is plain from their writings, that the Gospels were, before the end of the second century, gathered into an authoritative book. Other narratives on the same subject had been rejected as not equally authoritative. Now we may fairly ask, how could this process of sifting have taken place, had not the question of the authorship of the Gospels been freely discussed; and on what principle could these have been accepted and the others rejected, except that the authorship of the one was considered to be a guarantee for their veracity and authority, while that of the other was held to be uncertain?

A. But might not the contents of the other writings, which were discredited, have been such as to do harm to the cause of Christianity by the monstrous and incredible fables which they related?

B. Possibly; and that would prove that the spirit of criticism was to a certain extent alive among the rulers of the Church, and that a miracle was not accepted unless attested by good and reliable authority. But now, having traced the date of the Gospels into the first century, we are in the age of those who were the younger contemporaries of the disciples of Christ.

A. Stay; I must not allow you to proceed too fast. You are rather making assertions than proving conclusions.

B. Well, if I have shown that there is no probability that the Gospels were composed in the latter half of the second century; that there is a probability that one at least was written, and not only written but acknowledged as authoritative, early in the second century; if there is no ground for assuming that it was composed just before that time; and if the general impression was that the Gospels were of much earlier date;—I do not see, that it is very unreasonable to infer that they were the productions of men who lived in the time of the apostles; and who so likely to have written them as they who had witnessed the events which they recorded? There is as much reason for supposing them to be the writings of those whose names they bear, as there is for attributing other ancient writings to the authors whose names *they* bear. For if others had taken in hand the task of recording events which they only knew from hearsay, it is extremely probable, that they who witnessed the events would have considered it incumbent upon them to hand down, for the use of others, the correct narrative of the circumstances upon which they based a doctrine and a practice so new to the world.

A. But is it not possible, that the whole history is the result of an enthusiastic devotion in a few ardent minds, and that the real Christ and His teaching were as little like the Christ of the Gospels as we may suppose the real Socrates was unlike the Socrates of Plato's Dialogues?

B. What right have you to assume that Socrates did not teach what Plato ascribes to him? But even if you are justified in this assumption, the case is little to the point. Plato was an Athenian, a leading spirit in a nation of exceptional genius. The morality which he teaches, the doctrines which he inculcates, are elevated indeed; but they do not differ essentially from much of the wisdom of the foregoing philosophers; not so much as to compel us to view him as an entirely isolated thinker and moralist. But the notion that a body of uneducated Jews, living at a time when the Jews were regarded by other nations as in a state of degradation, moral and intellectual, when the whole of that people was in a condition of bitter and furious exasperation against their Roman oppressors, and perpetually engaged in bloody rebellions, should have invented a character so unlike a Jew as Jesus Christ; should have assigned to Him a system of teaching so elevated and ennobling as that which we find in the Gospels; should have devised a theory of a spiritual kingdom not connected with this world—a theory which, whatever its intrinsic merits, possessed a strength sufficient to cope with the power of imperial Rome, and to draw all nations to itself—this is a supposition so extraordinary, that no one who is not determined to close his eyes to the facts of Christianity can entertain it for a moment.

A. Yes; I allow it does appear extravagant; and when I take a general view, such as you have just indicated, I feel inclined to waive all objections; and yet, when my mind returns to details, I see objections innumerable which demand an explanation.

B. You have allowed that Jesus Christ did really live; you have now provisionally conceded that the Gospels may possibly be a narrative by competent writers; will you grant that the main outlines of the life of Jesus may be relied on?

A. Stay; is it not possible that men so aroused as these men were, may have been imposed upon, or that, convinced of the importance of their Master's life, they may have thought it right to present it to the world in an imposing dress?

B. I think I understand your meaning. You suppose that there is an element of truth in the history, but that the miraculous part of it is either a pious fraud or the result of superstitious susceptibility.

A. Exactly so.

B. If the writers of the Gospels had intended to make their writings attractive, they would not have adopted the simple narrative form. Remember that these histories are for the most part as simple as annals: there is no search for effect; the narrative is unadorned; the miraculous events are introduced as plain matter of fact; they enter in as naturally as the most ordinary circumstances; they are related as occurring in the sight of numbers of witnesses, some at least hostile.

A. But is it possible that such events should have occurred and not have gained a world-wide notoriety?

B. You must remember that they who opposed them believed firmly in the operations of an evil spirit; they held that the work which Christ was effecting was evil, as tending to the subversion of the religion of Moses. They therefore regarded Him as the agent of the evil spirit. So much for the Jews. As for the Romans, *they* counted the Jews as ignorant and superstitious barbarians; anything which was related as occurring amongst them would be simply laughed at as an oriental fable. The result is, that the Jews who could have borne witness would attribute miraculous works to an evil agency; and even if they had not done so, their testimony would have gained no credence in the world. Accordingly, the only witnesses who would have any interest in perpetuating the events were that knot of poor men who were personally attached to Jesus Christ. It is to them, then, that we must look for any trustworthy evidence.

A. But what warrant have we that they were not pious deceivers?

B. The warrant of their lives, spent in simplicity and honesty; the warrant of a doctrine, of which the essence is the hatred of deceit; the warrant that their preaching gained for them neither honour, nor riches, nor popular applause; but scorn, poverty, ignominy, persecution, and frequently cruel and lingering death.

A. All this sounds extremely well; but it is quite possible for men to profess a high regard for truth, and, on the whole, to act up to what they profess; to be willing also to lay down their life for their opinions; and yet to have so deluded themselves as to believe that the doctrines which they hold are essential to the well-being of society. Instances are abundant of persons in this condition. When once a habit of mind has been acquired, it matters little on what foundation it rests. It becomes a reality; men will suffer for it, fight for it, work for it, and lie for it; their mendacity is to a great extent unconscious; the institution or the faith for which they contend has become a necessity to them, and they conceive that its destruction would be an irreparable loss to the world.

B. Your observation is most just. Such cases are to be found; but you should observe, that they occur when institutions have already taken a deep hold upon the public mind. Such cases are the divine right of kings or the sacred rights of the people. But in a case when authority and prescription, the feelings of educated men, and the sympathies of the uneducated, are enlisted against an opinion; when, in fact, the whole tenor of public thought opposes it, your observation does not equally apply. You will find that, viewed historically, the propagation of opinions antagonistic to popular thought does not, as a rule, arouse such an enthusiasm as that which animated the early Christians.

A. What say you to the religion of Mahomet?

B. The opinions of Mahomet were, from the first, supported by powerful friends; they became the favourite doctrines of warlike and conquering tribes; they won their way by violent means, and can in no way be compared with Christianity, which was introduced by a few poor and despised men, and drew converts from the same class. The means of its propagation, for at least three centuries, were purely peaceful. They who espoused it, literally gave up all for its sake. They consented to be despised and persecuted by friends and relations; and this they did with their eyes open; for the first preachers of Christianity proclaimed, in the words of the Founder, that the father should betray the son to death and the son the father, and that a man's enemies should be they of his own household. But the fact is that the early Christians were earnest, not so much for *opinions* as for *facts*. If you will read St. Paul's language, as given in the Acts of the Apostles, you will find, that what he impresses upon his hearers is always the *facts* of Christianity. Now there is a considerable difference between vehement assertion of opinions and determined belief in facts. Opinions are impalpable, incapable of refutation except by reasoning, and therefore men may easily close their eyes to the other side. But facts are capable of verification. The early Christians embraced the Gospel under the idea that they witnessed miracles. The first converts received the new religion on the strength of actions, which they thought they saw performed before their eyes. It is, of course, open to you to say that they were deceived; but it seems impossible to imagine, that men would be willing to lay down their lives for facts which they had never witnessed, or at least supposed that they witnessed.

A. Yes; on the whole I think it probable, that the first preachers of Christianity must have believed the facts which they related. St. Paul must have been strongly impressed with a notion that he had seen Jesus Christ, and that God had spoken to him again and again; but all this may have been hallucination—the effect of hypochondria or nervous derangement. I can easily imagine a man of keen imagination, pondering painfully over the allegations of the Christians, impressed with their earnestness, and unconsciously drawn by his mental bias to their side. All the while that this unconscious agency was at work, an equally unconscious resistance to the impending mental change within him would operate: he would be urged on to more violent persecution in proportion to the growing sense of his cruelty and injustice; he would endeavour to still his moral sense by a more active discharge of his duties as an inquisitor. But the mental strain at length becomes too great; he is seized with an epileptic fit, and in his convulsions is convinced that he hears the voice of the God Whose followers he persecutes expostulating with him. On his recovery he becomes a Christian, and takes a pleasure in suffering for the cause which before he had oppressed.

B. Supposing that this were an admissible explanation of the circumstances to which you advert, you have yet forgotten an essential point. After his conversion St. Paul was blind for three days: at the end of that time he received his sight at the hands of a man named Ananias. This part of the event is circumstantially related by him. Here there is no question of hypochondria or delusion. The apostle declares that he was blind, and that he recovered his sight. The malady and the cure were both sudden; and we are told that the person from whom he received the cure was at first unwilling to visit him, but at length came to him by what he believed to be a direct command from God. How will you reconcile this with your theory of hallucination? According to your idea two persons, not personally known to one another, were almost simultaneously affected with unaccountable fancies: one was induced to change his whole manner of life, and to renounce what before he held most sacred; the other was prevailed upon to visit a man whom he knew to be a bitter enemy, and who had come for the very purpose of suppressing the opinions which he himself professed.

To trace such a coincidence to epilepsy or hallucination seems utterly impossible, or, at all events, a most desperate mode of solution.

A. But I imagine that the whole episode of Ananias and the recovery from blindness was part of the same transient mania.

B. In that case it seems strange that St. Paul, having had the opportunity of inquiring, should have embodied in his preaching things which were absolutely capable of refutation. You must bear in mind, that the whole current of the history tends to prove that St. Paul was looked upon with a certain degree of jealousy among the Jewish Christians; by many, indeed, he was regarded with a feeling akin to hatred. This we learn from those Epistles which are allowed by the most minute critics to be his writings. How strange, then, for him to repeat at Jerusalem and elsewhere, and to suffer his biographers to report, a thing which was capable of being turned against him with fatal force. Such an oversight is incredible. If he had wished to embellish his narrative with marvels, he would have chosen a safer subject than this. Neither as a deceiver nor as an enthusiast can he be supposed to have countenanced such a story.

A. But may not the Christians have agreed

to uphold this part of the narrative, on the ground that to discredit it was to injure the whole cause of Christianity?

B. You surely forget the enmity of some of the Jewish Christians against St. Paul. They would only have been too glad to seize upon any pretext to injure his authority. Your hypothesis will require, that St. Paul and Ananias must have conspired together to assert that an additional miracle had taken place, of which they alone were cognizant; and this miracle of a character comparatively unimportant, compared with others which they announced. It involves an elaborate deceit, contrived by men who before were unknown to one another, devised for a purpose which could not at the time have entered into their thoughts, viz. to countenance, in after-ages, the claim of Paul to a miraculous conversion. Thus you will have to multiply hypothesis upon hypothesis, purely gratuitously, in the face of the acknowledged fact, that the early Christians were men of blameless lives and extreme simplicity of character.

A. I confess that this is a most intricate impeachment; but will you allow me to hear how the supposed truth of the facts will assist you?

B. I say, that the Epistles of St. Paul represent him as strongly opposed by a party among the Christians, and therefore compelled to be circumspect in his assertions. However, it appears that he was on terms of intimacy with the leaders of the Christian Church, and learned from them the circumstances under which they had come to hold the views which they did respecting Jesus of Nazareth. Now the main point upon which St. Paul's teaching turns is the *resurrection of the dead.* His intercourse with the other disciples made him acquainted with many matters concerning this great doctrine. Among them he found many who had actually conversed with Jesus after His resurrection; they had seen Him die; they had witnessed Him, prostrate with weakness and suffering, undergo the punishment of the cross, from which no one was released until the official witnesses had certified themselves, that the sufferer was dead; in a few days they had held intercourse with Him again. Such at least was the testimony which they bore to Paul.

A. Pardon me; are you not assuming the reality of the history in the question, which is the point in dispute?

B. No, I think not. We have certain other documents besides the Gospels and the Acts of the Apostles. The most minute criticism seems to have decided that the four principal Epistles of St. Paul, those to the Corinthians, to the Galatians, and to the Romans, are proved by incontestable evidence to be his genuine productions. Now in these he asserts, that several of his predecessors in the Christian faith had actually witnessed the appearance of Jesus Christ after His death. He mentions His appearance to Peter, with whom Paul was on intimate terms, as well as various other manifestations of His resurrection; so that St. Paul is a genuine link between the earliest disciples and the more developed Churches; and his allusions to the Gospel facts bring us into the presence of the twelve Apostles of Jesus.

A. But may not they have deceived him, or have been deluded themselves?

B. As for their intentional mendacity, Paul himself was at one time an unwilling witness, that they were ready to die for their belief; and with regard to their being deluded, when he mentions the fact that Christ appeared in bodily form to above five hundred persons at once, it is very hard to assert that so many men could be at the same moment subject to the same ocular delusion.

A. The question then resolves itself into

this: can we believe testimony to such an incredible event?

B. That is a part of the question, indeed, but not all; you must add to this St. Paul's conviction, that he too had beheld the risen Jesus with his bodily eyes. But even then you have not exhausted the question. There is a passage in the Acts of the Apostles, in which an extraordinary manifestation of remarkable gifts is referred to. It is said, that a number of men were suddenly endowed with what is described as a gift of tongues. It matters not much what is especially intended by that expression, nor am I at present laying stress upon the history in that passage. Besides this, certain miraculous powers are attributed to various individuals. Now St. Paul, in writing to the Corinthians, evidently in answer to certain questions which they had addressed to him, refers to these miraculous gifts. The language which he uses is such as would imply that these phenomena were quite usual and common. He does not even lay great stress upon them, but sets them below other natural qualities not miraculous. Now any one would say that this simple way of alluding to these manifestations is a sign that very extraordinary phenomena had become so common among the Christians as to awaken little or no surprise; so that the question which you propounded just now is rendered more complex. The simple idea of the resurrection might possibly be thought to be the hallucination of an excited mind, but the addition of all these other phenomena complicates the matter very much.

A. But is not the existence and prevalence of these extraordinary phenomena altogether an argument against the whole miraculous narrative? I mean this: conceding the existence of very abnormal states of mind among the early Christians, may we not consider that they were more exposed to imposture and less ready to scrutinize what was miraculous than men in the normal condition? and that, accordingly, the extraordinary details in the narratives lose, rather than gain, in credit from the condition of the writers.

B. You are assuming that the writers of the narratives composed them under the influence of excited feelings. Such an inference is not warranted by the histories: they are, for the most part, as grave as annals; the writers betray no token of excitement, no aiming at effect. They were perfectly aware, that what they recounted was calculated to arouse astonishment, but they neither seek to enhance the wonder, nor even to make the most of it. Numbers of miracles are passed over in a verse or two of the Gospels. In such a case, it is fair to say, that so far as written testimony may go, these writers deserve credit, by reason of the simplicity and inornate character of their writings.

A. Truly, this is a goodly foundation to build Christianity upon, that the style of the narratives is not extravagant!

B. Nay, do not be angry; nothing that I now adduce is to be considered as a convincing argument in and by itself; still you ought to allow its own weight to each. Now, if it be an acknowledged fact, that men who have to relate extraordinary events, of which they have been witnesses, are apt to fall into extravagant language and to support their assertions by multiplied arguments and proofs; and if a writing is confessedly trustworthy, in proportion to the gravity and staidness of its composition, then the narratives of the New Testament, in this respect, deserve our attention. Nothing can be more grave and sober than the narrative; nothing can present fewer indications of a desire to commend itself by the structure and style. The ordinary events and the miracles are recorded alike in the simplest of language;

the failings as well as the virtues of the actors are calmly stated; in fact, if the miracles were not there, no one would deny that the narratives bear the stamp of truth.

A. But the addition of these, I suppose, makes little difference in the question.

B. Well; till the impossibility of a miracle is established on other grounds, we ought to allow this weight to testimony, that, when the writers are not guilty of extravagance, and write as they would in reporting ordinary matters, we ought to credit them with believing the truth of what they describe.

A. Clearly this is not an extravagant demand. I have no objection to exonerate the writers of the Gospels from the charge of intentional deceit. Nevertheless, you must allow me to say, that other miracles have been attested by evidence apparently as strong as that for the Christian miracles; the witnesses have seemed quite worthy of credit; their testimony has been most circumstantial; and yet, after all, the whole matter has proved to be either a mere fancy or an exaggerated statement of ordinary events.

B. Even if I were to grant that the evidence for other miracles is as strong as that for the Gospel miracles, I should be glad to hear what use you would make of the concession.

A. Why; may we not suppose, that the evidence for the Christian miracles might be disposed of equally summarily, if we had the whole case before us?

B. Your argument seems to amount to this: two witnesses are examined in different places respecting two distinct crimes, in no way connected with one another, except that they are of the same character. One witness is found to be untrustworthy, therefore you argue that the other witness is probably untrustworthy also.

A. I can hardly admit that to be a fair statement of my remark. The point is, that in a matter where men are especially liable to be deceived, to establish a similarity between two cases is to transfer any doubts attending the one to the other.

B. Yes; but there is a fallacy in your word *similarity*. The similarity to which you refer consists in the unusual nature of the events. Whereas the similarity which you require is of a different character. You must show that in both cases the influences under which the witnesses gave their evidence were analogous. Thus a miracle which occurs opportunely to support an established system exercising great sway over the minds of men, or a miracle which supports a failing cause, cannot be compared with miracles which appear to have no such tendency. Just in proportion as the assertion of a miracle is found to be obviously convenient, so is its evidence to be scrutinized more narrowly. For example, without entering into the question of later miracles in the Church, it is obvious that the opportuneness with which many supposed miracles occurred is rather a presumption against them. We can see an obvious reason for the promulgation of a religious fraud in such cases. If a certain bishop assembles a council, in which many of his open enemies are gathered, and during its session a part of the room gives way and swallows up the opponents, the obvious inference is that the whole was a trick; but the strongest opponent of the Christian miracles would not venture to assert, that they presented similar traces of opportune contrivance.

A. Still, if you are to accept testimony on such a matter, you must confess that you will find a difficulty in rejecting many notoriously false miracles.

B. Even if that be so, I do not see that it affects what I have asserted, that evidence *confuted by contrary evidence, or any way overbalanced*, cannot destroy the credibility of other evidence *neither confuted nor overbalanced*. The only thing which can destroy the evidence of testimony is, either that the witnesses are not competent judges of the facts to which they testify, or that they are under indirect influence in giving their testimony. But, if the early Christians saw the facts which they related, we cannot say that they were not competent judges. If they witnessed the cure of diseases, they were perfectly competent witnesses of the facts, for it does not require philosophical acumen but the use of the senses, to take cognizance of these things; for it cannot be too often observed, that the miracles of Christ were performed under the eyes of the most scrutinizing opponents; and though it may be said that it was not they, but His friends, who bore testimony, still it is plain from the narrative, that even *they* were only convinced by a repetition of unmistakable acts of power, performed utterly beyond their expectation. Since, then, the only reason to suppose that the narratives were not written by eye-witnesses is the occurrence of the miracles; since it is plain, that, in very early days, certain remarkable powers existed among the Christians; since they undoubtedly attested, with their lives, the facts which they related; and since those facts were such as they had every opportunity of scrutinizing carefully, we have, I think, a very strong reason for inferring, that they really took place at the time and in the manner asserted in the Gospels.

A. You said a short time ago, that the proofs of Christianity were manifold. At present our whole thoughts have been occupied with the probabilities or improbabilities of the Gospel history. I think I could raise many further objections; perhaps I might accuse your mode of argument of unfairness, in hurrying backwards and forwards from one part of the New Testament to another. I think also I could insinuate difficulties with reference to the Acts of the Apostles, which I have seen cleverly brought together in a very short compass. However, as my wish is rather to hear what can be said on your side of the question, than to enter into all the details on the other, I will ask you to furnish me with any other evidence which you may possess.

B. I should assert next that the fulfilment of prophecy is a very strong evidence in favour of Christianity.

A. My good friend, fulfilment of prophecy!

I should hardly have expected you to use this argument.

B. And why not, may I ask?

A. Why, have we not ourselves seen people utterly demented on this point, seeing in every minute event the fulfilment of things declared centuries before; twisting and contorting words and facts, so as to detect the shadow of a shade of coincidence between the two. I should have thought, that such an argument was injurious to your cause. Your adversaries will turn round upon you and say, that your process will make anything mean anything, distorts language, perverts history, and gives rise to every kind of error.

B. Suppose I grant that the interpretation of prophecy is very often utterly fallacious, I cannot see that that proves that the fulfilment of prophecy, in cases where the accomplishment seems obvious, is an argument of no value. I put the case to you in this way: if a revelation is possible, which is not denied, it amounts to a declaration of God's will made known for man's instruction. The relation of prophecy to revelation may be viewed as the indistinct, faint dawn which heralds the day. God's truth, though hidden, is by Him revealed partially and in glimpses before it is made fully known; such is the natural course of His operations. Great principles do not become evident all at once; indistinct apprehensions of them appear, long before the open recognition of them by men takes place. Now, if the prophets received a partial insight into the future, and announced, in language very general and to a great degree obscure, facts which afterwards were accomplished and principles which afterwards were recognized as true, we have a right to employ, as an argument in favour of Christianity, those predictions which correspond to it.

A. Yes; but consider, how very slight is the connexion between the things said to be foretold and the language of the supposed predictions. The method by which the connexion is made out is utterly unphilosophical and violent.

B. However, it must be allowed that the prophetical writers do plainly apprehend, that they are writing of something not yet accomplished. However indistinct the idea in their minds may be, you cannot read the prophetical parts of the Hebrew Scriptures without perceiving, that the writers have a strong conviction that they are foretelling events not accomplished in their times.

A. Such is my impression, I confess; but I believe it has been questioned, whether the peculiar genius of the Hebrew language will not allow of the use of the future to denote the past. There is an ambiguity in the use of the tenses of the verb, which renders it difficult to determine whether the writer, in apparently prophetic language, is not allegorically depicting the emotions of his own mind, or the fortunes of men of his own day.

B. I am quite ready to allow, that this difficulty does often occur. Nevertheless, no one who reads many consecutive chapters of the prophetic writings, can doubt that the Prophets do believe themselves to be speaking, in great measure, of the future.

A. I do not think it necessary to dispute your assertion. Whether the Prophets were vague, enthusiastic dreamers, or truly inspired, it seems quite evident that they *considered* themselves inspired; and however much their writings are the result of impressions derived from their own age, no one can deny that they frequently write as of persons and things not yet existent. But this in no way assists you in producing prophecy as an evidence for Christianity.

B. Perhaps not; but it may form an answer to an objection which is sometimes heard, that the application of prophecy to Christianity was an after-thought of the Christians to strengthen their position. Such an objection is altogether baseless, but I notice it here, lest it should in any way haunt us afterwards. The belief, that the prophets foretold future events, was held by themselves and was current to the time of the foundation of Christianity, so that it certainly was not invented by the Christians.

A. To that I make no demur.

B. Now I say, that in the Old Testament Scriptures, written by various authors, and at wide intervals of time, there is a progressive idea of a moral development of men, a notion, vague at first, and yet very definitely expressed in most unequivocal language, that the power of evil over the world shall at some time be broken. There is also a very distinct impression, that the author of this moral development shall be an individual man. Gradually this notion becomes enlarged; the idea of a kingdom to be established by this man—a kingdom over the hearts of men, that shall never end— is found to be announced by various Jewish writers; these ideas are finally grouped together, developed still further, and clothed in most definite language by two writers, Isaiah and Daniel, of whom the one announces, that at a certain time, specifically though obscurely intimated, the expected person should die, and the other, in a very elaborate account, describes the characteristics of the birth, life, and death of this person. Beyond this, there are not a few other references to a similar idea to be found in other writers. They are, it is true, extremely obscure and perplexing in their form; nevertheless, though the language is frequently metaphorical or allegorical, the thing intended is so clear, that long before Christianity a very general impression had come abroad that some great one was to be born. Men were constantly asserting themselves to be the Person thus foreshadowed, and misleading their followers into all manner of absurdities and enormities. So much so was this the case, that, when the Christians announced that they were the followers of the true Christ, this name had come to be notoriously synonymous with disorderly conduct and rebellion; and the men, whose lives are proved by irrefragable evidence to have been quiet and inoffensive, are styled by a grave and usually trustworthy historian "the enemies of the human race," in defiance of all facts.

A. I am perfectly aware that a very general belief was entertained, especially in the East, of the approach of some universal conqueror or deliverer; but the prevalence of such a belief would account for the Christians claiming that title for their Founder.

B. The point, which we are discussing, is not what could be made of such a belief, but that such a belief was prevalent.

A. I think there can be no question of that.

B. Suddenly, in the hill-country of Palestine, a young man, of humble parents and occupation, made His appearance. He was not educated, for His position and the place of His abode, a despised and infamous village, forbid the supposition. This man maintained for three years a war against evil in all its forms; His preaching and teaching, though most simple, drew vast crowds to hear Him; the sentiments to which He gave utterance were of the most exalted moral beauty. Amongst men given up to a literal service to, what may be termed, an unexpansive moral law, He taught a spiritual interpretation of its precepts, beyond which nineteen centuries have not been able to advance. His doctrine was not of an attractive or pleasing character; on the contrary, it inculcated the most rigid self-denial, an intense humility, and a profound disregard for what men most value. His teaching constantly brought Him into hostile contact with the leaders of the people, who eventually accused Him of the crime of aspiring to make Himself a King, and brought Him before the Roman governor. For this cause He was, though innocent, condemned to death and crucified with other malefactors. Shall you object to this account?

A. No; it seems mainly correct.

B. Now this history, remarkable indeed, but so far as we have traced it, not necessarily miraculous, is found to accord strangely with some of the prophetic declarations; and, what is more strange, it accords with those parts of them which men had hitherto overlooked. The very points in the life of Jesus which offended the people—His poverty, His origin, His shameful death—are those which most curiously accord with the prophecies of Isaiah. Even in most minute particulars the accordance can be traced. The result of the life of Jesus has been the foundation of a society which has endured ever since. Its principles have moulded the opinions, laws, and customs of all the most highly-civilized nations in the world; the spirit by which it has prevailed has been such as the Prophets describe as gentleness and patience; and the instruments of its success are such as to contradict all the maxims of ordinary experience. Yet the Prophets describe such a kingdom; and their language, frequently obscure, receives a fresh light, when compared with the facts of the Christian kingdom.

A. But, my good friend, though your argument sounds well in general terms, when you descend to particulars it is seen to be hollow; for in the first place, the agreement between the prophecies and the events is of the most general character; frequently in the same prophecy there are other points which do in no way accord with the supposed fulfilment.

B. If I understand you aright, you mean that, though a certain similarity exists, it cannot be traced throughout; is that so?

A. Yes.

B. Then we ought not to find any difficulty in this. If you were reading a certain political satire, such as "Reynard the Fox," or the "Tale of a Tub," and found certain points of similarity between events of which you knew, and the writings before you, you would not say that those events were not referred to, because you could not trace every point, but would rightly infer that the difficulty lay in your own ignorance.

A. But I should require a considerable amount of resemblance, before I acknowledged the accordance between the satire and the events.

B. No doubt; in fact you might never detect the resemblance at all, though it were as clear as the light to those who possess the clue. Nevertheless if the resemblance existed, your not seeing it would hardly alter the case.

A. To what end do you make this remark?

B. In answer to those who say that they see no resemblance between the prophecies and the events.

A. But if I can find other events, to which the prophecies are equally well adapted, may I not assume that it was these to which reference was made?

B. Yes, assuredly; but you must bear in mind, that you have no right to make hypotheses as to possible events, which were intended by the Prophet. You must only appeal to known facts. When the plain words of a prophecy apply literally to the history of Jesus, you have no right to suppose particular events, drawn from the general history of the Prophet's time, or to insinuate that possibly the Prophet was in a certain condition of mind, when he wrote the prophecy. You must meet historical fact with historical fact.

A. But it appears to me, that very frequently the Prophet has a simple idea in his mind, and your interpreters apply his plain words in a sense which they do not grammatically bear.

B. No doubt many Christians have done a grave injury to their cause, by pressing passages into their service which ought never to have been so used. I really believe, that the extreme repugnance to the use of prophecy as an argument, which many men feel, arises from this indiscriminate employment of materials. It is not hard to trace this to its source. Men who hold the central doctrines of Christianity as of vital importance, run the risk of seeing them where they do not exist. Their eyes see nothing but Christ; their minds are filled with the thought of Him; and not a line, not a word meets them, but it seems instinct with reference to Him. To men of well-balanced minds, such conduct appears irrational. A reaction sets in; and whereas men saw Christ everywhere, presently they see Him nowhere. This may be equally irrational. However, in reply to what you have just said, you must not forget that, if there is such a thing as prophetic writing, the proper analogy for it is not an original book, but a compilation from another man's materials. You must not compare prophecy with an edition of Aristotle, but with a *paraphrase* of Aristotle.

A. Pray make your meaning clearer.

B. I say, that as the paraphrast gives what he *conceives* to be the meaning of his author, so the Prophets, if inspired, wrote down the results of their inspiration, without completely fathoming the mind of Him Who inspired them. Hence it is perfectly possible, that they may have seen only a partial application of what they were inspired to relate; they *may*, indeed I will say they *must*, have known only in part: they could not have plainly seen all that their words convey. Hence it may often happen that their words have acquired a precision and definiteness, from the concentration of their mind on a single object, to which their language only imperfectly applies; while in relation to the grand subject of their prophecy, their eyes are partially darkened, so that they do not see it; and hence they lay the emphasis on parts of the idea which conform especially to circumstances of the times, passing over with slighter notice, and frequently introducing, as it would seem most inappropriately, ideas inapplicable to the present, but bearing very strongly upon the more distant events which they are commissioned to relate.

A. There is only one thing which vitiates your whole argument; you assume that the

Prophets were inspired to speak of things which they did not comprehend. This is the very point you have to prove.

B. No, I do not assume it; but I argue that if they were inspired with knowledge of the future, then these peculiarities of style might be expected; and I assert that these peculiarities do exist, and find a sufficient explanation in the analogies which I have suggested; but that, on any other hypothesis, they are totally unintelligible.

A. That is founding religion upon a hypothesis, which is utterly objectionable.

B. No; the Christian religion, at all events, lays claim to *facts* and not to *suppositions*, as its basis; and this hypothesis, as you are pleased to style it, is only one among many arguments in its favour. As I have said, every argument must be taken together with others. You remember the old fable of the king, who taught his sons the secret of strength in combination. I do not, indeed, allow that any of these arguments are like the twigs, which he broke with ease; but the whole taken together form a most powerful body of proof, which it is very difficult to resist.

A. You speak as if you have produced an endless chain of proof, whereas you have really only produced two forms of evidence.

B. You must not forget that the whole of our conversations from the first till now are evidences for Christianity. Every single point that we have established is comprised in the Christian faith. You will say that other religions have held these opinions besides the Christian. This may be true; but the Christian religion professes to hold all the truths which other religions hold, and to reject the errors. Everything, therefore, which appertains to the unseen world, to our relation to God, to our hopes and expectations for the future, as well as to our moral duties here, may justly be considered to form part of the Christian religion; and to this all our conversations have been directed. We have therefore traversed a very considerable line of proof in the course of these conversations. However, it is now necessary, as briefly as possible, to collect the main points of evidence. In so doing, I fear I shall, even more than before, engross the conversation; but I will ask you to interpose whenever you see objections to any of the statements which I make.

A. Let me hear your statement of the whole.

B. Well, then, imagine that you come to the study of the Christian Scriptures, in the spirit that you approach a romance or a tale of fiction; I mean without any thought whether the facts recorded are actual truths or not. You merely wish to collect what is the plot or argument of the whole. You find, then, a history professing to be from the most ancient times, relating events belonging to a period long antecedent to any other written history with which we are acquainted.

A. Pardon me for interrupting you thus early; but I must protest against the word *history* being applied to a series of half-mythical, half-allegorical stories, relating to what occurred before the Flood.

B. Well, I will not pause to discuss the exact nature of the records contained in the early chapters of Genesis. Possibly there may be less of a concession on *our* part, than we are willing to believe, in supposing that the earlier chapters of that book are mysterious moral lessons, rather than strict history. At all events, such a concession would not involve the overthrow of the Christian religion, though if it were made, it might necessitate a new interpretation of some parts of the New Testament. However, it appears that in very early times the consciousness was felt of man's relation to God a God eternally self-existent (Jehovah), and the ruler of the universe (Elohim); but that between the consciousness of that relation and its complete realization in religion, there was interposed a bar which kept man from God. This is *sin:* an inherent tendency of human nature, utterly unaccountable, and yet acknowledged by all thinkers in all ages. In those early times, when, upon the ordinary hypothesis of barbarism, nothing but a degrading condition of sensuality and lust should have been expected, there are some strangely clear traces of a conviction that purification from sin, or, as it it is expressed, victory over sin, should be attained by human suffering. Emerging from the darker tracts of primeval antiquity, we come upon records, which you will say are not historical, of the career of an Eastern Prince, Abraham, in whose touching history, whatever difficulties may occur in parts of it, there are distinct clear traces of the conscious intercourse of the soul with God, of an intense belief in the Unity of the Divine Spirit, of a trustful confidence in the dictates of the religious conscience. This man separates himself from his kindred, who have lost sight of the unity of God, and wanders away into distant lands, in search of a home which he believes that his God has promised to him. Let me pause for an instant to draw your attention to the moral beauty, the glimpses of intense nobleness in a character unsurpassed in the whole range of history.

A. I do indeed think the character of Abraham strikingly beautiful; and yet I see in it very many faults.

B. And can you fail to see that the presence of those faults in such a character is the best guarantee for the faithfulness of the history; or that, if Abraham had been morally perfect, the Christian dispensation might never had existed; for *one* at least of the objects which we Christians discern in the life of Christ, is the example of perfect moral beauty?

A. You do not then deny the existence of faults in Old Testament saints?

B. No; nor in New Testament saints either. It is not a part of Christianity to see perfection, except in *One*. Nor is there the least trace in the Scriptures of such an idea. However, to proceed. To Abraham a promise is made that his descendants shall inherit the land of Canaan; and a further promise is given, that from them shall proceed a blessing to all the nations of the earth.

A. But both those promises may have been inserted in the legends in after-times.

B. It is *possible*, of course, that they were. But observe this: the promise that they should inherit the land of Canaan, may indeed have been invented by one who wrote after the return from captivity at Babylon. But the interpolation of the other promise, at a time when the people were drawing more closely together, and isolating themselves more rigorously from all other nations, and the tolerance of such an interpolation by a nation so jealous of their privileges as the Jews, are things almost inconceivable. At all events, even if it be an interpolation, it is a most remarkable one, and points to an expectation, unaccountable except as a traditional heritage of the race.

A. There is something remarkable in this, I confess.

B. The history continues to relate the fortunes of the descendants of Abraham. They wandered into Egypt, and became slaves of the Egyptians, leaving memorials of their presence there in the brick buildings which they erected. From Egypt they returned to Canaan, where for several centuries they were settled. The one condition upon which they were to retain possession of their land, was the maintenance of the worship of the one God, and abstinence from the abominable rites of the heathen.

Should they transgress these injunctions, as the author of their books of laws foresaw that they would, their inheritance should be taken away, and they should become "an astonishment, a by-word, and a proverb among all the nations whither the Lord shall lead thee."

A. This again may have been inserted after the Captivity, to give force and authority to the enactments, which were promulgated as of ancient date.

B. Possibly. However, words of the same nature are found in the mouth of men, who lived contemporaneously with, or even subsequently to the Captivity. Indeed, as we approach nearer to the time of the later prophets, the threats held out against the people if they forsake the worship of God, and the promises of future rewards of a highly spiritual nature if they remain faithful, grow stronger. Moreover, about this time, a doctrine, which had every now and then appeared in the earlier writings, began to take a prominent place—the doctrine of a Messiah. We have before seen what was the nature of that opinion. However, it grew and waxed strong, and took firm possession of the nation. The voices of Prophets ceased through several centuries; yet still this opinion flourished, until it became the central expectation of the nation. They could not feel that the words of Prophets and Psalmists had received a fulfilment in the person of any of their historical heroes. God had promised a deliverer from the Seed of the woman; He had assured Abraham of a descendant in Whom all nations should be blessed; Jacob on his death-bed had seemed to speak of such an one; Moses had prophesied of one like unto himself, Whom they should hear. Balaam had indicated glories upon glories for Israel. David and the Psalmists had given utterance to mysterious words, which no torturing could make to fit their own case. The Prophets had taken up the burden of the song. Neither Samuel, nor David, nor Hezekiah, nor Josiah had seemed to come up to the promised glory. And so the burden of expectation was handed down from age to age. At last One arose, humble and despised, in the very lowliness of Whose lot the mysterious words appeared to find their fulfilment. But the Jews rejected Him— He did not meet their views. His humility, His boldness, the claims which He urged, and the latitude of conduct respecting legal ordinances, which He tolerated, offended them. He died a shameful death at their instigation, leaving behind, in the hearts of a few, the practical lessons of a perfect moral life, and the apprehension of still higher things, which enabled them to found a religion, which in the course of a few years grew to unexampled proportions, and leavened the civilized world. The Jews, who rejected it, were denounced by its Founder in language which reminds us strongly of the early Prophets. And both He and His followers have left on record certain prophetic indications of future events not yet accomplished. This seems to be a brief account of the connexion existing between the various parts of the Scripture dispensation.

A. And suppose that I had gathered this from the Bible, what then?

B. You would find that much of which we have spoken is certainly not impossible or incredible. There may be gaps, difficulties, even, if you choose, *contradictions* in the various matters recorded. But taken as a whole, there is much that is true and capable of corroboration; many things not incredible and falling in with the rest of the history. There is a general purpose in the whole, yet a purpose apparently concealed from the writers themselves; for the language of the Prophets not unfrequently betrays a more advanced condition of moral and religious thought, than the language of the earlier portions of the book; yet it seems plain that the writers are unaware of this. And this, by the way, goes far to dispose of the arguments of those who would trace the Pentateuch and earlier books to the times of the Prophets.

A. I agree with you in this.

B. Moreover, you will next be met with the astounding fact, that Christianity did establish itself on the very foundations which the Prophets predicted—a kingdom of righteousness; that it has withstood the shock of many centuries, and of countless enemies; and that the Jews, who rejected it, within a very few years ceased to exist as a nation; and yet that, instead of being absorbed among other nations, they have remained to this day despised, persecuted, and reviled, a distinct and marked race upon the earth.

A. But you surely cannot regard as miraculous the distinct existence of a race, whose laws forbid intermarriage with other nations, and whose customs compel them to remain separate from all others?

B. I might even not despair of showing that this isolated circumstance is intensely remarkable. But your explanation only accounts for the fact; it ignores, what is after all the important thing, that this isolation accords with words written at least two thousand years ago; and both the prophecies and the isolation coincide with a long dispensation of Providence of a peculiar nature towards that people formerly.

A. But with respect to the most momentous question, the references to a Messiah, it seems to me that, with few exceptions, the supposed prophecies would never have been detected, had it not been for the microscopic inspection of the middle ages, or of the early Christians. After the doctrine of a Messiah was once started, the Christian writers found references innumerable to Him in most unexpected quarters: references very startling to modern ears. If the word "*anoint*" occurs, immediately the commentator sees a prophetic intimation of the "*anointed:*" if a description of suffering is read, the foot-note says, "proleptically spoken of Christ:" if a shameful death is referred to, the phantom of the cross rises before the inflamed imagination. Take any of these passages alone, and compare them with the supposed accomplishment; and any reasonable man, if his mind were not preoccupied with a dread of blasphemy, would ridicule your credulity.

B. But as I have often said, in such a case it is not just to isolate the passages. And I will retort, that if any one says that the latter part of Isaiah does not *appear* to corroborate the Christian doctrine, his mind is unquestionably biassed on the other side: and I will willingly submit those passages to the person to whom you appeal—the fair unbiassed man of the world, not the philosopher who is determined that there *shall* be no miracles, and *can* be no prophecy; but to one, if you can find him, who has no propension, no predilection either way. With regard to the other isolated passages, I will only say that they are not easy to account for, and that, whatever their value or want of value, they had a great influence upon the Israelites. However, with reference to the whole argument, let me draw your attention to this, that monotheism, the worship of one God, moral purity, and all the most elevating principles of conduct have passed into the Western world through the instrumentality of a nation regarded by their contemporaries as ferocious barbarians; a people certainly possessed of a stern and savage earnestness, which, in all their history, plunged them into deeds of sanguinary violence. This nation, though it has given to us the heritage of a belief in God's unity, rarely maintained that belief itself in its purity; though it prided itself upon a literature remarkable at all events for its constant declarations of the universality of God's dispensations, this nation was seemingly unconscious of these liberal ideas, and fought against them in its public life, till it became hateful to every other people: cruel itself, it has become the herald of loving-kindness; remorseless itself, it has taught men to be merciful; faithless itself, it has enshrined in its literature the idea of faith to God; bigoted itself, it has been the propagator of liberal ideas; it has taught men that in the sight of God all alike are equal, and that before Him there is no respect of persons. Such are some of the services which this nation has been instrumental in conferring upon mankind. For Christianity took its rise among Jews, was propagated by them, and professed to be a completion of that which was before unfinished and rudimentary. It did, in effect, carry out such a scheme as the Prophets contemplated, whether their words were merely random guesses at the future, or the Christian religion the production of the combined energies of a few enthusiastic minds. And though you may say that the history is uncertain and unsatisfactory, the prophecies only the utterances of enthusiasm, occasionally indicating, by coincidence or by poetic instinct, the course of future events; though the life of Christ may appear to you only that of a wise, good man; though the founding of Christianity may seem the natural consequence of a world, tired of vice, hailing with delight some gleams of better things; though its rapid progress may be regarded as the result of purely natural causes; yet when you take the whole together and consider what has been done, the instruments employed, the connexion between the various parts, the utter incommensurateness of the means used and the results attained,—I think you will confess that Christianity is, of all things upon the earth, the most remarkable. Its history must not be put aside as a tissue of old wives' fables. The whole connecting web, which binds together the Jewish with the Christian world, merits from men of thought something better than the passing sneer, that without a miracle no one could possibly hold the Christian Faith.

DIALOGUE VIII.

ON A SUBJECTIVE PROOF OF RELIGION.

B. WITH the subject of our last discussion, these conversations might appropriately close. Yet when I review the ground which we have traversed, I am constantly reminded how imperfect has been my attempt to resolve your difficulties; and yet in my own mind I am more and more assured that the weakness lies, not in my subject, but in the way in which I have handled it. A fear comes over me, lest the cause of truth should have suffered in my hands; and as I hold others responsible for their intellectual gifts, so I mete out to myself that measure which I demand from others. If God's truth have suffered by my carelessness, by my neglect of things important to be set before you; if I have stated with stammering lips that which should be spoken clearly and with firmness; if I have omitted, through want of thought, to enunciate proof, which ought to have lain ready to my hand;

then am I responsible not only for my negligence, but for the assistance which I have failed to render to you. Or if, on the other hand, I have unconsciously used that for demonstration, which is but presumption; if I have evaded difficulties, or mis-stated facts, then, too, I have an account to render; and my heart shrinks at the thought, that in my endeavour to declare what I hold, from my soul, to be the very truth, I have unconsciously done evil that good may come.

A. My good friend, I think you are over severe to yourself. Surely if you have done your best for me, a righteous God will not hold you guilty of neglect. No man can do more than that. Besides, upon these purely intellectual questions, all that can be required is that you should state them fairly, and that I should judge them in a like spirit.

B. Ah! my friend; but the thought oppresses me, that I may all along have misled you as to the spirit in which these inquiries should be made. Perhaps if I had stated, at the outset, my conviction that in judging of the works of God, we have no right to use the judicial method of criticism, I might have influenced you more. We are God's creatures and His servants: and the clay has no right to say to the potter, Why hast thou made me thus? What if I have concealed from you the great central fact, that the only condition of religious inquiry is religious earnestness? What if I have encouraged you to think that we have a right to sit as judges, and not to fall as suppliants before the throne of the Invisible? And yet *without this spirit* religious inquiry is but mockery. The intellect may remain in suspense between the opposing difficulties; but the real subject of religion, the religious heart of man, may still remain untouched; and so the end will be the sad and mournful condition of those who end in doubt, with no inherent energy to guide them to the Source of truth and love, Who alone is able to afford them comfort and consolation in the trials of life and in the hour of death. What, I say, if I have been encouraging an inquiry about religion, without the necessary condition of a religious spirit of inquiry?

A. In that case I should say the fault is mine, not yours; for if I comprehend your meaning rightly, the religious spirit must spring from within, and it is not in your power, nor in the power of any living man, to implant this spirit in the heart of another.

B. Still, if you will bear with me a little

longer, I have somewhat more to say. I will ask you to listen, while I lay before you something of that process by which my own religious convictions have been matured. It may be that you will not be able to acquiesce in what I say. And yet it may not be without its value to you to learn the mental process, by which a fellow man has striven to be true to the *reason* which God has given him for his inward guide, to the *experience* on which his reason has employed itself, and to that *external revelation* which he holds to be Divine.

A. I will gladly listen to your account of your own religious development; only, if you will permit me, I will make such suggestions, or objections, as from time to time may present themselves to me.

B. By all means do so. Here then I will commence my analysis. I assume, then, as the first principle of my inquiry, that the Phenomenon of Religion is a thing to be investigated fairly, and not to be set aside on the ground that, the folly of the people and the interested designs of artful men, are sufficient explanation of its existence. This at least is the starting-point of my inquiry. I find religion existing in the world; the idea is not repugnant to my natural impulses; on the contrary it commends itself to me, and I see that in one form or another it has commended itself to the instincts of all mankind. Indeed it may fairly be said that, to use the language of scholastic logic, religion is an *inseparable accident,* if not *an essential part* of the definition of man.

A. All this seems fair enough and beyond dispute.

B. How then is it that we have this connatural idea of religion?

A. That is a hard question, and the subject of much discussion.

B. Well, I am not concerned to discuss it now; for in what I am now saying, I am presenting a subjective picture of the process through which my mind has passed. I assume that God exists, because I, for my part, never could think otherwise; and to me religion means the knowledge of God, of His will, and of our duties to Him. This knowledge we may learn from our own minds, from the voice of mankind, and from the course of the world. From these three sources we learn the Being and the attributes of God, our prospect of reward and punishment according as we obey or disobey Him.

A. But can we fairly be said to learn these things from these sources? Is it not plain that the majority of mankind do not thus learn the truth?

B. Yes; and the reason of that will become clear in the sequel. When the same question presented itself to me years ago, it perplexed me, as it appears to have perplexed you. But long and patient thought convinced me, that within the breast of man there resides an inward principle, dictating what is right, and sanctioning our obedience by the pains or pleasures which it attaches to our actions. The analysis of the developed conscience may lead us to consider it as complex, and formed of various converging faculties. But I felt that I had a right to assume, that what men of all nations and ages have instinctively recognized as a constituent element of their nature, what has impressed itself upon all language and embodied itself in the framework of human thought, is natural to man.

A. I shall not dispute your position: for to some degree I am prepared to acquiesce; moreover, I am now listening to your own subjective analysis of religion.

B. Conscience, then, I say, appeared to me to be a sense of duty: and I felt that it bore witness to a Master Who approves holiness and disapproves wickedness. But in so regarding

Him, we are looking upon Him as *a judge*. To this cardinal truth the natural instincts of the human race unconsciously direct us. Thus we acquire a notion of retributive justice. It is not the power, nor the wisdom, nor the knowledge, nor the benevolence of God, to which our original instincts especially bear witness, but to His justice. This is the aspect of God, which lies at the root of all systems of natural religion.

A. So it would seem.

B. The next point, which seemed plain to me was this, that, be our duties what they might, our *shortcomings* far exceeded our acts of obedience. But disobedience demands punishment. Hence arises the notion, universal in the system of natural religion, of an angry God.

A. And did not that stagger you?

B. No, I confess it did not. For I had, before that time, realized that to be angry is not necessarily wrong. To be angry at injustice and to desire that the unjust should be punished for their injustice is, if not a virtue, assuredly not a vice. But seeing that *personal malice* readily enters into the composition of our sense of anger, seeing, too, that beings sinful in themselves have not committed to them the task of avenging wrong upon their fellow-sinners, anger has justly come to be regarded as perilous and inappropriate to such a being as man. But in the All-Just no such excesses or abuses are to be apprehended; and stripping the notion of anger of these its extraneous accretions, I regard it as an essential part of the idea of justice. But since this is so, the consequence in religion becomes obvious.

A. What consequence?

B. How can natural religion regard man otherwise than as oppressed with a burden of *sin and sadness?* So it appeared to the ancients, and therefore some among their writers were offended at this gloomy aspect of religion. Such a one was Lucretius. Though we may not share his prejudices, we may employ him as an unimpeachable witness to the fact.

A. Your statement is precisely accurate. Nothing can exceed the loathing with which Lucretius regarded the dark and cruel religions of the heathen.

B. No, my friend, do not deceive yourself; it is not the *cruelty* which offended him: it is the *universal sense of guilt and sadness*, to which the general consent of man gives witness, that awakens his bitter animosity. It is not the *abominations* of their worship to which he objects, but the deep painful consciousness of *sin*, of which those abominations were the misguided acknowledgment. According to him that alone which deserves recognition by the reason of man is the supposed universal principle of love, which he typifies under the personal idea of "gentle Venus," who alone governs the order of the universe.

A. Such an idea of creative love would seem to me to be not unacceptable to the Christian Theology, which professes to recognize in its God the embodiment of transcendent love.

B. It is true indeed that Christianity does regard God as love; but it combines with that idea, as an essential element of its theology, the notion of a God of justice. Lucretius and his school if even in appearance they hold a doctrine resembling that of Divine love in the Christian religion, omit that no less fundamental idea, to which the universal conscience of men bears witness, that man is sinful, degraded, and separate from God.

A. But what induces you to assert that this is a natural feeling of mankind?

B. For proof of it, I appeal to the doctrines and practices of all nations; there is no natural religion upon the earth, nor, so far as we can ascertain, has there ever been one, of which this feeling is not the central principle. Wherever religion exists in a popular shape, it invariably presents its dark side to us. In its ceremonial practices, in the doctrines connected with those observances, the sense of sin is perpetually made apparent. Thus every sacrifice implies this, at least, that there is an *alienation* between man and God; and that to effect a reconciliation an *atonement* is required. Wherever there is a priest, there is the notion of *sin, pollution, and retribution,* there also is the idea of *intercession and mediation*.

A. But may not the intention of sacrifice be something less profound than this? Does it not often present itself under the form of a bargain with the Deity? "For so much expenditure on our side, God, as a matter of justice, may be expected to return an equivalent."

B. In some instances this may be the case. But by far the most universal notion is, that the sacrifice is a substitution of something offered, or some personal suffering, for a penalty which would otherwise be exacted. Of this idea the whole religious history of mankind in its earlier stages is a manifestation. The Hebrew Scriptures, ancient records, modern travels, all bear witness to this universal belief. It exhibits itself, we are told, in the centre of Africa and among the South-Sea Islanders, and has been found to exist among the Aborigines of Australia. Sometimes it is the mutilation of the person, which is thought acceptable; sometimes it is the sacrifice of some much valued possession; but in all, the same consciousness of sin, and of the need of atonement manifests itself.

A. But surely the idea is inconsistent with the dictates of that natural conscience, on which you lay so great stress. For if there be one thing more obvious than another, it is the sense of personal responsibility. "The soul that sinneth it shall die; the son shall not bear the iniquity of the father, neither shall the father bear the iniquity of the son;" this is the doctrine of the enlightened spirit. That which is past, is past; it cannot be undone. No personal repentance will restore what is lost; much less can the interposition of others on our behalf, or the sacrifice of anything, however precious, atone for the violation of our duty.

B. What you say is very true, and, for a time, it presented many difficulties to me. But on reflection I was led to apprehend that the two things are not irreconcilable. In the end each of us is responsible for his own acts; but, in the time of probation, it is not impossible, rather it is probable, that assistance may be rendered to us. The idea of atonement does not do away with human responsibility; it implies that in the intermediate period, which elapses before a final decision shall be passed upon human actions, men are, in some way, to make their own those opportunities which are offered them of reconciling themselves to the Divine will.

A. But were you not struck with the fact, that as men made progress in civilization, they shook off many of these primitive notions, and amongst them this doctrine of atonement?

B. Yes, I was; but reflection showed me, that what is called *progress* is by no means necessarily a development of the entire nature of man. As the intellect of the world advanced, I saw that it refused indeed to take cognizance of many things which were acknowledged in more primitive times. But I saw also that it gave no sufficient reason for so doing, save that, as it could not account for them, they were not subjects for human investigation; and then came the sequel that they were barbarous and exploded notions, and therefore to be rejected. But no sufficient explanation of their origin was given, nor could I find that the scorn of philosophy had ever been able to silence the voice of nature in the human heart. Therefore I argued that, though these intimations of the soul were less attended to now than of old, yet, in all reason, they demanded from accountable moral beings a recognition as being primitive declarations of the soul. I could not, without doing violence to my nature, extirpate them from my own mind; and, as men, who had no theory to uphold or to refute, maintained and handed on this doctrine, as it were, by natural impulse; since, too, it is found in various forms amongst nations widely separated from one another, and unconnected either by language or history, I held that there must be an essential underlying truth to which all these concurring evidences point. Or if I were led to conjecture that these notions were the inheritance of all the families of the earth, this, even more than the other, seemed a presumption that these notions were the result of some unrecorded events, of which the universal sentiment of mankind had embodied the remembrance.

A. Such a presumption is not according to

the canons of historic criticism : it is, however, not impossible.

B. I now pass to another sphere of information. When I had reached this point in the inquiry, I turned my eyes upon the system and course of the world. Being satisfied in my own mind that the established order of things is the work of an intelligent will, that is, of a personal Creator, I turned to look for His presence in the established order of things : that I must discern Him there was certain. But it was with a feeling akin to dismay that I found His action in this world so indirect. Then all those questions, which, in many of our conversations we have discussed at length, appeared like spectres to haunt me. Why is God so hidden from our eyes ? Why does He not write His moral nature upon the universe in letters which none can misinterpret ? Why are not all men guided to the knowledge of His will ? Why is it not an absurdity to deny His existence, His attributes, His providence ? Why does He not walk with us, as He is said to have walked with holy men of old ? Shall I say that God does not exist ? Shall I refuse to listen to His voice, when it seems to speak to me ? Is it a fancy that we see dim shadows of His presence in the affairs of men ? In this perplexity

I returned to my own inner consciousness. There I learned, as I thought, that God still exists; but I learned, too, another fact, from its disquietude, that I am alienated from Him; my sins "have divided between me and my God."

A. Again you are guessing, but there is a melancholy resemblance to the truth in your guess. But how could you account for such a growth of sin in a world coming from an All-Pure being?

B. That seemed incapable of explanation; but I could not perceive any ground to doubt the *fact*. Suffering, bodily and mental, seems to be the law of universe. Of the thousand millions of men upon the earth at this present time, who can calculate the aggregate misery? and if we add to this the sufferings of all the generations past, and of all those that may come after, it seems as if some being of malignant nature had gained possession of the fair universe. With this impression derived from reflection on the course of nature, all the popular traditions concerning the unseen state, all the superstitions of the ancient mythologies coincide. And such being the universal impression of mankind, I could find no other explanation, but that a malignant power was indeed at work to alienate man from his God. Furthermore, it seemed to me that, if we may conjecture the future from the past, there is reason to suppose that evil will never disappear from nature. For I saw that disobedience to the voice of justice was itself a misery, and one that man cannot evade; he carries it about with him wherever he goes, though in the delights of sensible objects he momentarily forgets it, yet it recurs again and again; and when the sensible pleasures are finally removed, I saw reason to apprehend that the sense of misery would remain with nothing to alleviate its pangs. Moreover it seemed beyond a doubt that the older a man grows the harder he is to change, no wishing can alter him, that therefore taken by himself, unaltered from his sinful condition, there is no prospect that he will rid himself from the misery which his sin has brought upon him. And this, combined with the conviction which possessed me, on grounds already explained, that the soul of man is an imperishable thing, threw a light upon the awful apprehension of heathen nations concerning a future state. I saw, that far from being a figment of Christianity, this apprehension was the irresistible testimony of the human soul to the eternity of the habits which it forms here on earth.

A. It is a sad and gloomy picture of religion which you are here tracing; indeed one may well call it repulsive. If this is all that natural piety can do for man, it is not to be wondered at that the nations of the earth turned away their faces from it, and preferred to rest in earthly things. And I must say that even the austerest Christian possesses incomparable happiness compared with this.

B. Doubtless it is severe, and as I have said natural religion wears its dark side outwards. But if you will examine it a little, you will find that even thus, there is much to comfort the soul of man.

A. How so?

B. For what reason it may be asked did men consent, even in the heathen world to forego pleasure, and voluntarily to undergo pain, except from the hope that their sorrows might be alleviated. There was, at least, a hope of future benefit to be derived; and, this hope in itself was a source of comfort. But beyond this, men had an earnest of this future good in the social happiness from which they were not debarred. With all their sufferings, they ever had much to make them thankful. The love which sweetens human life, which softens the hardest hearts in their better moments, led men to the conviction that they were not utterly cast off. In the sentiment of unselfish friendship, of the devoted love of parents to children and children to parents, of mutual good offices rendered in the simplicity of pure affection, men were led to see the workings of something beyond a severe justice. Moreover, amid all the difficulties of the material universe, the instincts of mankind have led them to trace something beyond a prospect of punishment for their shortcomings. Not only in Christian nations, or in modern times, have such principles as these existed, that treason never prospers, that honesty is the best policy, that the virtuous are happy, even though unfortunate. The principle which underlies all these instinctive utterances, is that in the end and on the whole, there is good for the good, and evil for the evil. And such a principle, however concealed in practice, has lain at the root of all national life in all ages, and has given the lie to those philosophies which see in the course of the world nothing but chance or physical law. They bear witness, in tones which refuse to be silenced, to an ineradicable conviction that there is a providence watching over human affairs.

A. I do not deny it; it is to me a source of

the utmost comfort to believe it, and to deny it would be to plunge myself in the blackness of despair.

B. And there is another matter to which my attention was drawn. Of all the natural facts which bear testimony to religion, the universality of prayer seemed to me the very strongest. There is no nation which has not felt, and embodied in its national life, the irresistible call to address the unseen in prayer and supplication. I do not say that the abstract difficulties as to the effect of prayer are not great. But, in spite of them all, prayer has ever been offered, and it is the natural address of a moral being to one who regards his supplication.

A. May we not regard prayer as simply an expression of man's wants without any reference to the possibility of having them supplied?

B. Even then it is an instinctive confession of his need of some one to supply them. But you must remember that prayer is not altogether petition. It is sometimes an expression of thanks for benefits already enjoyed; sometimes it is a simple outpouring of a heart full of inexpressible emotions which seek this mode of utterance; sometimes it takes the form of a declaration of the attributes of God. Any how the universal employment of prayer is a thing which appeared to me to present two alternatives. Either the instinctive tendency is to be utterly ignored as of no value, and called irrational, in which case we ought to see signs of a like habit in irrational creatures, which no one pretends; or it is to be regarded as based upon a primitive inclination of man to adore the unseen, in which case it is a powerful argument for religion.

A. But do you intend me to discern signs of God's hand in the absurd, fantastic, and contradictory adoration of heathen tribes?

B. By no means; what is *universal* has a distinct claim to be considered as part of man's nature; and such is the custom of worship. The fantastic and false developments of that spirit are to be regarded as the perverse or mistaken interpretations given by men to the principles which they find implanted in them.

A. Perhaps such a distinction is just.

B. Suppose that there is a God possessing such and such attributes, and you will see that it is certainly just; for if one form of worship is right, that which contradicts it must be wrong. Contradictions cannot be true together. However, to proceed. As prayer is natural to man, so the expectation of a revelation is natural. Every nation, rightly or wrongly, does in its primitive condition trace back its institutions, alike religious and political, to some supposed declaration of the Divine will. I do not mean for a moment to assert that the particular mode of revelation supposed, or the existence of the Divine founders of states and systems is to be allowed; but I say that the notion of a declaration of the Divine will is a connatural instinct of mankind, and so far to be accepted as a presumption in favour of the possibility of such revelation. No doubt the modes and circumstances of the supposed revelations are frequently utterly incongruous: and the reason of later ages has led men to reject them. But this does not alter the conviction that such events may have occurred, though by no means in the ways, or at the times supposed.

A. The possibility of a Divine revelation cannot be denied by any who believe in a personal God; even the probability of it may be conceded without doing violence to reason. Amidst all the perplexities of the human soul, the idea that God should enlighten it is a ray of light, comforting beyond measure to those who are distressed with doubt. The real difficulty lies in the fact that so many men cannot discern His revelation in that which is asserted to have come from Him.

B. It is; but as we endeavoured before to ascertain the reasons of this obscurity, we need not now recur to them. One remark more I will make respecting natural religion. It is an indisputable fact, that the notion of intercession on behalf of others has always manifested itself among mankind. Not only in heathen nations, but everywhere and at all times, men have regarded some of their fellow-men as purer, holier, nearer to God than themselves. Thus, in the Gospel, the man who said, "God heareth not sinners; but if a man be a worshipper of God, and doeth His will, him He heareth," spoke the conviction of the human race everywhere. And so the idea of intercession, on the part of the pure and noble, for the weak and sinful, is a part of natural religion to which all men bear witness. This, at all events, is a natural precept of religion, which commends itself to the generous-hearted among mankind, wherever they are found.

A It is, at least, a beautiful instinct, and lies at the root of all devotion to persons or causes, by means of which the noble lives of men have had their influence in purifying and elevating the human heart.

B. Such then are some of the principles of natural religion : the notion of the misery of sin, of the curse which it has inflicted upon men; the doctrine of atoning sacrifice; the expectation of future punishment, inseparable from the idea of future existence; the conviction of the agency of an evil spirit in degrading the human race, and setting it at variance with its Maker. On the other hand, the sense of a justice which, on the whole, awards to all according to their deserts; the instinctive tendency to prayer; the no less instinctive acceptance of a Divine revelation; the notion of personal mediation between God and man : all these things are found in the system of natural piety, however established, and form a remarkable preparation for the Christian religion. For that religion, though containing some things unknown before, yet, in the main, bases itself upon doctrines to a great degree coincident with those here enumerated. It was by virtue of the preparation worked in men's hearts by previous dispensations, whether Jewish or heathen, that men accepted with the utmost readiness the preaching of the Christian Faith. Those were a preparation, of which this is the completion. It does indeed add something to them; but in it nothing is to be found in essential contradiction to their principles. Bearing these things in mind, I felt when I came to the consideration of the Christian Faith, that I had not to deal with a system utterly unknown to natural religion; if I felt that it contained something hard to be understood, I saw, too, that the most difficult of these had already in outline suggested themselves to the unassisted human intellect; and if there were others of which this explanation could not be given, it seemed reasonable not to reject the whole, because I could not give a satisfactory account of a part. Such was the spirit in which I approached the intellectual side of the Christian religion. You will discern at once that the point of view of those who come critically to it, without the preparation of which I have here shadowed forth the outline, was not mine. For, indeed, to such persons, every single question resolves itself into one more remote; until eventually the point at which they arrive is, "Is there or is there not a personal God, Who speaks to the human heart by natural means, and inclines it, in some degree, to repose upon His fatherly kindness, His sympathy, if I may so speak, and His spiritual assistance?" Two systems of religion have pronounced in favour of this idea; or rather, I should say, two economics, one preparatory to the other, have instructed men in the various phases of this idea. Each of them in its main principles has exhibited the facts of natural religion in clearer and more precise delineation than the unaided reason of men has been able to discern. Each is based upon the sense of sin, and the possibility of relief from the misery of its degradation. Each has made the idea of an atonement a central element; each has encouraged virtuous living, abnegation of self, truthfulness in every department of the inner life; and one of them has been able to adapt itself to every phase of the human intellect, and to appropriate the language and the thought of those systems of philosophy, which have, in any way, travelled over the same range of ideas. The great problems of the human intellect remain, as they were, unresolved, so far as natural explication is concerned; nevertheless, they receive in this system a recognition, and are embodied as essential parts of the Christian doctrine. They who refuse to accept the doctrines are at least as far from explaining the difficulties as they who hold the Christian faith. And, moreover, they can positively give no satisfactory answer to the questions which the human soul is ever asking. The life of Christ and the love of Christ, if they fail to resolve the questions, at least suggest a way of life in which, so far as one may judge, every emotion which can ennoble the heart, every thought which can elevate the intellect has free scope to operate. The conquerors of the world are forgotten, and pass out of mind; but there is just one name, and one only, which seems never to be forgotten. It is the name of Him Who, nearly nineteen centuries ago, declared that the kingdom which He came on earth to establish was not of this world; whose power upon earth is felt by countless myriads of the human race, and evinces itself in lives of patience under suffering, contentment in poverty, humility in high places; which binds together in indissoluble bonds of brotherhood, the high and the low, the wise and the ignorant; which has fought the battle of humanity in evil times, till the philosophies which dimly longed for the results now attained by the weak things of the world, proudly claim the effects, while they repudiate the means. It is in this name that we trust; and looking to Him we feel that, in what form soever antagonists assail Him, in the end He will bring comfort, consolation, and if so be, victory to His faithful followers.

GILBERT AND RIVINGTON, PRINTERS, ST. JOHN'S SQUARE, LONDON.

www.ingramcontent.com/pod-product-compliance
Lightning Source LLC
Chambersburg PA
CBHW030323020526
44117CB00030B/709